COMPLEX Presents

Sneaker of the Year

The Best Since '85

Abrams Image, New York

Foreword by Marc Eckō 07

1980s
Air Jordan 1 (1985) 10
Converse Weapon (1986)...........22
Nike Air Max 1 (1987) 36
Air Jordan III (1988) 44
Air Jordan IV (1989)....................52

1990s
Nike Air Max 90 (1990) 62
Nike Air Huarache (1991)..........68
Vans Half Cab (1992) 76
Nike Air Force Max (1993)........86
Reebok Instapump Fury (1994) ..96
Air Jordan XI (1995) 104
Reebok Question (1996)...........114
Nike Air Foamposite One (1997). 126

Nike Air Max Plus (1998)........134
Air Jordan XIV (1999).............142

2000s
Nike Air Presto (2000).............152
Reebok Answer 4 (2001).........160
Nike SB Dunk (2002)...............168
Nike Air Zoom Generation (2003) 180
Nike Free 5.0 (2004).................188
Nike Zoom LeBron 3 (2005)...196
Nike Zoom Kobe 1 (2006)...... 204
Supra Skytop (2007).................212
Nike Zoom Kobe 4 (2008).......222
Nike Air Yeezy 1 (2009)...........230

2010s
Nike LeBron 8 (2010).............. 240

Nike Mag (2011) 248
Nike Flyknit Racer (2012) 256
Balenciaga Arena (2013) 264
Nike Air Yeezy 2 "Red October" (2014) 274
Adidas Ultra Boost (2015) 282
Adidas Yeezy Boost 350 V2 (2016) 292
Nike Zoom Fly (2017) 300
Nike React Element 87 (2018) 310
Nike x Sacai LDV Waffle (2019) 320

2020s
Off-White x Air Jordan V (2020) 328

FOREWORD

On the surface, the Air Jordan, Michael Jordan's inaugural signature model, was a commercial vehicle for fans to connect to the talent whose name the sneaker bore. But the 1985 release wasn't a landmark thanks only to Jordan's play, Nike's design, or the colors it wore. It changed an entire industry because, unlike any shoe that preceded it, it proposed sport as culture, with Jordan as the symbol of this convergence. The silhouette quickly moved beyond basketball, immortalizing the player and creating a new, wildly lucrative lane for companies and athletes alike.

In the thirty-five years that followed, brands would repeat this formula hundreds of times, often to great success. But something else happened: the players who attached their names to iconic sneakers became icons themselves, figures whose personalities could shape multinational companies from the boardroom down. Jordan—and Charles Barkley, and Allen Iverson, and dozens more—rose to a level that had once been off limits to athletes.

At the same time, for people like me, sneakers offered a gateway to a career in design. And for streetwear designers who collaborated with brands like Nike and Adidas on high-profile releases, they became a path to mainstream legitimacy, a Trojan horse that carried creators like Virgil Abloh from an overlooked corner of the exclusionary fashion industry to runways at Paris Fashion Week.

What began with Jordan wearing a pair of sneakers culminated in a moment of economic and social justice. It's a power shift we have never seen in any industry—and something we may not witness again.

by Marc Eckō

Sneakers predate the '80s, but the sneaker landscape as we know it today can be traced to one year: 1985. It was then that Nike released Michael Jordan's debut signature model and, as a result, surged past rivals like Adidas and Reebok to lead in the sports-footwear arms race. Those sneaker wars set the stage for modern sneaker culture. While there were signature models well before—for athletes like Jack Purcell and Stan Smith—it wasn't

until that first Air Jordan that brands realized how much a line based around a singular star could capture imaginations and spike earnings. And while there had been other footwear designers, it wasn't until Nike architect Tinker Hatfield started sketching sneakers around 1985 that the company's products were seen as functional pieces of art. This isn't quite where it all started, but it's where it all started to make sense.

1985 Air Jordan 1

Nike couldn't have come up with a better marketing strategy if it had tried. When the Beaverton, Oregon–based sneaker company launched the Air Jordan 1, it changed footwear. The man promoting it, Michael Jordan, was mesmerizing, both on the court and off. And the NBA banned one of the colorways, a combination of black and red sitting atop a white midsole, which drew more attention to the sneaker, upping the intrigue around and demand for a $65 basketball shoe. That model launched what is now a multibillion-dollar business for Nike and Jordan Brand and marked the dawn of contemporary sneaker culture. Never had the world become so enamored of an athlete and the shoes on his feet. For anyone who collects sneakers, the Air Jordan 1 is an absolute must-have—both to wear and to hold. Year after year, Jordan Brand drops both new and original colorways, and they sell out every time. It is a sneaker that has become timeless, a shoe that transcends fashion and looks good no matter what is currently trending. It was air personified, and the story behind the AJ 1 is as deep and complex as the man himself.

by Drew Hammell

It begins at the 1984 NBA Draft, when the lowly Chicago Bulls selected Michael Jordan with the third overall pick. To say the Bulls were lucky to grab Jordan with that pick is one of the biggest understatements ever. The NBA was a big-man's league back in the '80s, so players like Hakeem Olajuwon and Sam Bowie went before Jordan, mainly because teams prioritized centers above guards. Though Jordan wasn't the first pick, the Bulls were confident in his abilities and signed him to a seven-year, $6 million deal—the third-highest contract in league history at the time, behind Olajuwon and Ralph Sampson. The Blazers, who had the chance of a lifetime to draft Jordan, needed a center. It didn't make sense to them to pick the 6'6" Jordan when a big man was more of a priority. "So you play him at center!" former Team USA coach Bobby Knight once famously quipped.

After the draft, the race was on for the top sneaker brands to sign the Bulls' flashy new star. Nike was the top contender, though there was plenty of opportunity for Adidas and Converse to move ahead as well. On Nike's side, several key figures heavily influenced Jordan's decision to sign with the brand. Sonny Vaccaro was one of them; Vaccaro made a name for himself in the college basketball world by convincing coaches to ink deals with Nike so that big-market teams would wear the brand's sneakers and apparel on national TV. For a period, Vaccaro's advice was gospel for Nike, and he was all in on it signing Jordan. One of Nike's creative directors at the time was Peter Moore, who led the design of the first Air Jordan sneaker and the "Wings" logo.

If you notice similarities between the Air Jordan 1 and the Nike Dunk, it's because Moore led the design of that, too. Jordan's agent, David Falk, was a brilliant negotiator and made sure Jordan was getting the best deal. Another key figure in the Nike deal was Donald Dell, who was the president of ProServ. ProServ was a sports management firm that Nike worked with for the Air Jordan line initially.

Jordan was the real deal, but nobody knew for sure how great he would really become. Falk was confident and demanded a high price for whoever wanted to sign the prized guard. Nike certainly didn't have the deal in the bag at first, since Jordan was a big fan of Adidas (he loved the way the leather was broken in right out of the box). Jordan was ready to sign with Adidas, but Nike's team was more prepared and saw the huge potential of signing him. Converse certainly wanted to add Jordan to its strong arsenal of stars, which included Larry Bird and Magic Johnson. But Converse wanted to market Jordan alongside Bird and Magic, not set him apart. Nike's commitment to Jordan went so far that it even created a sneaker just for him, which was not common back in the '80s for basketball players. Only a chosen few athletes in any sport had their own sneaker, so the fact that Nike was willing to make one for a player who hadn't even stepped on a professional court yet proved how much it was willing to invest in the star.

Nike's connection with ProServ and Donald Dell was important because Dell was a professional tennis player; back then, tennis players were marketed more strongly than basketball players. For example, Arthur Ashe and Stan Smith both benefited from Dell's promotional prowess. Dell wanted to showcase Jordan in a similar fashion. Along with this approach came the signature sneaker Nike created for Jordan—a sneaker tailored just to him, down to a size 13½ for his right foot and a size 13 for his left. Nike and Dell threw around names for the shoe before they met with Jordan; one possibility was the "Prime Time." Obviously that name didn't work out, and the group agreed that "Air Jordan" was the best option.

The sneaker deal landscape of the '80s was far removed from what it is today. The biggest names didn't have the signing power that star athletes have now, and sneaker companies didn't have massive budgets for marketing, either. In 1984, Nike was a $25-million-a-year company, and it had about $2.5 million to spend on marketing. Like its competitors, Nike was considering signing multiple basketball players to promote the brand, but Vaccaro told Strasser to give Jordan everything. Nike listened but was somewhat skeptical, since it was such a huge risk.

Jordan was hesitant to sign with Nike as well—so much so that he wanted to cancel his meeting with the brand the night before he was scheduled to fly out to Oregon. Jordan's mother, Deloris, convinced him to get on the plane and listen to Nike's pitch. Phil Knight, Nike's cofounder and chairman, was kept abreast of the negotiations but was never all in on Jordan, either. In the end, though, he stayed quiet and allowed the deal to be done.

After Nike pitched its campaign along with the new sneaker just for Jordan, Falk went back to Adidas and Converse to see what their counters were. Jordan himself went to a Converse rep and told him it had

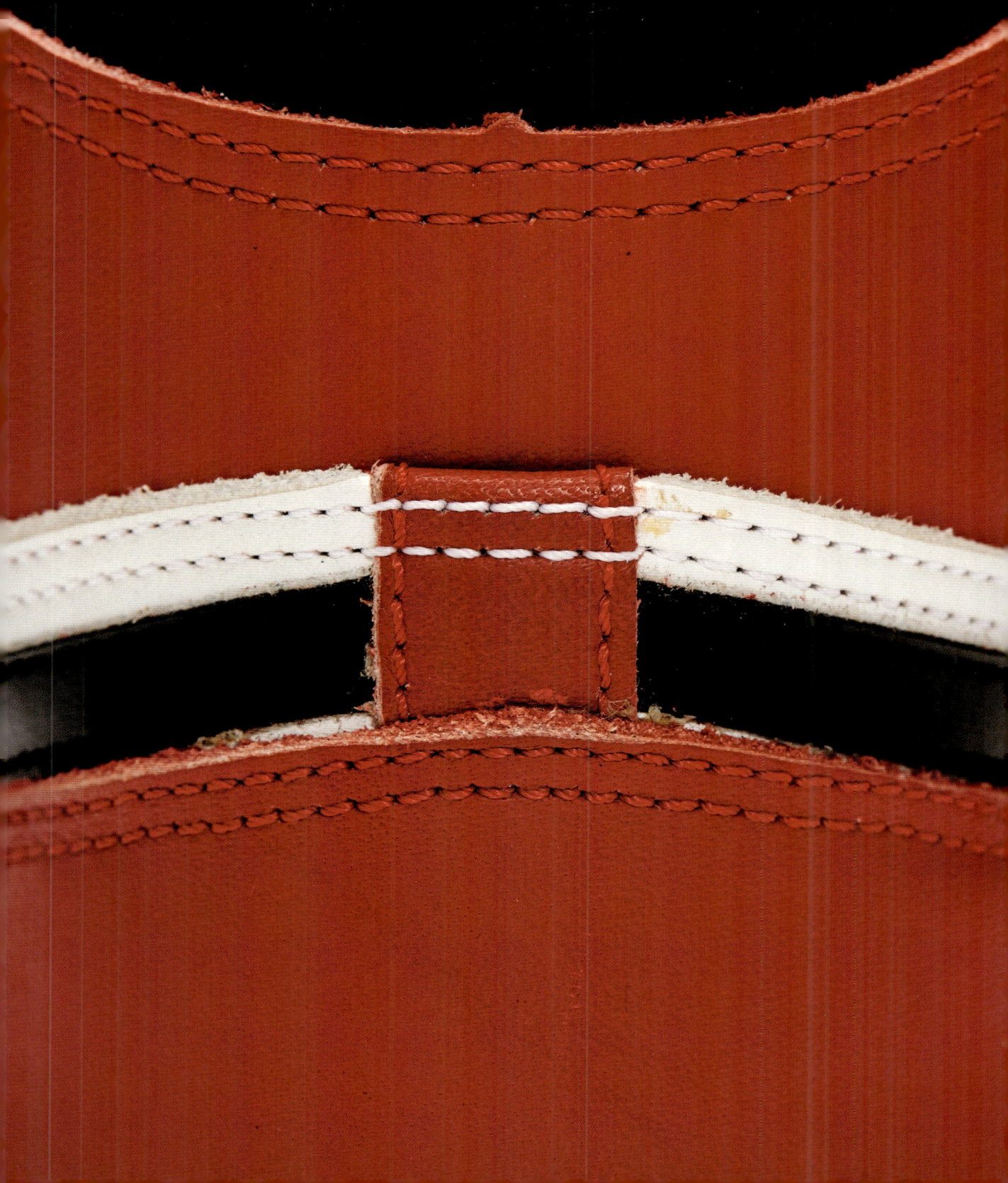

to get close to what Nike was offering in order for him to sign it. But neither of the two brands was willing to offer what Nike could for the future superstar.

Eventually, the deal between Nike and Jordan was signed: $2.5 million over five years, along with the agreement that Jordan would receive a 25 percent royalty for every Air Jordan sneaker sold (the originals retailed for $65). It was a huge amount of money for a rookie athlete, and it would mark the beginning of one of the greatest athlete/brand relationships of all time. After the Air Jordan sneaker released, Nike sold one million pairs in the first two months alone.

What a lot of people don't realize, though, is that MJ didn't start wearing the Air Jordan 1 at the beginning of his rookie season. He wore several models, with the Air Ship being the one in which he was most frequently seen. During a preseason game against the New York Knicks on October 18, 1984, Jordan sported the Air Ship in black and red. David Stern, commissioner of the NBA at the time, was at that game and apparently didn't like that Jordan's sneakers clashed with the primarily white and red models the rest of the team was wearing. The league threatened him with a $1,000 fine if he wore that color scheme again; the penalty would grow to $5,000 if he continued.

In the '80s, it was the norm for NBA players to wear primarily white sneakers with one additional color to match their jerseys. Because basketball is a team game, no one deviated from this, and it was understood that players' sneakers should match each other's. Jordan, with a little nudge from Nike, didn't seem to care. He valued camaraderie, and even went so far as to call the black and red sneakers "the devil's colors," but he also didn't mind standing out. The Bulls organization was concerned about this statement and the message it sent to the league. Did MJ think he was better than everyone else? With these revolutionary colors, what was his agenda?

According to sources, Nike planned to feature two primary Air Jordan colorways during Jordan's rookie season: the white/black/red model (now known as the "Black Toe") for home games and the black/red model (now referred to as the "Bred") for road games. The first models Jordan wore for a photo shoot with Chuck Kuhn had the words "Air Jordan" written by the ankle, as the classic "Wings" logo was not yet featured.

The "Chicago" colorway, which was primarily white and red, was apparently not intended to be an original color option. Because of the threat of being fined, Nike was forced to design an alternate colorway that met the NBA's strict sneaker regulations. Officially, Jordan first rocked the AJ 1 in the NBA on November 17, 1984, in a game against the Philadelphia 76ers. As the season progressed, Jordan went back and forth between the Air Ship and his signature model.

The legend of the "Banned" colorway has grown greater and greater over time. During the All-Star Weekend Slam Dunk contest in February 1985, Jordan broke out the black and red colorway and controversy ensued. Nike and Jordan knew he couldn't wear those colors in an NBA game, but the Slam Dunk contest didn't count, so he got away with it. On February 25, however, the NBA commissioner's office sent Nike another reminder that Jordan

was not authorized to wear this colorway in any games. Nike took advantage of Jordan's rebellious nature by hyping up the warning in a commercial. As Jordan stands against a gray backdrop, handling a ball, the camera moves down him as a voice-over explains: "On September 15th, Nike created a revolutionary new basketball shoe. On October 18th, the NBA threw them out of the game." With that, black bars appear over Jordan's sneakers to the sound of a thud. The voice-over concludes: "Fortunately, the NBA can't stop you from wearing them. Air Jordans, from Nike."

Jordan continued to wear the Air Jordan 1 into his sophomore season in 1985–86, but he broke his foot three games in. Nike tinkered with the model to help with his recovery by creating a hybrid Air Jordan 1 with an Air Jordan II sole and an Air Jordan 1 with a Dunk sole. It also designed a model just for him with special straps for added support.

Some thirty-five years after the inaugural Jordan's release, the "Chicago," "Black Toe," and "Banned" versions have proven to be the most popular Jordan 1 colorways of all time, though the "Shadow," "Black/Royal," and "Carolina" models also hold a special place in a lot of sneakerheads' hearts. The exact number isn't known for sure, but there were at least twenty-three different Air Jordan colorways released originally. Nike came out with low-cut models, metallic-colored Jordans, baby models, and a canvas version called the AJKO (some believe it stands for "Knock Off," and others believe it stands for "Knock Out"—a nod to canvas and boxing).

Nike waited ten years before releasing Air Jordan 1 retros, which came out late in 1994 and early in '95, with the return of the "Chicago" and "Bred" colorways. The first retro was not very popular, since most buyers still wanted shoes that were new, with updated designs and technologies like Air Max and Zoom Air cushioning. Jordan Brand waited another six years—after becoming a subsidary in 1997—to release the 1 again, and also released a new mid-top version.

Today, though, it's hard to keep count of the number of Jordan 1s to come out each year; there are hundreds of colorways. The model has seen serious collaborations, with figures like Travis Scott, Virgil Abloh, Dave White, and Anna Wintour, as well as brands like Levi's and Fragment Design, putting their stamp on it by way of some of the most coveted makeups to release. And even if you can't get those versions, you definitely have a go-to. It's a shoe that's become exclusive yet remains inclusive. The player who wore them first has inspired millions. But his footwear was more than an emblem of his achievements. The Air Jordan 1 signaled the beginning of athletes transcending the court—or field, or diamond—and influencing culture as a whole through their dress and taste. It must have been the shoes.

1985

Honorable Mention
Nike Dunk

Never has a shoe been so simultaneously unremarkable and bold as the Nike Dunk. From a design standpoint, the sneaker wasn't entirely unique when it arrived in 1985. It owed many of its clean lines and roomy, uncluttered panels to the Air Force 1, a genre-defining performance basketball model that preceded it by just a few years. Those same lines overlapped closely with the Air Jordan 1, a shoe that arrived a few months before it and one that has long eclipsed the Dunk in many ways. And still, the Dunk is an indelible icon that has been a cultural canvas for different generations that understand the power of footwear.

Where the Jordan 1 splashed a few colors across the league, the Dunk, a collegiate model dubbed the "College Color High" before its release, painted the entire NCAA with its full palette. Thus was born Nike's "Be True To Your School" series of Dunks,

by Brendan Dunne

an original set that remains the most recognizable of the franchise. There was a black pair shining with a school bus yellow made for the University of Iowa. The Kentucky Wildcats version, a rare iteration of which featured the team's logo on the tongue, had a rich blue. And well before the Fab Five made Michigan's Wolverines a household name, the 1985 Dunk designed for the school made maize and blue a potent mixture for footwear.

    The Dunk would have been a significant shoe if its legacy ended there, at the conjunction of collegiate sports squads and sneaker sponsor money. For a while, it looked like it might—the shoe disappeared in 1988 and didn't pop back up until 1998, when it found a home in Nike's burgeoning retro offerings. It was then that the Dunk unlocked its true potential as a vehicle for collaborations and projects that just didn't make sense on other silhouettes. The Wu-Tang Clan flipped the original Iowa colorway into a grail by adding its logo to the heel. This blueprint would resurface endlessly through Nike SB, Nike's skateboarding division, which leveled up the Dunk by soaking it in ever more colors. Certain pairs referenced musical artists or adult beverages without proper legal clearance, creating a new lane for storytelling in sneakers and a cottage industry of resellable releases. The Jordan 1, too indebted to its own heavy history then to be quite so playful, couldn't do it. Nike's other basketball shoes from 1985 and beyond, mostly forgotten in retro runs, couldn't do it. The Dunk did it.

1986 Converse Weapon

Magic Johnson didn't want to make the commercial. Going all the way to some place called French Lick, Indiana? Just so he could shoot an ad for a new pair of sneakers with his archrival, Larry Bird? Hard pass, Johnson thought. Adversaries dating back to their days in college, Bird and Magic weren't supposed to be seen together during the off-season, especially not in front of the cameras, filming an ad for some sneakers. In the 1980s, camaraderie between players on different teams wasn't exactly a thing.

by Adam Caparell

Today's athletes are more likely to be cool with each other, frequently dapping one another up before and after games and refusing to hide their friendship away from the court. But three decades ago, just as the NBA was morphing from niche professional sports league to an association full of superstar athletes who were also cultural trendsetters, you didn't fraternize with the enemy. And you surely didn't film a commercial with him. The idea that Bird and Magic, widely believed to be bitter enemies, would ever team up for *anything* seemed preposterous.

The truth, it would later emerge, was different. Because the day Bird and Magic spent taping their famed commercial, still considered among the greatest ever made for a sneaker, thawed whatever antagonism and false assumptions the enemies on the court had about each other off of it. Shockingly, a friendship blossomed while the rest of the NBA sat stunned, staring at their TVs, trying to figure out what the hell they were witnessing in the name of selling sneakers.

Converse created a sensation with that commercial, the foundation of which was a pair of its new signature sneakers, called the Weapon, which would eventually rank among basketball's most revered. Converse needed to keep up with the increasingly competitive athletic sneaker market of the mid-'80s, and the Weapon's innovation, aesthetics, and impact on the industry still resonate nearly thirty-five years later.

"Internally, it is one of those unique, iconic Converse models," said Sam Smallidge, Converse's archivist. "As much as I would love for people to know our more obscure models from the '80s, it is the Chuck Taylor, the Jack Purcell, and the Weapon."

While the Chuck Taylor All-Star and the Jack Purcell are usually the first sneakers people associate with Converse, the Weapon is largely considered the brand's third-most-important model. During All-Star Weekend in 1986, a year after Nike dropped the Air Jordan 1, Converse introduced the basketball world to the Weapon as it was engaged in an arms race with competitors, trying to maintain its status among the most popular sneaker brands. With a campaign that featured five future Hall of Famers, two legendary college coaches, and plenty of print ads, the company created a sneaker that was practically a classic from the moment it dropped. The Weapon was *the* definitive basketball shoe from the Boston-based brand in the '80s.

"That was the Converse shoe to wear back then," sneaker historian Russ Bengtson said.

Manufactured with injury prevention as its priority, the Weapon evolved from the brand's Maverick and Cimarron models into something much sleeker and more technologically sophisticated than anything Converse had produced. Incorporating the Y-Bar Ankle Support System, the Weapon was engineered to give players a sense of security, with extra padding around the ankle, while offering a level of comfort and traction ideal for the hardwood. In one of its infamous "Choose Your Weapon" print ads featuring Magic and Bird, Converse touted that the Weapon was "incredibly cushioned" thanks to "the Center of Pressure outsole and a shock absorbing EVA midsole." The sneaker was "mechanically designed to help players play their best." And back in the mid-'80s, no two other players were on the level of Bird and Magic. Both were in the middle of their legendary

careers in 1986, having faced off in the NBA Finals three times during the decade, adding epic and dramatic chapters to the Celtics-Lakers rivalry, to this day the league's most revered. Bird was named the 1985–86 NBA MVP during his sixth season after averaging 25.8 points, 9.8 boards, and 6.8 assists per game. The Celtics won an astounding 67 games on their way to being the number-one seed in the Eastern Conference playoffs and won the franchise's sixteenth NBA title, beating the Rockets, 4–2, in the Finals. Wearing a pair of black-and-white Weapons, Bird had a triple-double (29 points, 11 boards, and 12 assists) in the series clincher and was named Finals MVP for the second time. Magic, in his sixth season, would finish third in the MVP voting. In Lakers-colored Weapons, Johnson averaged 18.8 points, 5.9 boards, and 12.6 assists per game. He led Los Angeles to 62 wins in the regular season and the number-one seed in the Western Conference playoffs. The Rockets would upset the Lakers in the Western Conference Finals, preventing a third-straight Celtics-Lakers Finals.

With Michael Jordan having just finished his second season in the NBA, Bird and Magic were undoubtedly basketball's biggest names and, luckily enough for Converse, brand endorsers. They were also complete opposites, and their teams had engaged in absolute battles on the basketball court. Johnson, certainly the more gregarious of the two personalities, has joked that, while he was always open to being friends, Bird wasn't having it. So when they teamed up for an ad pitching sneakers, no one saw it coming.

On paper, Bird and Magic were different for a million reasons, starting with the fact that Bird was from a farm town in southeastern Indiana, while Magic hailed from Flint, Michigan. The two had played together and against each other in the amateur ranks, but by 1986 their rivalry was on a different level. They had already battled for an NCAA championship in 1979 (Magic won) and faced off in the NBA Finals in 1984 and 1985 (Magic won in '84, Bird in '85). For the big-budget ad campaign Converse cooked up for the Weapon, the brand wanted to play up the rivalry between the superstars and how they needed to load up for their battle on the court. The Weapon, of course, is what they would choose to wear into battle. Somehow Converse had to convince Johnson to trek to Bird's hometown to make the vision a reality.

"I did not want to go to Indiana," Johnson told David Letterman in 2012. "I'm going to his home, too. I protested. I didn't want to go."

The commercial's backstory, and how it fostered an unexpected friendship, was told most definitively in Jackie MacMullan's 2009 book *When the Game Was Ours*, further explored in the *Magic & Bird: A Courtship of Rivals* documentary from 2010, and summarized hilariously in the Letterman interview. The story goes that, despite his reservations and hesitance, Johnson showed up to the shoot without much, if any, expectation of becoming buddies with Bird.

"We didn't say too much when I arrived," Johnson told Letterman. "We had actually never interacted with each other."

After the two were done filming the first half of the commercial and it was time for lunch, Magic thought he would head back to his trailer to eat alone. Instead, he was invited back to Bird's house. The story goes that Bird's mother prepared lunch for the pair and welcomed Johnson with a hug that melted all the tension.

"His mom just greeted me at the door with a big hug and that sorta just calmed me down," Johnson said. "I said, 'Wow, I'm getting a Mom Bird hug,' like my mother would hug me. Then she told me I was her favorite player."

The last line was a joke, but when the ad debuted in 1986, it was shocking. The commercial starts with a shot of a black limousine—bearing a blue California license plate that reads "LA 32"—flying down a dirt road in French Lick. It sticks out severely among the vegetation and rural setting of the Indiana town known for its mineral springs that sits an hour and fifteen minutes outside of Louisville, Kentucky. Next, we see Bird, proudly sporting the glorious blond mustache that was his signature during the '80s, grab a basketball and look up toward the ruckus rumbling down the road. The window rolls down, and there's Magic.

"I heard Converse made a pair of Bird shoes," Johnson says as the camera pans down to a pair of black-and-white Weapons on Bird's feet, "for last year's MVP."

"Yep," Bird replies in a midwestern drawl.

"Well, they made a pair of Magic shoes for this year's MVP," says Johnson, the camera zooming in on his Lakers-colored Weapons hitting the pavement after he exits the limo.

The second that Magic finishes tearing off his warm-up pants to reveal his full Lakers uniform, Bird, wearing a Converse

T-shirt, flings a basketball at his adversary. Gritting his teeth, Bird growls, "OK, Magic. Show me what you got." The 30-second spot ends with a voice-over imploring viewers to "Choose your Weapon."

The commercial was a hit and is revered as one of the greatest a sneaker brand has ever produced. But the most interesting subplot in it is that a Bird-Magic bromance began when the two realized they were way more alike than different. They shared similar values, had both grown up poor, and had built themselves into superstars through hard work. On that shoot, Johnson told Letterman, "I got to know Larry the man, and he got to know Earvin the man." When word got around that archrivals Bird and Magic actually became pals while making the spot, it floored their teammates.

"We know on the court they were trying to beat each other's brains out," said Mychal Thompson, Johnson's teammate on the Lakers for five and a half seasons. "It was kind of weird to see those two rivals come together and have such a friendly commercial and hear how well they got along off camera."

Converse didn't limit the marketing of the Weapon to just its NBA headliners. Mirroring what it did with Magic and Bird in print, which readers started to see in publications like *Sports Illustrated* and *Rolling Stone* in the spring of 1986, the brand produced an ad featuring Denny Crum, then the head coach of Louisville, and Bobby Cremins, then the head coach of Georgia Tech, standing back-to-back and holding up the Weapon like a pistol. All the different colorways of the sneaker were displayed, and the tagline read: "Some of America's most respected leaders are turning to the Weapon."

While it would never fly in today's world, Converse went all in on the gun/duel theme to sell the sneaker—the children's version of the shoe was called the Revolver. For another print ad, the brand rounded up three-time NBA All-Star Mark Aguirre and future Hall of Famers Isiah Thomas, Kevin McHale, and Bernard King—along with Bird and Magic—to show off the colorways each player would wear and flaunt its star power. During the '80s, Converse had seven of the ten NBA MVPs on its roster, including Julius Erving, who did not appear in any Weapon ads, since he was a year away from retirement.

The ad featuring the six stars read: "More and more of the NBA's big guns are wielding a new weapon." The copy described the sneaker's technological features below a picture of the six stars either holding the sneaker or draping it over their shoulder.

"For the brand, the print ads served as a way to educate people more about the technology," said Smallidge, "and the video component was more a means to showcase this marketing savvy around rivalries and pitting the two greatest players in the league against each other. It was the perfect marriage of innovative basketball shoe and killer ad campaign."

To top it all off, there's also a thirty-second TV spot in which all six players are rapping about what the Weapon can do for them. Some would argue it's the better and more iconic TV spot than the Bird and Magic ad, since it represents one of the first popular culture crossover moments that saw basketball and rap merge. If that weren't enough to cement its legendary status, you get to hear Bird rhyme in it. Sans mustache, Larry Legend ends the spot first hoisting up a pair of black Weapons, followed by the MVP trophy, bragging, "Y'all already know what they did for me / I walked away with the MVP." The Weapon, along with its clever and popular ad campaign, was arguably the pinnacle of Bird's and Magic's reign as sneaker influencers, thirty years before the term became ubiquitous.

"That was the closest they ever got to doing 'signature stuff' for Magic and Bird up to that point," said Bengtson. "They had just kind of worn whatever. I don't think there was ever any effort to sell a particular Larry Bird shoe. That was the first case where they put out a shoe that [was] directly identified with [Bird and Magic]."

For Converse at the time, the Weapon was *the* sneaker, as evidenced by the fact it appeared on the first page of the company's product catalog in 1986 and '87. After Bird debuted it in the 3-point contest during the 1986 All-Star Weekend in Dallas, the Weapon was touted as the most advanced sneaker when it dropped, and it soon became a bestseller.

"This shoe was created for us to win the basketball market," said Smallidge.

Engineered and manufactured in response to the increasingly competitive sneaker market in the '80s, the Weapon first took shape for Converse when the brand opened its biomechanics lab, because it knew it had to innovate or be left behind. While the company had offered performance enhancements from the Maverick, the first sneaker to feature the Y-Bar Support System, Converse set out to make something even more impactful with the Weapon.

To put it succinctly, the Weapon was fresh. Its most dominant feature, besides the Y-Bar, was its distinct colorways. But print ads played up all of the sneaker's enhanced performance features, like "natural rubber outsoles for traction" and a "shock absorbing midsole for cushioning." Extra padding was added around the sneaker's collar for increased comfort. Sitting between a high-top and a low, the Weapon looked sleeker than the Maverick.

"The Weapon was one of their first shoes that kind of acknowledged the whole shift in the way basketball shoes were going to get made," said Bengtson.

Unlike the majority of today's sneakers endorsed by basketball's biggest stars, who are intimately involved in the design of their shoes, the Weapon did not evolve based on the input of the brand's band of ambassadors. As best he can tell, Smallidge believes the Weapon's creation "was never driven by the athletes." It was internal, and its innovative features weren't limited to the nuts and bolts of the sneaker. The solid-color-blocking patterns that became a signature of the Weapon were relatively new in the mid-'80s. When Converse received its first batch of the green colorway from the factory manufacturing the sneaker, Smallidge says it actually wasn't happy with it. The green was slightly lighter than it should've been, but they still went to market. Converse requested a deeper, darker green for its second run, and that, said Smallidge, is when the manufacturing process really took off.

While its design was unique and made in response to the growing competition between companies like Adidas and a fledgling Nike, the Weapon will always be closely associated with, and likely remembered because of, its ad campaign and its plethora of colorways. Always featuring a solid-colored toe box, the sneaker had the chevron star silhouetted in its secondary color, giving it a distinctive look compared to Converse's previous basketball shoes. Because it was so versatile and Converse's factories had the ability to manufacture numerous variations, the Weapon became a very popular shoe for college teams.

"The Weapon, the way I look at it, was like, 'Oh, shit. If we don't do something in the vein of Jordan, we're going to get left behind,'" said Bengtson.

Internally, there was also a distinct desire for the Weapon to double as a lifestyle sneaker that cool kids and influential individuals would rock away from the hardwood.

"This shoe was our entryway into that broader sneaker culture that was bubbling up in the '80s," said Smallidge. "As iconic as the ad campaign was in terms of putting it on the court, it was also about putting it on kids' feet that go out into the world."

While Smallidge said no individual gets credit for creating or designing the Weapon, like Tinker Hatfield does for numerous iterations of the Air Jordan, somewhere out there is a Converse pattern maker who deserves recognition. It's just never coming because "no one can remember exactly who it was," said Smallidge.

The Weapon was retroed in 2014. The most recent version was updated slightly from the original, as Converse touted that the newest Weapon was lighter and featured a slimmer midsole. It experienced upgrades

in its tongue construction and placement of padding, and the inclusion of memory foam. The 2014 Weapon also featured a different silhouette, since the original version had a distinct heel rise that was left off almost thirty years later. The more noticeable tweaks were bolder branding and colorways that the creators of the OG would have never imagined, like the Patchwork that was as chaotic as it was colorful. In 2012, designer John Varvatos released a premium leather version of the Weapon, meant to give it a vintage look.

Sure, in its impact, the Weapon will always pale in comparison to the Air Jordan 1 and a few other basketball sneakers released in the '80s. But its historical standing will never be lost on connoisseurs and enthusiasts alike. Perhaps its most notable moment since the mid-'80s came courtesy of Kobe Bryant. Bryant wore pairs of Lakers-colored Weapons during the 2002–03 season, when he was a sneaker free agent, just after his deal with Adidas ran out and just before he signed with Nike.

The debate as to precisely where the Weapon stands in the pantheon of iconic basketball sneakers will continue forever, but its influence and ubiquity can't be denied. Worn by some of the best players of the '80s and pitched to the masses in unforgettable ads, the Weapon was a huge hit for Converse—it even set up a toll-free "Weapons Hotline" shortly after the sneaker's release so consumers could find the nearest retailer carrying it. It's a hit Converse hasn't quite been able to replicate since.

"It was huge to sell 1.8 million pairs in a two-year span for a brand that had gotten used to the Chuck Taylor being its shoe for so long," said Smallidge.

Honorable Mention
Nike Sock Racer

By 1986's standards, the Nike Sock Racer is hardly a sneaker. In 2020, though, its design language looks familiar. At the time he conceived it, Bruce Kilgore, who also designed the Air Force 1 in 1982, wanted to create a minimalist shoe for runners in search of lightweight footwear for racing. And he turned that idea up (or down) to 11.

The Sock Racer isn't just bold in its design—it has a Roshe Run–esque midsole that sits atop a mesh upper with two straps and no laces—but also in its color choices: yellow, black, and white. Nike designer Wilson Smith, best known for the Air More Uptempo, created a pair of special socks for the Sock Racer called the "Bee Socks." As their name suggests, they were yellow with black stripes.

by Matt Welty

Nike knew how outside the box the Sock Racer would seem to the public. It ran an ad that said, "Still crazy after all these years." (Nike was only fourteen years old at the time.) Not only was the look of the shoe not everyone's ideal, but, being a racing flat, it wasn't built for everyday wear. In the same ad, Nike put in small text: "The Nike Sock Racer. A serious racing flat with a full-length Nike Air midsole. Definitely not for everyone."

The sneakers weren't all talk, either. Norwegian Olympian Ingrid Kristiansen won the 1986 Boston Marathon in a pair of Sock Racers. Nike even joked that if God wanted your feet to run fast, they'd have come with a pair of Sock Racers on them. The shoes' actual performance record suggests there's some truth to that.

The Sock Racer is significant not only because of this, but because of its influence on modern footwear design. Nike has billed it as the godfather of its Free technology, which it built around the concept of natural motion in running shoes. The idea holds up today, and Nike acknowledged this lineage in the Genealogy of Nike Free collection in 2014. Sock sneakers would become a trend nearly thirty years after the model was introduced. But brands opted for knitted versions, which often looked cheap and missed the point altogether. It's safe to admit that Nike nailed the concept from the start. The Sock Racer wasn't an athleisure model; it was a real performance shoe.

So, then, how do you wear the Sock Racer if you're not running marathons? Likely with no socks and a pair of shorts. Or you buy a pair just to admire it as a piece of history.

1987 Nike Air Max 1

Tinker Hatfield damn near lost his job at Nike because of the Air Max 1. Imagine one of the greatest athletic footwear designers of all time hitting the unemployment line over a model that changed the look of sneakers and the Swoosh's fortunes in one fell swoop. What sounds improbable today almost occurred in the mid-'80s as Hatfield carved a tiny window into the soles of running shoes to birth the Air Max 1.

by John Gotty

Nike's Air technology wasn't new. It was developed by former NASA engineer Frank Rudy, and the company began using it for support in running shoes as early as the Air Tailwind in 1978. Running enthusiasts loved it, even if they didn't know exactly what it was. Up to that point, the tiny bubble units were hidden inside polyurethane soles. Hatfield knew the Air technology could offer more if it could be seen as well as felt.

Nike occupied a much different space compared to the pole position it sits in today. Dwindling sales and strong competition from other footwear brands pushed the company to look for solutions that would turn things around. As Hatfield recalled to *Sneaker Freaker*, former executive Rob Strasser told him, "You guys better do something, because this company is going down!" Hatfield took the directive and set out to create one of his most radical designs to date.

Hatfield is known as someone who looks outside of shoes for inspiration. Random items—sports cars, gym bags, or buildings—informed his designs, which was a drastically different approach at the time. A trip to Centre Pompidou in Paris provided Hatfield with the idea to show people there really was Air in Nike shoes—that it wasn't just a marketing gimmick. The building gained notoriety for its "inside-out" design, with a facade showing its staircases and hallways. This ultimately inspired Hatfield's decision to remove a portion of the midsole foam to reveal the cushioning system of the Air Max 1. "I came back from that trip and I was immersed in working on some new products for Nike, essentially the entire Air Pack," Hatfield told Complex in 2008. "As I was working on the running shoe, which was going to have a bigger Air bag, and I thought, 'This bag is getting so big, it's getting closer and closer to the edge of the midsole on both sides,' I said, 'Why don't we just cut a big hole in the midsole and let the bag kind of be exposed?' In many ways, it almost eliminates the need to talk about it, because now you can see it. The Centre Pompidou was clearly an instigator for me, or an inspiration."

He shared the initial sketches with fellow designer Mark Parker, who later rose to the position of company CEO, and the two hunkered down alongside a few others in a workspace away from the company's main campus. Not everyone supported the idea of a special group being allowed to work in isolation on what appeared to be a bunch of wild ideas that wouldn't amount to anything substantial. Others resisted the idea of exposing the Air unit, calling the move too risky. They imagined tons of defective shoes being returned once the Air units popped, either from using the shoes naturally or because of curious customers who deflated the bubbles themselves.

There was enough concern at Nike that an internal push arose to give the special group pink slips. But Strasser and Peter Moore, another well-respected designer for the company, shielded Hatfield and Parker from anyone looking to derail their creative process. While others sought to get them fired, Hatfield and his co-workers kept moving right along toward refining the initial idea to make Air bigger, better, and visible.

Exposing the Air unit wasn't the only radical change coming with the new model. The bright red material wrapped around the

shoes served as another eye-catching element of the Air Max 1. Leading with a bold color choice went against the conservative wishes of the Nike sales team and retailers, who subscribed to the notion that more neutral colors like white, gray, and navy sold better in stores. But an incremental change would only lead to a small growth in sales, which the company couldn't afford. In essence, Nike bet big on Hatfield.

Despite the mounting number of naysayers, Hatfield knew the shoe would be a hit as soon as he had the final version in hand from the factory. He and Parker could hardly contain their excitement on the flight home from Asia after weeks spent finalizing the product. "I remember sitting on a plane with Mark and we didn't want anyone else to see it, because we were fresh out of the factory," he told *Sneaker Freaker*. "I'd look at it and he'd look at it and we'll look at each other and go, 'Man, this is wild!' I remember both of us pretty much thinking the same thing: 'This is crazy, but this is going to work, and people are going to go nuts!' Sure enough, it just exploded."

The Nike Air Max 1 finally released on March 26, 1987. Despite the detractors, the nylon mesh and synthetic suede mix of the sneaker resonated the most with buyers. "People were looking for something different," Hatfield said in an article published

on Nike.com about the consumer climate at the time. Runners took to the model naturally. What no one could have predicted was how the sporty model transcended its intended market. An influx of non-athletes—entertainers, city dwellers, weekend warriors, rappers, teens, and others—bought the shoe thanks to a new wave of marketing genius. The Air Max 1 connected with a swath of people like no running shoe before it.

The advertising campaigns associated with the model, created by agency Wieden+Kennedy, gave buyers a fresh perspective on Nike products. The company's first television commercial came out in 1987 and featured the shoe, along with superstar athletes like Michael Jordan, Bo Jackson, and John McEnroe, with the Beatles' "Revolution" providing the soundtrack. The spot connected the worlds of music and sports, forming a union that remains as strong as ever today. The print ads drew attention to the newly exposed Air unit by illuminating it and using taglines like "A revolution in motion."

Suddenly, shoes weren't just objects made of rubber and leather whose sole purpose was protecting the feet. They took on a level of personality and importance. They morphed into status symbols that accorded cool to their wearers. Along the way, Nike emerged as the designated purveyor of that cool.

The Air Max 1 holds a high rank in the sneaker world decades after its first launch. The model has been released in countless colors and material mixes, and a variety of forms. Visible Air remains an essential part of Nike footwear across multiple categories and sports. Those once-tiny bubbles have grown in size, shape, and color over the past thirty-plus years. The technology helped spawn countless running models under the Air Max umbrella—the Air Max 90, Air Max 95, and more—each with its own identity, but always with Air as a key element.

Hatfield's gone on to attach his name to too many other silhouettes to count, many of them constructed with the same design ethos he tapped into for the Air Max 1. "Generally something that's actually a little more progressive, and well designed, is either loved or hated," Hatfield explained to Complex in 2008. "There's no middle ground. I look for that kind of design result. People will either love it or hate it. If they're kind of in the middle, I think that means you didn't do too much. That means you just sort of maintained some status quo. That's simply not my job; that's not what I care to do. I don't want to be a status quo designer that skates by with the lowest-common-denominator work."

What started as an experiment in design and cushioning morphed into a career-defining creation for Hatfield and turned Nike's business around. The Air Max 1 challenged the status quo in 1987 and changed the course of sneaker history forever in the process.

Honorable Mention
Nike Air Trainer 1

"You cannot be serious!" This phrase from John McEnroe's infamous outburst at the 1981 Wimbledon tournament is what most casual tennis fans probably remember the '80s star for. He was also a nine-time Grand Slam winner and one of the best players of his era, but his temper made him a household name. To others, particularly those into sneakers, McEnroe is known for his footwear—more specifically, the "Chlorophyll" Air Trainer 1.

    Designed by Tinker Hatfield, the Air Trainer 1 made its retail debut in 1987. But the public's first glimpse of the model took place unexpectedly a year earlier, when McEnroe laced it up on the tennis court. Nike had sent him a prototype, and he was told not to wear it in any tournaments just yet. He loved

by Mike DeStefano

it so much that, true to his rebellious behavior on the court, he disregarded Nike's wishes and wore it anyway. Once he laced the Air Trainers up, they were his go-to. McEnroe kept winning. It wasn't official, but the Air Trainer 1 was essentially his signature shoe, years before Andre Agassi made a statement of his own on the court with his Air Tech Challenge series.

The Air Trainer 1 was billed as the first-ever cross-training shoe, a concept Hatfield drummed up after he noticed people in his local gym switching footwear when going from running to weight lifting. It was made to straddle the line between a runner and a basketball sneaker. As the name suggests, the Air Trainer 1 featured Air cushioning in the heel for comfort. The silhouette's other standout design elements included a forefoot strap for additional lockdown and a lateral outrigger. Its signature black, white, and green "Chlorophyll" colorway was also influenced by Hatfield's gym visits, as he recalled all of the equipment at his particular establishment being black and white with green text.

While McEnroe became notorious for wearing the model, two-sport athlete (baseball and football) Bo Jackson was the official face of Nike's new cross-training division. The partnership birthed the iconic "Bo Knows" ad campaign, and would go on to introduce other popular silhouettes like the Air Trainer SC High and Air Trainer III.

Many more colorways of the Air Trainer 1 would release over the years, Nike's SB division would adapt it for skateboarding in the 2000s, and Hiroshi Fujiwara's Fragment Design even dropped a pack in 2015. But, to collectors, no person means as much to the sneaker as McEnroe, and no colorway beats the original.

1988 Air Jordan III

Just how critical was the Air Jordan III to Nike's legacy? So critical that it's known as "the shoe that saved the brand." The honeymoon phase between Nike, Michael Jordan, and everyone else involved came to an end after Jordan injured his foot very early in his second season in the league. Adding to that was the fact that the Air Jordan II design was nowhere near the hit that the Air Jordan 1 had been. Peter Moore, who designed the first two models, left Nike in 1987.

by Drew Hammell

Then Nike's VP of marketing, Rob Strasser, left as well. The two of them ended up collaborating on their own new sneaker brand, Van Grack. With these two key figures gone, the production timeline for the Air Jordan III slowed down significantly. To make matters worse, Jordan's first contract with Nike was coming up for renewal. Moore and Strasser still had a good relationship with Jordan, and there were no stipulations forbidding the two from speaking to him about switching over to Van Grack and starting his own line.

Fortunately, Nike had a pool of talented designers who were perfectly capable of creating the next Air Jordan model while the company hammered out details of the contract renewal. The designer who rose to the occasion was former University of Oregon pole-vaulter and architecture major Tinker Hatfield. Hatfield happened to be in the right place at the right time. He was on a roll after designing the Air Max running shoe, the Air Trainer 1, and the Nike Mag, which was featured in the hit film *Back to the Future Part II*. These three sneakers were revolutionary for Nike, and that opened the door for Hatfield to work on the Air Jordan III. "It was six months behind schedule by the time [the Air Jordan III project] was given to me," Hatfield recalled in the 2017 documentary series *Abstract: The Art of Design*. "So it had to be another hurry up, no sleep for weeks and months, traveling back and forth to Asia with all the developers and getting a prototype in."

It turned out Hatfield was the perfect designer for the task, as he genuinely wanted Jordan's feedback on the sneaker. Hatfield was so good at interpreting critiques from Jordan and other athletes in part because of his college track-and-field coach: Nike cofounder Bill Bowerman. Like Bowerman, Hatfield was fascinated by the athlete's foot and how it moved. When Hatfield met with Jordan about his next model, he wanted to know what he was looking for. Jordan ideally wanted a mid-cut shoe instead of the typical high-cut sneaker players were wearing at the time. He wanted a shoe that was comfortable, one already broken in, with soft, supple leather. He also liked shoes that were flashy but sophisticated. Hatfield absorbed all that information, and he was ready come presentation time.

Hatfield, Phil Knight, and several other Nike execs flew to California to meet with Jordan and his parents for the big AJ III presentation. MJ was four hours late for the meeting because he was out on the golf course with Nike competitors Strasser and Moore. The two were pitching the idea of Jordan leaving Nike to create an even greater legacy on his own with their new brand. Apparently they did a good job, because by the time Jordan showed up for the Nike meeting, he was in a bad mood and didn't plan on staying long.

Knight handed the meeting off to Hatfield, who began asking Jordan if he remembered the conversation they'd had months earlier about the kind of sneaker he was looking for. Jordan did and began to soften up as they continued talking about his ideal shoe. Hatfield eventually pulled away a shroud from the Air Jordan III prototype, and Jordan fell in love. It was exactly what he was looking for. There was sleekness, there was a new lower-cut height, there was soft, supple leather. There were things Jordan hadn't seen before, like the exotic elephant print and his own logo right on the tongue. Hatfield designed that Jumpman logo, inspired by the famous image of Jordan leaping into the air, and he displayed it on the tongue to ensure everyone knew Jordan was the face of the brand. After the meeting, it was over for Strasser and Moore: MJ was staying with Nike.

Few would dispute that the Air Jordan III is one of the line's most elegant designs and popular models, and that it set a new standard for style and technology. The silhouette was both advanced and sophisticated (and the $100 price tag in 1988 proved it). Its aesthetics—including the "Nike Air" logo on the heel and the absence of an oversize Swoosh on the side, along with its colorways—were eye-grabbing. And like its predecessor, the Air Jordan II, the Air Jordan III was the real deal, both in style and performance. But unlike the previous model, it was the hit Nike needed to propel it, and Jordan, to the next level.

One of the fondest collective memories of Jordan in the AJ III comes from the 1988 NBA All-Star Game in Chicago. While that wasn't the first time he'd worn it—he'd been seen in the "White/Cement" model in several games in November '87—it's a major part of the model's lore. The most important moment of the weekend arrived in the Slam Dunk Contest, which he won for the second-straight time with his signature foul-line dunk. In the All-Star Game itself, Jordan wore the "Black/Cement" colorway in front of 18,403 fans. He wowed the crowd and poured in 40 points, along with 8 rebounds, 3 assists, and 4 steals. That would be the only time all season Jordan wore the black colorway in a game.

That weekend couldn't have gone much better for Jordan and Nike. MJ took home All-Star MVP honors, and on his feet was the Air Jordan III. The fact that Jordan rocked both new colorways was ample marketing in and of itself, but Nike bolstered it even further by premiering Air Jordan III commercials during the second half of the All-Star Game. The commercials featured Jordan alongside a young Spike Lee, aka Mars Blackmon (Lee's character from his film *She's Gotta Have It*). The nerdy, loudmouthed sneakerhead sidekick to Jordan went on to costar in four straight Air Jordan ad campaigns. Nike also bought a two-page ad in the 1988 *Sports Illustrated* Swimsuit Issue that featured Jordan and Blackmon. Those ads, which were produced by the marketing agency Wieden+Kennedy, immortalized catchphrases like "It's gotta be the shoes" and one of Jordan's nicknames, "Money."

"Loved it," Lee said of the Jordan III. "I mean, I loved Jordans from the beginning. That's why Mars wore them in *She's Gotta Have It*. That wasn't product placement. Mars wore Jordans because that shit was hot."

Officially, the "White/Cement" and "Black/Cement" Air Jordan IIIs released in January 1988 for $100. Jordan rocked the white/cement model for the rest of the 1987–88 season before switching to the "Fire Red" colorway for the '88 Playoffs and also to begin the 1988–89 campaign. There was also a fourth OG colorway—nicknamed "True Blue"—which Jordan didn't wear on an NBA court in the '80s. He did, however, wear them during an exhibition game versus Team USA in 1988. He also sported a special PE version that featured a few tweaks in 2001 during his time with the Washington Wizards.

Over the past few decades, it's been tough to keep up with the amount of Air Jordan III retros to come out. By far, the "White/Cement" and "Black/Cement" colorways have been the most popular retro releases over the years, returning for the first time in 1994. Both the OG "True Blue" and "Fire Red" colors have retroed as well.

In 2010, Jordan Brand released a special "Doernbecher" version of the AJ III designed by Cole Johanson, a patient of the children's hospital for which the shoe was named. Along with a red tonal upper, it included plenty of special touches like Johanson's favorite foods (spaghetti and chocolate) written behind the heel tabs, and "Strength" and "Courage" written on the insoles. Like all Doernbecher sneakers, this silhouette was extremely limited, and demand for it was high. Jordan released the model again in 2013, but canceled orders due to a high purchase rate by bots.

The following year, former Oregon Ducks football player Jason Williams partnered with Hatfield, an alumnus of the University of Oregon, to design a Ducks-inspired AJ III. The sneaker was nicknamed the "Pit Crew," a nod to the crazed 1,500 fans who scream in the student section at home games. The Oregon "O" was stitched onto the tongue, while webbed duck feet appeared on the heel. A similar Hatfield PE design came in 2018 in very limited numbers; the shoe featured a nearly all-green upper and a Swoosh inspired by Hatfield's earliest designs of the AJ III. The pairs, which are extremely rare and very valuable, set a new standard for college-affiliated retro creations from Jordan Brand.

Jordan Brand has continued to release both new colorways and OGs over the past few years, including the "Black/Cement" in 2018 with the original "Nike Air" branding on the heel, again demonstrating its commitment to collectors. After the slight dip in popularity brought on by the Air Jordan II, and the shaky handoff from head designer Moore to the young Hatfield, the Jordan line took off with the help of the AJ III. Hatfield went on to design one hit after another for Jordan over the next ten years. The Air Jordan III was the first to feature the Jumpman logo, as well as the first Jordan with a visible Air window. The sneaker helped MJ earn his first MVP and Defensive Player of the Year awards, etching it into the mind of every sneakerhead. Unlike today's players, Jordan primarily wore one colorway for the majority of the season. Everyone knew what he'd be wearing each night, and all eyes were glued to his feet. It was a genius design by a brilliant designer, and the beginning of the greatest designer-athlete partnership in the history of sports.

Honorable Mention
New Balance 576

New Balance owes much of its notoriety, and profits, to the 574 sneaker. For a lot of people, it's the first sneaker they owned from the brand. But the 574 owes its whole existence to the 576.

The 576 was a top-tier New Balance running shoe, built for performance, when it was released in 1988. It had multiple layers of sole absorption, a heel cap, and a suede and mesh upper. Designed by Steven Smith, the sneaker falls neatly in line in his New Balance history, behind the 997, 1500, and 995. It's a shoe that's remained a favorite among connoisseurs, often as a part of the brand's Made in the USA production line, other times manufactured at its Flimby factory in England, and

by Matt Welty

frequently the basis of memorable collaborations with European retailers like Hanon and Solebox over the years.

Popular versions of the shoe include Solebox's "Purple Devil" and Hanon's "Northern Soul" series, which commemorates the popular music genre in the UK. London's Footpatrol has remixed the 576, a version that saw a ten-year rerelease. UK footwear maker Grenson put brogueing on the shoe and gave it a menswear touch. The shoe has taken on bright suedes and mismatched materials, but some argue that it looks best in its original gray and navy.

By contrast, the 574 was, until recently, seen as the New Balance shoe that hard-core fans of the brand like to forget—the mainstream moneymaker collectors didn't want in their rotation. And for good reason. The brand bastardized the shoe. Foot Locker notoriously sold the sneaker via two-for-$89 deals in the 2000s. It was viewed as a discount model from a company that prided itself on quality and craftsmanship. Everything the 576 was, the 574 was not.

The irony of the differences between the two shoes, many of which go unnoticed by the average consumer, is that Smith is often credited with creating the 574, despite having been more accurately responsible for its premium older sibling. His explanation in the past was that the 574 was something of a watered-down version of the 576, a shoddy Frankenstein stripped of its premium pieces and produced by someone else at New Balance. Yes, the 574 has been loads more popular over the years, but those in the know agree that the 576 is the model of that ilk truly deserving of the spotlight. It's the sneaker that's everything the 574 has ever wanted to be.

1989 Air Jordan IV

Legendary performances on the basketball court have always played a key role in the success of an Air Jordan sneaker. One of Michael Jordan's first seminal moments was "The Shot" in 1989. Whether you're a Bulls fan or not, you've seen the clip of Jordan rising up into the air over a flailing Craig Ehlo and sinking that dagger deep into the heart of every dejected Cavs fan. What followed was an ecstatic Jordan, leaping and pumping his fists with those black-and-red sneakers on: the Air Jordan IV.

by Drew Hammell

That mid-air ballet stance Jordan was immortalized in for his Jumpman logo isn't the only floating figure of his burned into the memory of '80s babies.

Since then, everyone from Eminem to KAWS to Travis Scott has put their stamp on the IV. Back in the day, rappers like Jay-Z and Ice-T wore the original models. But the IV wasn't just for hip-hop artists. Doogie Howser, M.D., was known to sport them from time to time as well. The Air Jordan IV was another masterpiece in sneaker design that transcended age and race—primarily and most importantly because of the man who wore it first.

After the overwhelming success of the Air Jordan III, the project lead for the next model was a no-brainer: Tinker Hatfield. But the designer faced a new challenge: How would he follow up one of the greatest sneakers of all time with something even better? The answer was simple: make some tweaks, but keep the overall design in line with that of its predecessor. When Hatfield designed the Air Jordan IV, he kept many of the elements the same. The "Nike Air" logo was again featured prominently on the heel. The Jumpman logo was back on the tongue, with the addition of the word "Flight" underneath. There was a shiny, visible Air unit in the heel, and an encapsulated, responsive Air unit in the forefoot as well. Like the AJ III, the first two colorways to debut were again "White/Cement" and "Black/Cement."

There were some clear differences in the design of the Air Jordan IV, too. After striving for elegance and sophistication with the Air Jordan III, Hatfield opted for a more utilitarian approach with its successor. To enhance performance, Hatfield added "over-molded" mesh paneling to promote breathability. The urethane-coated mesh netting was dipped in soft plastic, then Air was blown through the mesh to clear out the plastic in between. In theory, this new technology allowed the foot to breathe more compared to sneakers with fully leather panels.

Along with the mesh paneling was a synthetic leather called Durabuck on the upper, which was more cost-effective and animal-friendly. The AJ IV also featured multiport lacelocks and wings, which had extra holes on each side of the shoe for a more tailored fit. The sneaker could be laced in different patterns for a more customized look. The words "Air Jordan" were also stitched inside the tongue, upside down. Wearers could flip the tongue down (kind of like the way Jordan stuck his tongue out) so that "Air Jordan" could be read right side up. The design, more complicated than the III's, foreshadowed and set the tone for a decade of techy-looking shoes to come. Lines became more angular, shoes more decorated—the Jordan IV played a big part

Air Jordan IV

in this shift. Though Jordan wouldn't debut the IV until the NBA All-Star Game in February 1989, there was a "first look" image of both the "White/Cement" and "Black/Cement" in the November 16, 1988, issue of *Sports Illustrated*. Sitting on a desk with both colorways, Nike cofounder Phil Knight is seen smiling and holding up the "White/Cement" model.

The official debut of the AJ IV came when Jordan laced it up for the All-Star Game on February 12, 1989, in Houston. MJ rocked the "Black/Cement" colorway in the main event and scored 28 points. Just like the previous year, Nike dropped commercials featuring Jordan and Spike Lee, aka Mars Blackmon, during the game.

And also like the previous year, Nike bought an ad in the *Sports Illustrated* Swimsuit Issue, showing the model. The Air Jordan IV released in the "White/Cement" and "Black/Cement" colorways that month for $110, which was $10 more than the Air Jordan II and Air Jordan III. It was the first global release for an Air Jordan model and was a roaring success.

Adding to the new model's lore was "The Shot," which, on May 7, 1989, sent Jordan and the Bulls into the second round of the 1989 NBA Playoffs. Incredibly, during the timeout before Jordan made history, coach Doug Collins drew up a play to have center Dave Corzine take the final shot. Collins believed the Cavs would never expect Jordan not to get the ball. But Jordan quickly put an end to that plan by slapping the clipboard and shouting, "Just give me the fuckin' ball!"

Jordan credited his focus to a pregame locker room ritual that included listening to "Giving You the Best That I Got" by Anita Baker, a song that inspired him and his teammates to give it their all because they had nothing to lose. "We're going to New York, baby," the twenty-six-year-old Jordan confidently proclaimed after the victory.

That summer, a sample pair of the "White/Cement" Air Jordan IV appeared on the feet of Buggin' Out in Spike Lee's film *Do the Right Thing*. With Lee continuing to link Jordan Brand to hip-hop, the cement was hardening for the rise of sneaker culture in the '90s and beyond.

The next NBA season, two more colorways of the Air Jordan IV released: the "Military Blue" and "Fire Red" versions.

Like the Air Jordan III, the Air Jordan IV has retroed a dizzying number of times over the years, initially returning after Jordan's second retirement from basketball in 1999–2000. Along with the OG "White/Cement" and "Black/Cement" colors, Jordan Brand also released three new colorways over the course of late 1999 and early 2000, first among them the "Columbia" in August 1999. All three featured distinct changes from the originals, including leather paneling instead of mesh and a Jumpman logo on the heel instead of the standard "Nike Air" branding. Though the design variations were not drastic, the new colorways were the first non-OGs to release, ushering in the era of classic Jordan silhouettes presented as "lifestyle" models instead of just performance sneakers. Their success proved that consumers had an appetite for classic silhouettes with a modern twist. This opened up a huge revenue stream for Jordan Brand, which has applied countless new colorways to heritage models in the twenty years since.

In August 2006, Jordan Brand released the "Thunder" and "Lightning" Air Jordan IV models. Both sneakers were sold on jumpman23.com—signaling how sneakers would be bought and sold less than a decade later—and were bundled with matching merchandise, which raised the price of each. The "Thunder" colorway, black with yellow hits, was packaged with a varsity jacket and retailed for a total of $500. The "Lightning" colorway was yellow with hits of black and was packaged with an Air Jordan "Flight" T-shirt; it retailed for $250. Both models were rare when they released, which drove up hype and demand. In 2012, the "Thunder" returned, but the "Lightning" has yet to release again.

The Air Jordan IV has also served as a canvas for artists and brands for decades. The Air Jordan IV "Undefeated" released in 2005, with only seventy-two pairs made. Eminem's Air Jordan IV "Encore" was limited to just fifty pairs back in 2005. His Carhartt release was extremely limited as well in 2015. In 2017, Jordan Brand also teamed up with KAWS, aka Brian Donnelly, to drop a cool grey/black version of the IV. JB retroed a friends-and-family-only "White/Cement" Air Jordan IV, commemorating the movie *Do the Right Thing*, in 2017. In 2018, Travis Scott collabed with Jordan Brand to release his own version of the IV.

More than thirty years after its release, most sneakerheads would rank the Air Jordan IV among the five greatest silhouettes of all time. The design was flawless, and the shoe was easy to wear in any setting. Jordan's game kept on evolving at lightning speed, just like the shoes Hatfield was creating for him. MJ continued to dominate the game in the AJ IV, being named to his fifth consecutive All-Star Game and winning the league scoring title for the third-straight year. Though the Bulls came up short against the Detroit Pistons in the Eastern Conference Finals, Jordan put the league on notice that the team was close to getting to the NBA Finals. His run on the court and in the sneaker world was just getting started.

Honorable Mention
Reebok Pump

Some might have fallen in love with the Reebok Pump when they saw Atlanta Hawks star Dominique Wilkins tell Michael Jordan—through the camera—to "Pump up and Air out" in a 1989 commercial in which Reebok took a not-so-subtle jab at its competitor Nike. Maybe it was when Dee Brown covered his eyes and took flight in the Omni in the 1991 NBA Slam Dunk Contest. Those a little younger might have begged their parents for a pair after watching *SmackDown* and seeing WWE star John Cena pump up the tongues on his pair before hitting a Five Knuckle Shuffle on his opponent back in the 2000s. Whatever your introduction to the sneaker was, there's no denying the significance of the Reebok Pump.

    The technology, which has been used in many designs over the years, debuted in 1989. The high-top basketball sneaker

by Mike DeStefano

designed by Paul Litchfield came with a $170 (about $363 today) price tag, which is expensive even by current standards, but found no problem flying off shelves behind the endorsement of some of the NBA's biggest stars of the era, like the aforementioned Hawks forward and Dennis Rodman. Its selling point, of course, was the basketball-shaped Pump on the tongue, which could be used by wearers to inflate an inner membrane with air for a customized fit. The idea was inspired by an Ellesse ski boot with an inflatable liner—Reebok had recently bought the sportswear company—said to have been suggested by Paul Fireman, Reebok's president at the time.

Reebok's answer to Nike Air was as much a genuine performance tool as it was a fun novelty for kids to mess around with. The brand pulled no punches in addressing its competitor, either. One of the more notable instances arrived by way of a commercial showing two bungee jumpers hopping from a bridge, one wearing Nikes, the other Pumps. The former was implied to have died because his sneakers, at the end shown hanging from the cord, were too loose, as a voice-over said, "The Pump, from Reebok. It fits a little better than your ordinary athletic shoe." The ad was later banned.

The Pump also made notable cameos in cult classic '90s films like *Juice*, *Above the Rim*, and *Wayne's World*. Its overall success prompted Reebok to implement Pump technology across its lineup over the course of the decade in other popular models like tennis pro Michael Chang's Court Victory, the Instapump Fury, and Shaquille O'Neal's Shaq Attaq.

Calling it Reebok's biggest technological achievement might not do it justice.

At the end of the 1980s, sportswear manufacturers realized they could convert prospective buyers into full-on fanatics if they presented them with the proper specs. So, in the decade that followed, brands took full advantage, making shoe designs increasingly complex. Carbon-fiber plates under your foot ensured your athletic maneuvers, if that's what you were actually using the shoes for, were precise. Foamposite uppers ensured

your metatarsals would survive the apocalypse. Casting a long shadow over the 1990s in every chamber of pop culture was Michael Jordan, the omnipresent salesman. Alongside him, though, were athletes like Charles Barkley, Allen Iverson, and Shaquille O'Neal, on whom brands placed similar bets. If the '80s were when sneaker culture began, the '90s saw it proliferate, slowly seeping into the mainstream.

1990 Nike Air Max 90

If you've only worn one pair of Nike Air Max sneakers, there's a high probability it was the Air Max 90. Designed by Tinker Hatfield and released in, as its name suggests, 1990, the shoe wasn't the first Air Max sneaker in the line, but it's certainly the most mainstream—the unsung hero of Nike's Air Max empire. But, while popular, it's still a shoe that's not as currently heralded as other models in the line (mainly the Air Max 1, Air Max 95, or even the Air Max 97). The story of the silhouette isn't something people can recite at the snap of their fingers, or something that Nike even tells at length itself. But it's something worth knowing. And the sneaker's original colorway is perhaps the greatest Nike color scheme of all time.

by Matt Welty

The Air Max 90 doesn't differ a lot from the Air Max 1. It has a slightly bigger Air unit, more construction on the upper, more padding on the tongue. More support. And it upped the ante on how bright a running shoe could look.

The Air Max 1 wasn't just an exercise in creating the future of running shoes, with its Air unit inspired by the see-through structure of Paris's Centre Pompidou building, but it also broke through the barrier of boring, gray running shoes designed for old men. The first two colors of the shoe—white/red and white/blue, as dull as those seem in 2020—were unlike anything else on the market in 1987. And Nike knew that. The ads for the shoe put it simply: "Nike Air is not a shoe. It's a revolution. A revolution that works."

"Most running shoes were either white or dark blue or white and black and gray. There was a lot of gray. Bright colors hadn't hit the traditional running shoe market. When I first drew this one up, I grabbed the brightest color in my felt pen box and drew it up," Hatfield said in an interview floating around YouTube. "I knew I had done the right thing when a shoe reviewer had gotten ahold of this particular model in Great Britain and lambasted it for its bright and garish use of color. And that no one would wear such an abomination. I love to hear that sort of thing, because you're on the right track when people start to criticize."

The bright red was controversial on that shoe even at Nike, and Hatfield had to fight to get it on the first Air Max.

Three years later, there were several other Air Max sneakers under Nike's belt, but none of them seemed to have the cultural resonance and marketing success of the Air Max 1. The Air Max Walker is a shoe that many forget about (it's never been rereleased), and the Air Max Light is a cult favorite, but it doesn't hold up in the lineage of the Air Max line. Then the 90 came.

Its introductory men's colorway, "Infrared," is still the most popular makeup of the shoe to date. It's the right balance of bravado and function. It's a white, gray, and black sneaker, but it also has hits of the brightest red the world has ever seen. It's a color that's not only associated with this sneaker from Hatfield, but also another sneaker he designed a year later, the Air Jordan VI, which Michael Jordan wore when he won his first NBA Championship. In the popular consciousness, it's a color for winners.

It's crazy to think that Hatfield had to fight to get a much more toned-down red on the first Air Max sneaker, and then, when it came time for the Air Max 90, originally referred to as the Air Max 3, that Nike turned the red even brighter. By that point, however, Hatfield was in much different standing with Nike. He wasn't just the left-field thinker who wanted to change the way the sneaker industry worked—he had a proven track record. He had helped bring Jordan back to the brand in 1988 with the Air Jordan III and was the biggest name in footwear design.

In the years following its release, the Air Max 90 transcended sport, becoming a significant sneaker in hip-hop and across subcultures, including grime music, and among core footwear collectors. Eminem, a big fan of Air Max sneakers in general, had a limited-edition Air Max 90 collaboration in 2006, with only eight pairs manufactured, the proceeds from which went to charity. He's not the only artist to put his stamp on the sneaker. Grime pioneer Dizzee Rascal received his own "Tongue n' Cheek" Air Max 90s in 2009 to celebrate his album of the same name. To some, this is one of the best artist collaborations that Nike has ever executed. The details on the shoe, the tongue-colored tongue, the see-through outsole, character on the heel, and input from British design guru Ben Drury all make it one of the most coveted Air Max sneakers, regardless of model.

"[Air Max] was, like, the hood uniform. Trainers were, like, one of the things I was always into as a kid. People were like, 'What trainers you got? What trainers you getting?' It was always a thing," Dizzee Rascal said in a 2019 interview with Complex. "Those are the type of trainers people wore in the areas that we come from." He called the collaboration "a no-brainer."

"That one was real smart—the colors and all that," he added. "The pink tongue was the touch; it was a bit of genius. They were, like, $200 when they came out. Now I saw one on eBay for $8,000. That's mad, because I didn't keep any. I was just giving them away. And I feel like an idiot."

Another person who heightened the legacy of the Air Max 90 was Dave Ortiz, then the owner of Dave's Quality Meats, a New York City skate boutique. His 2005 project with the sneaker was inspired by his favorite breakfast food, bacon, and has become a cult favorite.

"They told me to design a shoe, and they give me three months, four months to do it. And I had no idea. First they asked me, 'What shoe would you do?' And my whole thing is function before fashion. If I'm going to make a pair of shoes that I'm gonna have in my store all day, I might as well have a pair of shoes that I can fucking wear all day that aren't going to hurt my feet," Ortiz said in a 2018 interview with Sneaker News.

"I got an email and they said, 'If you want that shoe, you need to submit it by Monday,'" he added. "It was Saturday and it fucking hit me like a ton of bricks. I was starving and I went to the deli to get a bacon, egg, and cheese, and that was the 'a-ha' moment. I was like, 'What if I designed a shoe to look like bacon?' I was like, 'Everybody loves bacon.' I was like, 'Who's going to hate on it?'"

The sneaker became an underground success and is still one of the most desired Air Max 90s of all time.

Kanye West, ironically, also became one of the faces of the Air Max 90. In 2013, before he separated from Nike, he was spotted wearing multiple pairs of the "Independence Day" Air Max 90 Hyperfuse that came in all red, white, or blue. He even got in a tussle with a paparazzo while wearing them. The shoe had been out for months at the time and even went on sale, but became one of the most valuable Air Maxes on the resale market and was widely bootlegged.

In the years before and since, the Air Max 90 has seen many changes. Hyperfuse uppers. 360 Air Max units. Leather editions. Limited editions. Lightweight editions. Bootie editions, with a pair reworked by Hatfield himself. It's been thirty years since the shoe first came out, and it shows no signs of going away. Need a pair? Just walk into your local sneaker store. Unlike other shoes from its era, you'll find one.

Honorable Mention
ASICS Gel-Lyte III

ASICS may not have the name recognition of Nike or Adidas, but it has long been known for crafting some of the best performance running sneakers on the market. While it's seen primarily as a lifestyle silhouette today, the Gel-Lyte III fit the bill as a performance shoe when it debuted back in 1990.

It was the third model in the brand's Gel series. It boasted a Gel cushioning setup in the midsole, along with an ultra-lightweight upper, and introduced a thicker tri-density sole as well. Designed by Shigeyuki Mitsui, its most notable feature was its unconventional split tongue that aimed to increase comfort by eliminating the movement of a traditional tongue. The design still stands out, but coupled with

by Mike DeStefano

the bright colorways that ASICS dressed it in, like citrus and green, the Gel-Lyte III was unlike any other runner on the market in the early '90s. While it was popular in Europe, there's a good chance that people stateside became familiar with the design in the 2000s and 2010s, thanks in part to premium collaborations with boutiques like Concepts, Solebox, and Atmos. But the number-one collaborator, the man who "made ASICS cool," was Kith founder Ronnie Fieg.

Fieg's first Gel-Lyte IIIs released before his boutique and brand Kith even existed, exclusively at noted New York City store David Z, in May 2007. The multicolored "252 Pack" designs were eye-catching, and the limited trio sold out in less than twenty-four hours after a photo of them was featured on the front page of the *Wall Street Journal*. Other Fieg creations, like 2011's "Salmon Toe" or 2013's "Miami" and "New York" iterations, remain coveted. The designer's infatuation with the Gel-Lyte III started by accident during his childhood, when his mother refused to buy him a pair of the most expensive Reebok Pumps.

"I wanted the Reebok Pumps," Fieg recalled in an episode of the *Complex Sneakers Podcast* in 2020. "My mom bought me a pair of ASICS Gel-Lyte IIIs that were a lot cheaper, and I wore them till I had holes in the soles."

To date, Fieg has designed more than fifty pairs with the running brand, and it all started with the Gel-Lyte III. While he isn't solely responsible for its status, his collabs were instrumental in solidifying the Gel-Lyte III as not only one of the most popular models in the history of ASICS, but one of the most recognizable silhouettes in sneakers.

1991 Nike Air Huarache

"Have you hugged your foot today?" It was the perfect slogan for the futuristic-looking, white-and-neon-colored running sneaker with the big chunky sole and external heel cage. The Huarache was the right sneaker to welcome a decade full of wild new designs and the brightest colors ever seen in fashionable footwear. But what was Nike thinking, removing the Swoosh altogether? That logo was its moneymaker. And why was there so much neoprene? Was the world ready for a Swooshless water-ski bootie sneaker? How was this ever going to sell?

by Drew Hammell

The brainchild of designer Tinker Hatfield, the Air Huarache featured a sock liner whose fit around the foot was without precedent. Bright neon colors were in, and the Huarache sported plenty of vibrant options. The outsole was chunky, like an SUV, but the sneaker itself was light, like a sports car. The Huarache offered something for everyone, but it took some getting used to.

"Only fifty pairs were booked by maybe only one store," Hatfield told Sole Collector in 2012. "[Product line manager] Tom Archie believed in that running shoe so much that he ordered 5,000 pairs, and he didn't even have the authority to. Then he was kind of, in a sense, on the hook for these 5,000 pairs. [*Laughs*.] He took them to the New York Marathon, put them in our booth at the New York Marathon, and started selling them. He sold them all. Now there are 5,000 pairs out there, and the orders just start rolling in. And then the rest is history for that running shoe that, I think, at the end of that first year had sold 250,000 pairs."

The inspiration for the Huarache came from some unlikely places: indigenous Mexican sandals and water skis. Once, when Hatfield was water-skiing, he found himself staring down at the neoprene booties that were securing his feet to the slalom skis. "They just sort of conform around anybody's ankle. The neoprene bootie in a water ski fits a bunch of different people, so I'm thinking, 'That's kind of cool.'"

It was this function and fit of the neoprene bootie that got Hatfield thinking about its use for other types of footwear—maybe something you could run in. As some of the early marketing booklets explained, the vision behind the Huarache was "form follows function." Hatfield wanted to strip the running shoe down to its bare essentials and build it back up, with only the most necessary elements included. For Nike, the function of a shoe is always the same: performance. Nike's goal is always to help the athlete run faster, jump higher, look better, and land softer. These ideals led to advances such as Air Max cushioning and the stretch revolution of the Huarache fit. The Huarache epitomized the philosophy of "less is more" to the athlete.

To coincide with this minimalist tech philosophy, Nike also eliminated the side Swooshes altogether with the Huarache line. In fact, the basketball, running, tennis, and trainer Huarache models barely had any Nike branding on them. "It didn't need a Swoosh, because people knew that only Nike could think of this crazy idea and then pull it off," Hatfield said in a post published on Nike.com.

Internally, at Nike, there were debates about the Swoosh removal. This was a risky move by Hatfield, but, if anything, the lack of a big Swoosh drew even more attention to the Huarache.

Not only was there no Swoosh logo, there was also no visible Air bubble. Hatfield's original sketch featured a visible Air unit in the sole, but the final model ditched the window. This was a somewhat puzzling direction for Hatfield to move in because Nike was becoming famous for its massive visible Air windows, which differentiated the brand from its competitors. Why not build on its success by continuing to use that window? Ultimately, the decision to scrap the visible bubble was the right move, as the final product was eye-catching and extremely cushiony.

Hatfield certainly wasn't the only one working on the Huarache and experimenting with different designs. In fact, some of the most legendary designers of all time were involved in the Huarache creative process. The godfather of Nike SB, Sandy Bodecker, also had his hand in the creation and naming of the shoe. "The first sketch sort of showed this neoprene idea with this exoskeleton over it, and Sandy, he thought it was really cool, and in a red pen, he just wrote, 'Sneaker of the Gods,'" Hatfield told Sole Collector in 2012. "Like, it looked like something that Zeus would wear—like a sandal, kind of like a sandal. I was not thinking sandal or Huarache or anything at the time; it was Sandy who wrote 'Sneaker of the Gods,' and [he was] kind of thinking, 'Yeah, this is what Zeus would wear, or Mercury or somebody.'"

It was this ability to brainstorm and think outside the box with his colleagues that allowed Hatfield to come up with ideas for a shoe that had never been considered before. Hatfield, ever the sponge, was always learning from his experiences and incorporating lessons he learned into his designs. In a way, he was sharing a story with his designs.

"So I came back. I'm going, 'It's sort of like a sandal.' And then I'm going, 'I don't want to call it a foot sandal or something,'" Hatfield told Sole Collector in 2012. "So a lot of us had been to Mexico, and I'm thinking, 'Instead of calling it a sandal, I'll call it a Huarache.' So that's how the whole thing got started."

A "huarache" is a leather-thonged sandal worn by indigenous Mexicans, and was popularized in the United States by '60s hippie culture. In the late '80s, it was Hatfield and Bodecker who bounced different concepts off each other to modernize the term.

Along with Bodecker, Hatfield credits Michael Donohue and Mike Quinn with the design of the Huarache runner. The group quickly realized that they could apply the sneaker's ethos to other major categories, like basketball and cross-training.

To handle the basketball model design, Hatfield handed the reins to Eric Avar. "He was still pretty young at the time, so it was just sort of given to him to finish it all off," Hatfield told Sole Collector in 2012. "So he finished his design, put in some of the other little details, and he did the outsole, too. I didn't do that particular outsole. He took it to its conclusion, and that was because I was busy working on the cross-trainer. He was doing this one, and the running shoe was kind of just up and rolling. So that's really how it got sort of birthed."

Just like the runner, the basketball model took off in popularity, with Dream Team member Christian Laettner sporting it on the '92 US Olympic team, the Fab Five players rocking it at Michigan, and Scottie Pippen wearing it in the pros.

To hype up its latest footwear breakthrough, Nike's print ad campaign was equally bold and in your face. "Have you hugged your foot today?" asked one of the ads. "The future is here. In sizes 6 to 15," said another. And, "Yo Buck Rogers. Your Running Shoe Is Ready," referring to the character in the novella *Armageddon 2419 A.D.*

Along with the print ads came a legendary commercial for the Huarache line produced by marketing agency Wieden+Kennedy. For the commercial, W+K wanted to use John Lennon's hit song "Instant Karma!" For that to happen, however, it needed permission from Lennon's widow, Yoko Ono. Nike had gotten itself into some hot water in 1988 when Apple Records sued the company, its ad agency, and EMI/Capitol Records over their use of the song "Revolution" in a famous commercial featuring Michael Jordan, John McEnroe, and other athletes. So, to avoid a similar outcome, Nike execs went to New York to meet with Ono and her attorney to discuss the brand's newest campaign for the Huarache line. After they presented the concept for the ad, Ono gave permission for the rights to "Instant Karma!" The fee was the largest licensing deal for music Nike had ever paid.

The commercial, featuring athletes like Michael Jordan, Scottie Pippen, and sprinter Michael Johnson, was a hit and aired during prime-time sporting events like the '92 European Cup soccer final and the Wimbledon final. Ono was so pleased with the ad, she even wrote a letter to Nike attorney Mark Thomashow after it was released, sharing how touched she was. Directed by David Fincher, the commercial won the prestigious Cannes Bronze Lion award at the 1992 Cannes Film Festival.

Along with the initial running, training, and basketball models, the floodgates opened for other models to use the Huarache neoprene bootie. The Mowabb, the Huarache Light, the Huarache International, the Huarache Plus, the Air Revaderchi, Andre Agassi's Air Challenge Huarache, Scottie Pippen's Air Dynamic Flight, and, of course, Michael Jordan's Air Jordan VII

all incorporated the Huarache language into their designs. Toward the mid- to late '90s, the Huarache would go into hibernation as visible Air Max technology and Zoom Air took center stage. In the early to mid-2000s, though, Nike would begin to release some retro models. It also created a revamped basketball version called the Air Zoom Huarache 2K4, which had great success thanks in part to stars like Kobe Bryant sporting it. Starting in 2012, Nike swapped out the famous big sole for a more minimalist option and debuted the Huarache Free running, basketball, and training sneakers. Many of the original models returned to retailers, with the popular running, training, and basketball iterations leading the way. Today, it's difficult to walk down the street without spotting two or three people wearing a Huarache running shoe or a sneaker owing to Hatfield's water-ski-bootie-inspired design. Of all the sneakers Hatfield has designed over the years, the Huarache was one of his biggest risks. "You take these risks. You go to a new place. You really don't know if it's going to work," Hatfield said in an article published on Nike.com. "The Air Huarache validated to us that sometimes you can take a bigger risk, and if you work hard, everything else falls into place. It changed the way that everybody thought about shoes."

Honorable Mention
Air Jordan VI

The Air Jordan VI will always be a crucial part of Jordan Brand's history. Its design tells the tale of Michael Jordan's love for sports cars and speed, complete with a fire-red spoiler on the back. And it carries Tinker Hatfield's signature aesthetic, which looked to unconventional sources for inspiration.

But that's not what makes this silhouette so special. Jordan wore the shoe when he and the Bulls took down the Magic Johnson–led Lakers in 1991 to notch Jordan's first championship, beginning his flawless 6–0 Finals record. The importance of that win, which transformed the narrative around the Bulls superstar, to Jordan's legacy as a basketball player cannot be overstated. The same goes for the sneakers he wore, which were immediately imbued with a new weight, his legend growing.

by Ben Felderstein

In 1991, the VI debuted in a "White/Infrared" colorway that was soon followed by a "Black/Infrared" counterpart, as well as the "Maroon," "Sport Blue," and "Carmine" iterations. Today, the "Black/Infrared" makeup—the one MJ wore in the title-winning game—is regarded as one of the best original Jordan releases of all time, having been retroed four times since its initial drop, in 2000, 2010, 2014, and 2019. In its retro lifecycle, the shoe was adopted by Kanye West and his circle of Chicago creatives, who were particularly drawn to that makeup.

Like other models, the Jordan VI has further immortalized its namesake player's story, highlighting major moments in his career through its design flourishes. Drops have paid homage to his first ring, his championship celebration, his endorsement deal with Gatorade, his "Black Cat" nickname, and more. The shoe also made an appearance in the '90s anime series *Slam Dunk*, which was referenced by Jordan Brand in a special-edition pair in 2014.

The Air Jordan VI has also been sold in a handful of two-sneaker packs, including the Defining Moments Pack in 2006, a Countdown Pack with the Air Jordan XVII in 2008, an "Infrared" Pack in 2010, and again in a Golden Moments Pack in 2012, only proving the shoe's popularity.

The VI remains sought after, anchored not just by retro returns but high-profile collaborations with the likes of Travis Scott, stylist and model Aleali May, and French football club Paris Saint-Germain. Though it's not currently as lauded as more iconic models like the Jordan 1 and the Jordan III, the Air Jordan VI is an essential collector's piece and a legit artifact of sports history.

1992 Vans Half Cab

by Anthony Pappalardo

In 1992, the market for skateboarding footwear seemed narrow and niche. Vertical skating—once the most popular and profitable discipline—had experienced a downswing as street skating eclipsed it. The shift was a bit of a mirage, though, as skateboarding itself had scaled back and the industry hit a lull, with larger companies becoming doughy and antiquated as nimble, skater-owned brands produced graphics and shapes that mirrored what was on the minds of street skaters.

The shoe category was small, with Vans, Airwalk, Etnies, and a once-dominant, now-dormant Vision Street Wear owning most of the market. With the exception of Vans, which was still selling the Era and the mid-top Chukka boot, a model that had caught on via legendary street skater Matt Hensley, most brands were mainly producing high-tops, riding the insight that they offered more stability and ankle support. Not only was this later proven trivial by many shoe designers, but many street skaters, especially those driving innovation, eschewed highs for lower-profile shoes, often looking for deadstock from Adidas, Nike, and Reebok, none of which were in skate as a category at the time.

Those given product by the skate-centric brands took to modifying the high-tops in their boxes, cutting them into lows or mids, often masking the seams with stickers or duct tape, or even sewing them. With many shoes mimicking the silhouette of the Air Jordan 1, there was a logical cut line on models like the Airwalk Enigma and the Caballero Pro, Steve Caballero's signature shoe. But it was the Cab that caught on and became an integral part of the evolution of skate footwear.

Though Caballero's original Vans shoe was instantly popular, the second iteration of his model crystallized the shift to skate footwear specifically aimed toward street skating. From 1989 to 1992, skateboarding was changing so rapidly in both style and product development that each year was almost a distinct era. Because Caballero had intuition and access to Vans's production capabilities, he was able to react to that change and keep skaters away from the scissors and the department store sale racks. In its original form, the Caballero Pro was iconic, but the Half Cab, released in 1992, signaled a sea change in skate shoe design.

But it started, indirectly, with the Air Jordan 1. With its thin sole, padding, and leather construction, the Jordan matched skating's needs, but its price point—$65, or roughly $150-plus in 2020—was prohibitive, especially for those who had access to Vans outlet stores or department stores where similar-looking high-tops went for less than half the price. It wasn't until an overproduction of Air Jordan 1s led to the legendary sneakers landing on sale racks at a price comparable to those of Vans that skateboarders began to adopt the shoe. The most visible to do so were Powell-Peralta's Bones Brigade, due to their contest dominance and the exposure offered by the emerging medium of skateboard videos, pioneered by the brand's cofounder, Stacy Peralta.

Dubbed the Bones Brigade in 1979, the core pros who defined the team were '80s riders Steve Caballero, Tommy Guerrero, Tony Hawk, Mike McGill, Lance Mountain, and Rodney Mullen. Though the Brigade's list of alumni runs deep, the aforementioned members were constants in the brand's string of videos, which elevated them to stars. Despite their rise in skateboarding and penetration of pop culture, most of their revenue came from board royalties—roughly a dollar per deck—not the footwear contracts that would outweigh hard good sales in skateboarding's modern era.

As the last-remaining and longest-tenured member of the original Bones Brigade, Caballero is an anomaly in skateboarding. He's maintained the same board sponsor for his entire career—a rarity in the industry. In 1989, Caballero became the first member of the Brigade to receive a signature shoe. But he was not the first pro skater with his own model. Etnies, a French company, had earlier released shoes for Natas Kaupas and Pierre André Senizergues in Europe. But, at least initially, neither design saw great popularity stateside.

Since signature models were uncharted territory, Caballero's approach to his own shoe was almost blasé—he'd had his name on skateboards for years, so what would be the difference with a pro shoe? After an initial disagreement with Vans over his contract, Caballero took the advice of Bones Brigade teammate Mountain and signed the deal.

"I didn't think anything was lacking [in skate shoes]," Caballero said. "I just wanted to design something good for skateboarding. At that time, we were really stoked on the Air Jordan. I brought the design to Vans and they had already been working on something that was similar to my drawings, so instead of using my initial drawing, I used what they presented to me. I was just happy to be getting a shoe. I wasn't that opinionated."

During Vans's restructuring in the '90s, two women would become integral to not only the brand's reemergence but also to the creation of Caballero's first two models with Vans. "Adaline Harrell and Bunny Caminiti, one of the early developers for Vans. Bunny, who was a pattern maker, designed the Half Cab, Caballero, and Mountain Edition," Vans's senior director of global footwear design, Rian Pozzebon, told *The Editorial Magazine* in 2017. "Before there were designers, there were just pattern makers who would generate designs. Bunny was the main pattern maker, so she would talk about the design with somebody and then she would go make the shoe. If you look back at our history, at the Mountain Edition, the Full Cab, and the Buffalo Boot, you'll see that they are similar patterns. Basically, they would just remove a panel from the pattern and it would be released as a different shoe."

In 1984, Vans had filed for bankruptcy, and eventually emerged from its $12 million debt to creditors in 1987. By 1988—the year it signed Caballero—it was ready to recommit itself to skateboarding. That gap, however, allowed Airwalk to establish itself, with Hawk on board, though it didn't initially release a signature shoe with him. Vans—specifically Caballero's pro shoe—was instantly not only more visible, but offered functionality germane to street skating's progression. Airwalk's designs often employed layers of rubber and adornments that added little more than weight. Many have mentioned altering the shoes to remove the cardboard insoles to make them more pliable.

With its vulcanized rubber waffle sole, the Caballero Pro was essentially a flexible Dunk or Jordan 1, so a few minutes with a pair of scissors or a razor blade could turn the high-top into a lower-profile shoe that offered both grip and mobility.

"Around 1990 or 1991, people were cutting them down," said Chet Thomas, a former pro and the owner of Darkstar Skateboards. "The first person I saw doing it was either Eric Koston or Danny Way—maybe they were both doing it at the same time. I noticed it at contests, originally. Alphonzo Rawls comes to mind, too—he might have been one of the first as well. The reason why everyone chose that shoe was because the Cab was a great shoe, but the high-top had one layer of foam that was easy to cut down. You just drew a line and put one layer of duct tape over the exposed foam, fold it over, and there you go. It was quick, easy, and it achieved what you were after. And the toe was super good; it didn't wear through super quick. They nailed it."

While he was known for his vertical skating, Caballero had always been an all-terrain skater. So after noticing pros and amateurs skating his cut-down pro model, he communicated the idea to Vans. Roughly six months later, Caballero's second shoe was released as the Half Cab—an homage to the truncated version of his namesake trick, the Caballerial. The most notable changes, other than the shoe's height, were the branding and materials, leaving the core design mostly intact, save for minor tweaks to the toe and sidewall. Abandoning the reptilian leather accents, the original Half Cab opted for an all-suede construction to allow an even break-in and replaced the dragon-inspired typeface with "Half Cab" embroidered on the upper with a Jumpman-esque icon of Caballero performing the move, later changed to a sewn-on tag still offered on the shoe today.

"They didn't give me any grief," Caballero said of bringing the idea to Vans's design department. "It just worked out. There were no problems in presenting the idea—it all fell in place really quickly. [Having a signature model] wasn't a thing. Once they saw my shoe was doing well, a lot of other companies jumped on the bandwagon."

The Half Cab became skateboarding's

de facto street shoe. Few riders were receiving checks from shoe sponsors, giving them the leverage to wear what they wanted without consequence. Unlike Caballero's original model, which was offered in only a few colorways, the Half Cab came in multiple colorways and with various midsole colors, as well as in customizable makeups, allowing the shoe to feel individualized despite its popularity.

"I always dug the support Half Cabs provided because of the extra suede and being a mid-top," said former Bones Brigade member, professional skater, and musician Ray Barbee. "My flat feet need it."

Videos and skate periodicals were rife with people skating the shoe, and the profiles of its supporters propelled it to canon. Eric Koston, Mike Carroll, Salman Agah, Rick Howard, Julien Stranger, John Cardiel, Kareem Campbell, Danny Way, Ray Barbee, Kris Markovich, Guy Mariano, Fred Gall, and Keenan Milton—most of whom didn't officially skate for Vans—logged footage or landed covers in the shoe. In 1993, the Half Cab was featured on at least six of *Thrasher*'s twelve covers. Carroll—cofounder of Girl Skateboards, Royal Trucks, and Lakai Limited Footwear—has released several models inspired by or at least referencing the Half Cab, including his first and only signature shoe for Vans, which updated the design with mesh and cord lacing, and the Mike Carroll 4 and Mike Carroll Select Mid with Lakai. Carroll's Vans model was retroed in 2011 through a collaboration with Supreme.

Most important, with skaters ranging from Mark Gonzales to Jeff Pang sporting it in mags, the Half Cab never felt like a shoe only one *type* of skater wore. Also, for as much attention as street skating was receiving, vertical skating was feeding off its energy, with Way, Colin McKay, Bucky Lasek, Bob Burnquist, Alphonzo Rawls, and others bringing technical street tricks to transition. Rawls would actually go on to become a successful footwear designer, beginning with his contributions to Kastel and later DC, Duffs, Axion, Gravis, Osiris, Adio, Fallen, Globe, Circa, and others.

Though the original Caballero Pro was itself retro-inspired, the lift felt less obvious in 1992, as the Jordan franchise was still of its time, with Michael Jordan himself playing and dominant. A new Jordan release ostensibly rendered the prior model obsolete, or at least out of vogue, so by 1992—before the retro craze began—Air Jordan 1s were seen as relics and so far out of the public consciousness that few connected the Half Cab to the past. Conversely, Etnies and Airwalk picked up on the shoe trends partially sparked by the popularity of the Beastie Boys' *Check Your Head* and the interest in old-school sneakers and vintage clothing it inspired and delivered takes on Puma Prowlers and Adidas Gazelles and Campuses, while the Half Cab and Vans in general built on the heritage design tenets of grippy rubber and classic lines. Through that lens, the Half Cab answered a need in skateboarding for a street-oriented shoe with its own identity, contributing to its timeless standing in skateboarding. Caballero himself doesn't overthink its success, crediting it to serendipity more than marketing.

"If you look back, there wasn't much push for it—it's always been a sleeper in their line," he said. "The design has stood on its own without any extra promotion. There's not much you can do with that design to make it better—it doesn't need anything."

Vans's senior director of footwear design, Nate Lott, echoes Caballero's take on the Half Cab's longevity, describing the lengths to which the company goes to preserve its legacy. "The Half Cab really does revitalize itself. It's such a unique shape and stance that people gravitate toward every few years," he said. "We make sure to get Steve's approval for collaborations, and we've made it a policy to keep the labeling/branding consistent on collars."

Even as competitors upped their mid and low offerings, the Half Cab remained a staple years after its introduction, with little marketing other than organic endorsements and a few print ads. The shoe's popularity continued into the mid-'90s, with many skaters choosing a "tongues-out" approach, often lacing them up to the logo and pushing the tongue out at the rivet and sometimes stuffing an additional tongue behind the existing one to make it more pronounced. Just as they did with the original Caballero, some went as far as to perform minor surgery by opening up the top of the tongue and adding padding or a (hopefully clean) sock into the sleeve for effect. Even as companies such as DC and éS focused on technology, adding air bubbles, thicker insoles and outsoles, and taking influence from athletic brands, the Half Cab stayed in vogue and true to its original design. Caballero and Vans eventually introduced the Low Cab, Half Cab Two, and Half Cab Lite, but the original iteration of the shoe has remained, with few tweaks throughout its twenty-five-plus-year existence.

The Half Cab has also been the foundation of high-profile collaborations and customizations, arguably making it the first model co-designed by a professional skateboarder to see that kind of treatment.

For Caballero, one of the most important milestones associated with the shoe calls back to the band he's often credited with introducing to skateboarding—a then-burgeoning Bay Area thrash outfit called Metallica. "I heard them first through [pro skater] Tom Groholski—he gave me a tape," he said. "I was into punk rock, but when I listened to them, they were a metal band that seemed to have a punk edge. When I started getting into them, I noticed that Cliff Burton would wear a Misfits shirt, so I knew they were into punk. You could just tell they had that feel. The music was really driving and went well with vert.

They were one of my favorite bands for the longest time, so doing a signature Half Cab with them was neat—working really close with them, getting to know them, to the point where I got to interview James Hetfield for Vans. To look back on that—having a shoe attached to Metallica [released in 2012] is amazing."

Caballero's talked about his desire for the Half Cab to have its own devoted team to carry on the shoe's legacy, but its presence remains as organic as its origins. For the next generation influencing and shaping skateboarding, the shoe's relevance stretches past its functionality and look. "Half Cabs have always been special to me because they were made for and by a legend," said Baker Skateboards professional and Vans team rider Kader Sylla. "And they just feel good when they are on my feet."

Honorable Mention
Reebok Shaq Attaq

Reebok landed the athlete of a lifetime when it signed Shaquille O'Neal to an endorsement deal before his rookie season. The game-changing center, selected first by the Orlando Magic in the 1992 NBA Draft, made perfect sense to become the brand's first athlete with a signature sneaker. And in the ensuing years, O'Neal's footwear franchise yielded a few noteworthy models, perhaps none greater than his first, the Shaq Attaq.

After it inked O'Neal's deal in June, Reebok tasked designer Judy Close with one big order: building a shoe for Shaq to wear for his first NBA season, set to begin that October. As if the time constraints weren't enough, Close had to construct a shoe that could withstand O'Neal's size 20 feet and look good enough for a consumer who wore a more standard size to buy. Thankfully,

by John Gotty

the player was an enthusiastic collaborator. "He basically gave us direction for what he liked and where we should go," Close told Sole Collector in 2017.

The model arrived with uppers done in leather and suede, and featured Reebok's Pump system, which gave it a customizable fit. Underneath, a Graphlite plate created extra support in the midfoot while streamlining the shoe in the process.

Reebok took a simple approach to colorways for the original release, opting for looks that complemented the Magic's uniforms: a tonal black pair with azure blue accents and a white-based pair with measured amounts of black, azure blue, and steel gray. The shoes didn't require fireworks; O'Neal supplied enough excitement with his play on the court. Each game produced new highlights, with the big man banging on opponents left and right. He put rims in danger and broke backboards in games against the New Jersey Nets and Phoenix Suns.

Those vicious attacks inspired O'Neal's logo, which, while similar to another famous flying logo, was unmistakably his own. "The emblem was based off of Michael Jordan's emblem and the way he dunked," O'Neal explained to *Sports Illustrated Kids* in 2013. "I dunk with two hands and knees up. I patented that in high school, patented it as well in college. I patented it then because I knew if I became big time, that that would be my emblem."

As big as he was, Shaq's exuberant personality and million-dollar smile made him the perfect pitchman for a slew of companies. He embraced the role by wearing Shaq Attaqs in every commercial, movie, and TV appearance he made. In turn, fans, especially young ones, fell in love with the player and his shoes.

1993 Nike Air Force Max

Nike earned much of its current cachet as the world's leading sportswear brand through the shoes it produced in the early 1990s and from the athletes who wore them. And while the company created sneakers for almost every sport imaginable, it built the bulk of its reputation on basketball courts across America. By the early '90s, Nike regained its position as the leader in athletic footwear after losing the spot to Reebok some years prior. When it came to basketball, Nike dominated from the pros to collegiate ranks, and no other brand came close. "Nike's association with elite US athletes dwarfs that of any other company," *Sports Illustrated* reported in 1993. "Of the 320 or so NBA players, 265 wear Nike shoes, eighty-two of them by contract. Half the teams that have won the NCAA basketball championship in the past ten years have worn Nikes, and more than sixty big-time colleges are 'Nike schools' because their coaches are Nike coaches."

by John Gotty

Sure, other brands like Adidas, Reebok, and a handful more existed. It's just that Nike offered the most outstandingly designed and innovative shoes.

Nike simply worked with the best of the best in basketball. The list begins with Michael Jordan but also includes '90s hoops heroes Charles Barkley, David Robinson, Scottie Pippen, Penny Hardaway, Alonzo Mourning, and more. The majority of the aforementioned players wore shoes from either the Flight or Force series. Agile guards and wingmen with games built around quickness and finesse leaned toward the Flight collection. All of the models in the Force lineup were built to support workhorse types and to withstand the endless banging those players might put the shoes through during the course of a game.

Of the two groups, Barkley held a membership in the Force family dating back to when he entered the league playing for the Philadelphia 76ers. As his game grew, so did his role as an endorser, until he eventually became one of the key faces of the Force. Throughout his career, he had eight shoes, six of them official signature models. While the Flight and Force are both great, the Air Force Max deserves recognition as the shoe Barkley wore when he hit the pinnacle of his game.

Designed by Steve McDonald, who also cofounded Nike's ACG category, the Air Force Max was built for the brutish performance of someone like Barkley. The upper consisted of leather for the two white-based models and a soft Durabuck for the black colorway. A midfoot strap provided the lockdown fit many athletes preferred at the time. The EVA overlays extending from the midsole further locked the foot in place, but they served a dual purpose, since the three "teeth" also gave the model a more menacing look. From a design perspective, the Air Force Max best exemplified Nike's basketball footwear of the '90s: hulking, aggressive, and functional.

But the most notable technical feature of the sneaker was the actual Air. At the time, the 270 Air unit stood as the biggest version of Air Nike had implemented in a basketball shoe. The Force Max's oversized bubble wrapped around the heel, providing a clear look into the cushioning. Nike applied the new and improved cushioning system to several runners released around the same period, like the Air Max 93 and oft-forgotten Air Burst. It represented the continuous evolution in technology from Barkley's previous shoe, the Air Force 180. As his shoes evolved, so did Barkley's role, both as a player and an endorser.

Nike preached how improving the athlete's performance drove every innovation the brand developed. But by the mid-'90s, the company also specialized in the marketing of athletes and products far better than any sporting company had done before. The Air Force Max coincided with one of Nike's most memorable marketing pushes of all time. In the world before social media and influencers, footwear brands were more limited in how they—and the athletes they sponsored—could push their products. And Barkley thrived as one of Nike's main pitchmen.

But "Sir Charles" didn't act as kindly as his royal nickname would have people believe. He never minced words when asked his opinion and racked up fines from the league for run-ins on and off the court. He even threw an occasional person through

a glass window if he got really rankled. He served as the antithesis to Jordan, even though the two were great friends. Jordan operated above the rim; Barkley used a ground-and-pound attack on his way to the basket. Barkley's fiery nature contrasted MJ's cool and controlled demeanor. One was the perfect spokesperson, while the other was far from it.

Barkley made headlines in 1993 when he appeared in a black-and-white commercial, created by Nike's longtime agency partner Weiden+Kennedy, for the Air Force Max. In the spot, he delivered a stiff dose of reality to the world: "I am not a role model. I'm not paid to be a role model." The future Hall of Famer reminded viewers that his job was to "wreak havoc on the basketball court," not mold their children into productive members of society. "Parents should be role models. Just because I dunk a basketball doesn't mean I should raise your kids."

For all of Barkley's bluster about not being a role model, he performed like a player any coach would love to have on the roster. During the same 1992–93 season, he won the league's Most Valuable Player award, averaging nearly 25.6 points and 12.2 rebounds per game while leading the Phoenix Suns to a 62–20 record. The team made it to the NBA Finals, where they eventually lost to the Bulls in a six-game series. But Barkley was a valiant foe for MJ's Bulls, putting up 42 points in Game 2 against Chicago's vaunted defensive unit.

What Barkley did for Nike and the Air Force Max on the pro level, the Fab Five replicated and amplified in the college ranks.

The Fab Five consisted of University of Michigan basketball players Chris Webber, Jalen Rose, Juwan Howard, Ray Jackson, and Jimmy King, five freshmen who shook the basketball world when they all started in the 1991–92 season. Wolverines coach Steve Fisher made an unprecedented but not unwarranted decision, considering four of the five were McDonald's All-Americans coming out of high school. The whole group played with a level of cockiness matched only by their talent. Like Barkley's, their brand of basketball was brash, unapologetic, and in your face at all times. But fans loved the rambunctious, fun-loving approach from the new kids on the block.

The Fab Five did everything in their own style. Thanks to Nike, the Michigan crew sported quite a few revered '90s hoops shoes, like the Air Maestro, Air Max Strong, and Air Unlimited. But their legacy remains firmly attached to two models: the Air Flight Huarache, a sneaker recognized for its sock-like bootie and a shape built for movement, and the Air Force Max, the black version of which matched the edginess with which they played during that second season together. They cut an intimidating figure when they marched onto the court wearing baggy maize shorts, black socks, and black Force Max.

"I remember [equipment manager] Bobby Bland. He distributed the shoes. He came in the locker room, and drops a lot of Nikes out on the floor," Rose said, recalling when new shoes arrived for the team. "We picked them up, tried them on, and kicked the tires a little bit. We were like, 'We aren't wearing none of them.' He was looking at us like we were crazy, but we were serious.

"We realized when we signed the letter of intent, we basically signed a shoe contract. So we said, 'You get on the phone, call Nike, and tell them to come correct.' They didn't have any Jordans, Deions, Bo [Jacksons]—what's going on? So a week later, I can't even front, they came correct. They stepped up. He came back with a big duffel bag and dropped them all on the floor. He had the Barkleys, the Huaraches, all of them. We wanted those."

Michigan's freshmen weren't the only ones who wanted the shoes. The quintet's on-court attire crossed over to the streets. While older generations turned their noses up at the group's garb, every kid in America converted to knee-length shorts and trashed their white socks in exchange for black ones, just like the Michigan starters.

By their sophomore year, public sentiment had shifted and the babyface ballers soon became the bad guys to some segments. "The Wolverines' extraordinary accomplishment of last year, reaching the NCAA Finals with an all-freshman lineup, has evolved from cuteness to disdain, mostly because of the scowling, macho swagger that has become a part of their unprecedented success," the *Baltimore Sun* wrote in 1993. The team's taunting and trash-talking were seen less as fun banter and more like obnoxiousness from a group that hadn't won a title. Their passion was called recklessness as the racial undertones of the critiques rose to the surface. Webber commented on it in the *Washington Post*, explaining that if he were at any school other than Michigan, with its all-Black starting five, things would be much different: "They'd say, 'Look, he's always smiling, he's got such personality, such heart! He's a mean player, but a good mean player. He's enthusiastic and he understands the game. That's what Bobby Knight wants from his kids.'

"Or if I went to Duke? They'd be saying, 'He's such a smart player! Look at the way he pushes Bobby Hurley! Look at how he gets everyone pumped up!'"

The Fab Five were part of the first generation of ballers who grew up on rap music, so they were drawn to the stories and perspectives embedded in the lyrics of artists like Public Enemy, N.W.A, and 2Pac. Likewise, the artists were drawn to the team. "They brought, like, our attitude to the court," Ice Cube said about the team in ESPN's *The Fab Five* documentary from 2011. "The Fab Five let people know it's not how old you are as long as you can play."

The Michigan squad—and Barkley, too—reflected these shifts and represented a new version of Black manhood, one in which these men were unashamed of being their natural selves even under massive public scrutiny. They gave American society a glimpse at a side of Blackness it wasn't used to seeing. Much like Barkley, the Michigan team came in second. They lost to the University of North Carolina in the 1993 NCAA Championship game, but did so in the most dramatic way possible, finishing 77–71 in a battle that came down to the last minute.

Losing championships dooms most second-place finishers to being footnotes in history. Not so with the Fab Five. For a team that never actually won a title—not even a conference one—they managed to leave an indelible mark on college basketball. They were hailed as the gold standard for recruiting classes for many years to come. And no other group at the college level has matched their influence on style. In their wake, the start of the NCAA basketball season and March Madness resembled the footwear version of the fashion runway, with new models on display. Throughout the '90s, perennial contenders like the Arizona Wildcats, North Carolina Tar Heels, and Georgetown Hoyas influenced generations not just with their styles of play, but with how they looked.

On the professional level, Barkley served as the dominant face for the Force franchise before eventually earning a series of signature models, and Webber arrived for his rookie season wearing his own shoe: the Air Max CW. Barkley's marketability opened the door for other notable Nike athletes like Gary Payton, Kevin Garnett, and Alonzo Mourning. Blue-collar types reconstructed in the image of good endorsers spoke to consumers in a way not seen before Sir Charles.

The Air Force Max ushered in a new era for basketball footwear. The model defined the look of basketball: mid-top sneakers made functional for the court and fashionable enough to be worn off of it. Nike applied the shoe's aggressive design cues and massive Air units to predominantly black- or white-based basketball sneakers for years before any major design shifts occurred. The look dominated retail store shelves, the streets, and courts for decades. The model set the trend for the hundreds that came after through the use of fully visible Air units.

Nike has rereleased the Air Force Max several times since the original in 1993. The black/silver colorway has made multiple appearances over the years, while the two white-based pairs have retroed fewer times but are well received when they do return. The Air Force Max reflects the golden era of Nike Basketball—a time when the personality and character of players informed the shoes they wore.

Honorable Mention
Nike Air Max 93

A milk jug might not be the first thing you think would inspire a sneaker design, but that's exactly what Tinker Hatfield and Bruce Kilgore referenced when they created the Air Max 93.

At the time, the model was one of the most significant leaps in innovation for Nike's popular Air Max line. It continued where 1991's Air Max 180 left off by placing an even larger Air unit in the midsole. The 270-degree bag that wrapped around the heel was the biggest Nike had crafted to date, and the model was originally referred to as the Air Max 270 (not to be confused with the silhouette that debuted in 2018) for this

by Mike DeStefano

notable feature. Nike achieved the bulbous Air unit through a blow-molding process similar to the one used on the Air Max 180, in which gas was injected through an external tube to allow for the bubble to be molded.

The revamped cushioning system was not the only feature introduced with the Air Max 93. Hatfield and Kilgore also included a neoprene inner bootie for an improved fit. Though a first for the Air Max line, it looked strikingly similar to the liner found in the Air Huarache, which debuted two years prior. A combination of mesh and leather made up the rest of the upper, while plastic overlays in a vibrant "Dusty Cactus" hue were used for the Swooshes on each side panel and heel counter. Like other sneakers in the Nike archive, the 93 is synonymous with this bright splash of color. The model also marked the first time color had been applied to the inside of the Air bubble, something that would become commonplace on many models that followed.

In an email shared by the late sneaker historian Gary Warnett in 2014, Hatfield called the 93 "one of my personal favorites. Probably the best running shoe of the lot." While the tech might not hold up in comparison to the running shoes on the market today, the 93's unique build has helped it transition into the lifestyle space easily.

Nike has not kept the Air Max 93 on the shelves with as much consistency as other models from the era, but it did give it some shine in 2018 to help introduce the Air Max 270. Still, its innovations and importance should not be overlooked. The fact that Nike took cues from its design twenty-five years later shows just how ahead of its time it truly was.

1994 Reebok Instapump Fury

The Reebok Instapump Fury looks more at home in 2020 than it did in the year it came out, 1994. The sneaker, with its split-sole design, red/black/yellow colorway, and Pump unit, was like nothing else on the market when Steven Smith designed it. It was also a sneaker that Reebok wasn't ready for at the time, although it would prove to be one of the brand's defining designs more than twenty-five years later.

by Matt Welty

Reebok Instapump Fury

Before the Instapump, there was the Reebok Pump, which was unveiled in 1989 in the form of a bulky basketball model that had a Pump bladder inside it that made the shoe tighten or loosen on the foot. The technology, developed by Paul Litchfield, became a pop-culture phenomenon. The sneakers were worn by Dominique Wilkins, and were positioned to rival Nike's Air Max technology, which had begun to dominate the footwear industry. In a commercial for the shoes, Wilkins is seen holding a pair of Nike Air Command Forces and saying, "If you want to fly first class, Pump up and Air out," as he tosses the Nike sneakers off the screen.

Tennis star Michael Chang also endorsed Pump technology, opting for the Court Victory shoe, which was designed for his sport. In the same brash fashion, he aimed fire at the rock 'n' roll star of his sport, Andre Agassi, and in a spot similar to Wilkins's, tossed out Agassi's Nike Air Tech Challenge shoes.

Reebok wasn't afraid to use the Pump to make a performance product, ruffle a few feathers, and give itself a leg up on the competition. "We were in a competition with our competitors to become the preeminent supplier of basketball shoes," Litchfield said in a 2015 interview with Bloomberg News. "We looked outside of the athletic footwear industry and looked at what they were using in skiing. We looked at what they used for air splints. We looked at how they created a snug fit. We settled on this new and novel concept where they used an air bladder. To make the bladder work, it ended up bringing the price of one component to what the shoe was. We weren't sure if a consumer would embrace a $170 shoe. Out of the gate, there was a lackluster order."

Pump technology had its most important pop cultural moment when Boston Celtics guard Dee Brown laced up a pair of Omni Lite sneakers for the 1991 NBA Dunk Contest and executed a dunk with his left arm cocked back and his right arm covering his face and blocking his vision. That highlight made the shoes. Reebok has referenced it for decades and continues to rerelease the black, orange, and white sneakers over and over again.

The Instapump Fury was a departure from the earlier shoes in the Pump line. Its minimalist design and mesh upper were a far cry from leather basketball and tennis models from previous years. The shoe was also designed, though, to bring down the cost of the Pump and make the sneaker more functional from a production standpoint.

"When I first got to Reebok, we were working on building this innovation team that didn't exist before," said Smith. "[We were wondering], what do we do with Pump from here on out? Pump bladders were, like, 15 bucks a pair, and why are we building a complete shoe and then stuffing it inside of it? The Pump bladder was more expensive than the rest of the shoe, because it was being made in Massachusetts, [where Reebok is located].

"We were like, 'Let's get rid of the rest of the shoe.' We sat a Pump bladder on a sole unit—like, 'Let's just do that.' We were doing experiments with how to have [the Pump] be the outside of the shoe with fabric layers and things laminated to the urethane films. I was sitting in this boring meeting and I doodle this thing in my notebook, and it was the bladder flattened out. I nudge Litchfield, and I was like, 'Look, fuck, that's it.'"

Smith sketched the design out, and it ended up being close to what the sneaker

became. When he was going through the process, he knew how important the model would be in the grander scheme of things. "The [sketch] is pretty true to what the shoe came out to be," he said. "The sketch board page would have been lost to history, because the lawyers took everything [when I left Reebok], but I ripped that page out 'cause I knew the shoe was important."

The Instapump's split-sole design offered maximum padding in the forefoot and heel, with Hexalite cushioning in the rear of the shoe. The carbon-fiber plate in the arch also gave support, while the mesh upper made the shoe breathable and lightweight.

While the design of the shoe is what inspires the strongest reactions these days, its colorway was the biggest hurdle for Smith to overcome internally. At the time, a red, yellow, and black color scheme was jarring, and was met with resistance from conservative-minded marketers at Reebok. The colorway, as Smith tells it, was inspired by punk rock, his involvement in the straight edge scene, and his desire to make an "in-your-face statement."

"Running shoes didn't look like that. They definitely didn't have those colors. They were white with a color pop," Smith said. "When I showed [them the Instapump], they were like, 'We can't sell that.'"

This stirred up a feud between Smith and the marketer who would be responsible for making his sneaker sell or sit on shelves. "The marketing guy was like, 'Well, we'll put it in our line, but I doubt we'll move any. If we do, we've had to do it in a conservative colorway: blue, silver, black,'" Smith said. "And I was like, 'What are you talking about? That's not what this is. You don't do the Dodge Viper and not make it red.' I was like, 'You don't fucking get it.' So I went home and spray painted [a pair] with gray automotive primer. I brought it back. I went to the marketing dude. I'm like, 'This is what you're thinking.' He says, 'Oh, yeah, that I can sell.'"

Smith eventually went over the marketer's head and talked to Paul Fireman, who purchased North American rights to Reebok in 1979. "I went up to Paul Fireman and was like, 'The marketing and running team says they're not going to do this colorway, that they need to do it in, like, a subtle gray.' He said, 'You fucking tell them they're doing it,'" Smith said. "I went back down, and I was like, 'I was up talking to Paul, and he said you're fucking doing this color.' He was like, 'Oh my God, I can't believe you would talk to him about it. OK, we'll do this colorway, but I guarantee you it will be a 60/40 sales split, if we're lucky.'"

It turned out to be the complete opposite. The red/black/yellow colorway sold 60 percent and the gray/black/blue pair sold roughly 40 percent of the total sales of the Instapump Fury.

The model became something of a cult shoe, especially in Japan. It would have major moments thanks to the likes of Björk and Jackie Chan, with Reebok even rereleasing a colorway of the shoe that Chan wore in subsequent years.

One of the most mythical versions of the Instapump Fury was a pair that Chanel designed, which featured shades of gray and the interlocking C's logo of the fashion house on the heel of the sneaker. It was created in 2000 and appeared in Chanel's runway show. How the shoe happened, though, is a bit of a mystery to Smith.

"I wasn't paying attention to a lot of the streetwear side of it at that point. You know, it was like, 'Oh, there's another variation of it,'" he says. "It's always a surprise when you see your thing show up in the fashion world."

That sneaker got a second life in the world of limited sneaker collaborations when Concepts, a boutique founded in Cambridge, Massachusetts, revived the design in 2017. Although it wasn't a true one-to-one version of the Chanel Instapump, which has found its way into museums, it was close enough for a lot of connoisseurs.

"Rhett [Richardson, who was our designer at the time], always had this inclination to do this design. We knew it was kind of a unicorn and not many people knew of it," said Concepts creative director Deon Point. "We wanted to get it [as close to the original as possible]."

A few years prior, in 2014, Concepts was able to work on another Instapump Fury collaboration, which resulted in one of the most hyped versions of the shoe. The sneaker, which was inspired by prints on silk Versace shirts, became the most coveted of a slew of collaborations that Reebok released that year.

"The reason I did the Versace thing was because I thought of 1994 and I'm like, 'What was happening back then?' Obviously it was the Bad Boy era, or it was on the come-up," Point said. "We went back and found a montage of different patterns and materials. That's how that whole Versace thing came about. So there was a rhyme and reason to it. I just didn't throw a bunch of shit together."

The pairs of the sneaker were limited and created an instant demand on the resale market, due to Point and his team underestimating the popularity of the Instapump. "The reason why the resell is probably so high is that we undershot the unit," says Point. "I think we only did 350 of those, where typically we would have done something like 1,200 or 1,800, or something like that. That is about 15 percent of what we typically would do. People are hitting me up. I was like, 'Oh, shit. They went for a lot.'"

The shoes would resell for around $800, and they've held a strong value as of late. Decades after its release, the Instapump is still the legend that it was back then, with its history growing bit by bit. It was also the centerpiece for the first Adidas and Reebok collaboration, where it received a Boost sole. And it's no surprise to Smith that the shoe became an icon. "When you saw it on the wall, it looked like nothing else," he said. "That was the intent: to disrupt and make a statement, and that's what this thing has done."

Honorable Mention
Nike Diamond Turf 2

Anyone who grew up in the mid-'90s has a little Deion Sanders in their DNA. How couldn't he sway the youth when he appeared to have it all? The profile, nicknames, jewelry, gear, hair, and footwear.

Nike released Sanders's second signature sneaker in 1994, when he played for both the San Francisco 49ers and Cincinnati Reds. The two-sport star talked the talk, famously saying, "If you look good, you feel good. If you feel good, you play good. If you play good, they pay good." And he walked the walk in his trademark shoes.

Nike designer Tracy Teague built on the construction of Sanders's previous model. The silhouette shared the flowing lines common to most of the Diamond Turf line, which evoked a sense of speed. "I love fast things, like a Lamborghini," Sanders

by John Gotty

explained on Complex's *Sneaker Shopping* in 2017. "If you know a Lamborghini, it sits up high in the back and it slopes down low. So that gave me this look."

The second iteration of the Diamond Turf embodied that statement. The design pattern created momentum with the lines arching forward, starting at the midfoot and accelerating into the forefoot. Sanders opted for a three-quarter high-cut for ankle protection and stability, with encapsulated Air units providing the necessary comfort and support. Teague added a larger forefoot strap and an internal sock bootie for a lockdown fit as tight as Sanders defended helpless receivers. One of the most popular colorways of the shoe used an intense shade of varsity red that complemented both the 49ers' and the Reds' uniforms. Gold-colored mesh running underneath the strap and along each side of the midfoot added breathability to the shoe while serving as a nod to the NFL Hall of Famer's taste for jewelry. A special logo showcased both Sanders's football and baseball jersey numbers, and stands as one of the best signature icons in footwear history.

The Diamond Turf 2 arrived at a time when Nike, from design and marketing standpoints alike, tapped into both the athleticism and personalities of its athletes. Sanders's shoe was able to transition from one sport to the next, and then to the streets. "In those days, it was either cleats or tennis shoes or cross-trainers," Sanders said on *Sneaker Shopping*. "I said, 'Nah, I should be able to wear the shoes I'm kicking it with on the field.'"

"Neon Deion" made those shoes come to life through his play, and every base he stole or high-stepping pick six he pulled in the Diamond Turf 2 helped Nike sell another pair.

1995 Air Jordan XI

Whenever the newest Air Jordan releases, you know it's going to be loaded with the latest and greatest technology, and you know it's going to turn heads. Sometimes the model is a hit; other times, it takes a little getting used to. The Air Jordan XI took no getting used to; it was eye-popping and head-turning from the very first time we saw it.

by Drew Hammell

Michael Jordan always had to be different with his footwear. Back in the early '90s, MJ kept mentioning to Tinker Hatfield that he wanted a sneaker that was shiny—something you could wear with a tuxedo. He was looking for something fancy, something with flash. How that would actually be done was up to the master designer. This was the inspiration behind one of the most recognizable Air Jordans of all time. The Air Jordan XI had pizzazz. It had polished patent leather. This shoe was perfect for Jordan—it would stand out more than any other on the basketball court. There was only one problem: MJ wasn't in the league anymore.

In 1994, Hatfield continued working on future Air Jordan models, even though Jordan was on a bus riding around the Bible Belt snagging fly balls for the Birmingham Barons minor league baseball team. After retiring from basketball in 1993, Jordan had left the sneaker world in disarray. He was the face of Nike, the biggest shoe brand on earth. In the wake of his retirement, Nike had to figure out how to carry the brand forward without its main spokesman in the spotlight.

By this point, Hatfield had worked on every sneaker Jordan had worn starting with the AJ III. Hatfield certainly had his work cut out for him, since Jordan wasn't playing basketball while he designed the AJ XI. Which direction should Hatfield take? Should he create a sneaker that's more fashion-forward and can be worn on the street? Or should he continue testing footwear boundaries and design a tech-heavy shoe meant for the court?

Industrious and wise as ever, Hatfield kept pushing the limits of what a basketball sneaker could be: a full-length Air sole ran through the midsole of the Air Jordan XI for plenty of cushioning. A new carbon-fiber shank plate inspired by soccer and football cleats stabilized the foot and launched it forward as the wearer leaped through the air. And the new patent-leather mud guard was both flashy and functional, as it helped secure Jordan's foot during his sharp cuts and pivots. Also worth mentioning was the mysterious Greek-style font with the cryptic letters across the tongue, and the number "23" (or "45") on the heel. What did those letters say? Jumpman? Jordan?

Hatfield first presented his newest creation with a team of designers and execs at Jordan's condo in Scottsdale, Arizona, in late 1994 while MJ was playing in the Fall League for the Scottsdale Scorpions. There was a full line of apparel to go along with the shoe—an ongoing effort to portray Jordan as more than just a basketball player: a global icon.

When Jordan first tried on the XI, it had a wraparound tongue like Dennis Rodman's Air Shake Ndestrukt. It had straps, instead of laces, to lock down the foot. The prototype also featured a black upper with white patent leather, just like Hatfield's early drawings. Jordan took off his black velcro Deschutz sandals and slipped his foot into his newest sneaker, with Hatfield explaining all the benefits the XI had to offer. Jordan shared his feedback with the team, and Hatfield listened, as always.

Flash-forward to the spring of '95: Jordan, after plenty of cajoling by friends and former teammates, couldn't resist returning to the NBA. When he first retired in '93, he all but guaranteed he'd never go back to basketball. But that itch and competitive fire just wouldn't die. When Jordan got back in March '95, he sported the Air Jordan X for the regular season, and then in the first round of the playoffs, against the Charlotte Hornets.

Jordan and his Bulls easily disposed of Charlotte, but faced a much bigger test against the Orlando Magic in the second round. For that round, Jordan chose to switch to the Air Jordan XI, despite Hatfield's plea not to. It was still a prototype, and was not ready to be mass-produced for the public. Of course, Jordan couldn't resist an opportunity to wear something new and more advanced—especially with that shiny patent leather.

During Game 1 of the series, MJ rocked the XI now commonly known as the "Concord," which featured a white upper with black patent leather and the translucent outsole. The sneaker got the name Concord because of its purple accents—MJ's favorite color. On the heel was the number "45"—the number MJ wore in honor of his older brother Larry when he returned to the league.

He wore them again in Game 2, but was told by the league that he had to wear a shoe that matched his teammates' black sneakers and that he would be fined for his violation. So, for Game 3, he inconceivably switched to Penny Hardaway's Nike Air Flight One and cut off the "1" on the heel. He then switched to a mostly black colorway with Concord purple hits and a "45" on the heel for Games 4, 5, and 6.

Incredibly, Shaquille O'Neal, Penny Hardaway, and the rest of the young, talented Orlando Magic squad took down the Bulls in six games. One of the key moments came during the final seconds of Game 1, when Jordan dribbled the ball up the court but was stripped by Nick Anderson, who passed to Hardaway for a breakaway dunk. "Number 45 is not number 23," Anderson famously remarked. Because of that, MJ switched jersey numbers and went back to 23 during the series.

Going into the offseason in '95, Jordan was on a mission to make sure the embarrassing early exit never happened again. At the same time, he was also filming *Space Jam* in LA. To stay in shape while he was on set, he had a court built with a dome over it and invited NBA players to scrimmage with him. During that time, Jordan wore the Concords.

In the actual *Space Jam* movie, MJ sported the Black/Concord XI colorway again, but this time with a number "23" on the heel instead of "45." These have since been referred to as the "Space Jams."

As fall approached, Jordan and the Bulls were ready to go on a run unparalleled in the NBA. Armed with extra support from Dennis Rodman and Ron Harper, the Bulls went on to win 72 games during the 1995–96 season. During every one of those games, MJ had the Concord XIs on his feet. During the All-Star Game, Jordan switched to an all-white and "Columbia Blue" model.

In the playoffs, Jordan moved to the black/red model, now famously referred to as the "Bred." He wore two different low-cut models briefly, and primarily sported the mid-cut model with black patent leather. The Bulls stormed through the playoffs, and ultimately defeated Shawn Kemp, Gary Payton, and the Seattle Supersonics in six games on Father's Day, with Jordan falling to the floor in the locker room sobbing as he thought about his father, who was killed a few years earlier. That 1995–96 Bulls team was one of the most dominant teams ever, and for every single game MJ was wearing the Air Jordan XI on his feet. The XIs were already special, but that season made them iconic.

But that year, Jordan and some of his teammates weren't the only ones to rock the XIs. Players like Kevin Garnett and Anderson were sporting them as well. And in the NCAA, Hoyas guard Allen Iverson famously wore them during his time at Georgetown.

Not that Nike needed to market the XI that much, but there were several print ads for the AJ XI, including a "phone ad" featuring the Concords on a white background with a red Swoosh and phone number at the bottom. Jordan also filmed a commercial for the XI in which he was in an old gym staring at a hundred-foot rim. As he prepared to storm toward the rim, there was a close-up shot of the Concords before he launched forward and up into the air.

Aside from the original four mid-cut colorways, a low-cut model was also released in a white/grey/cobalt colorway and a black/red version—but the design of the low didn't mirror that of its mid-cut sibling. Overall, the low-cut model shared plenty of features with the mid, but the upper design and lacing were different. The white/grey model was also officially called the Air Jordan XI Low "IE," though the meaning of "IE" has never been confirmed or clarified. The most common theory is that it stands for "International Exclusive."

The first Air Jordan XI to release to the public was the white/Concord version back

in November 1995. It was popular right off the bat—there was no conversation about it being too out there or ugly. The Air Jordan XI was so popular, in fact, that it took only five years for the sneaker to retro for the first time in 2000, with the return of the classic Concord colorway. The black and varsity royal "Space Jam" colorway also released in 2000.

Early in 2001, the white/Columbia blue colorway returned and the "Cool Grey" model debuted. As 2001 progressed, seven new low-cut patent leather XIs arrived, along with the "Bred" OG model, which closed out the year. Nike never released a low-cut patent leather XI back when the original colorways launched in 1995–96. The only low-cut patent leather model before the '01s was seen on the feet of Jordan himself briefly during the '96 playoffs, when he wore a black/red version, and then in the '96 Championship parade, in which Jordan sported the "Concord" lows. The success of the '01 low-cut models opened the door for more colorways down the road.

Since 2008, it has been tradition for Jordan Brand to drop at least one colorway of the Air Jordan XI during the holidays. Sometimes the XI release is an OG colorway, like the "Bred" and Concord, and sometimes it's a new one, like the "Gamma Blue" or "72–10." Sometimes the release causes some controversy, as with the 2011 rendition of the white/Concord, which featured a lower-cut patent leather, or the 2012 "Bred," on which the patent leather was not as thick, meaning no white stripe was visible. These deviations were subtle to the average sneaker enthusiast, and most did not mind as long as the OG versions made a return. Others, however, criticized the models, arguing that the shoes should remain as true to the originals as possible. Regardless, the hype surrounding the Holiday XI release is always huge, with sneakerheads anticipating significant additions to their collections that week. Though Jordan Brand never releases official data on units sold, a record number of XIs continue to be available every holiday season, and those units always sell out quickly. Long lines are no surprise for most big Jordan releases, but for the XIs, they're a given. And in some instances, fights have broken out over the sneakers—most notably in 2011 for the Concord release.

Beyond those releases, over the past few years, Jordan Brand has responded

to what consumers have been asking for, remastering the classics so that the look, shape, and feel reflect those of the very first models. Of course, sometimes even Jordan Brand takes some liberties—for example, when the "Space Jam" model returned in 2016, it kept a "45" on the heel. In the movie, however, the sneaker had a "23" in the same spot. The new version came out with full *Space Jam* packaging, but was technically the player exclusive model MJ first wore in the 1995 NBA Playoffs, against the Magic. The release was huge, with pairs selling out almost instantly.

Over the years, countless more versions of the Air Jordan XI have dropped in high and low cuts. Jordan Team members like Randy Moss, Warren Sapp, Derek Jeter, Darius Miles, Ray Allen, Chris Paul, and many others have all rocked their own PE versions as well. The XI has become a timeless silhouette that continues to sell out almost immediately when an OG colorway releases. The combination of patent leather and mesh was a brilliant concept by Hatfield, and the sneaker looked absolutely perfect on Jordan's foot the moment he stepped on the court with it.

Honorable Mention
Nike Air Max 95

After the Air Max 1, the Air Max 95 may be the most recognizable member of the popular running shoe family. The model has been widely bootlegged, turned into a thigh-high boot, appeared in comic strips, and more. It's also been at the center of violence, with owners assaulted for pairs. Regardless of form or controversy, though, one thing is certain: with the model, Sergio Lozano crafted an indisputable classic in 1995.

From a design standpoint, Lozano looked to the human body for inspiration, linking elements of the sneaker to the ribs, vertebrae, muscles, and skin. At the same time, the shoe's gradient colorway, which starts out as black on the bottom via the midsole and works up to progressively lighter shades, had a

by Ben Felderstein

concrete intent for the wearer. Lozano's idea was that the black bottoms would help hide dirt that accumulated on the shoe during trail runs, especially in Oregon, where Nike is based.

The 95's original "Neon" color scheme remains its most memorable, a fact to which its ten retro releases (1997, 1998, 1999, 2003, 2006, 2008, 2010, 2012, 2015, and 2018) attest. Given how many times it's arrived in stores, it's nearly impossible for you not to have a pair in your collection. While the overall appearance of the "Neons" hasn't changed much over the years, some of these drops have overlooked an original detail that helped the model stand out: the PSI indicators that Lozano included on its sole, showing off the cushioning in the then-newly engineered Air bubble.

Still, that hasn't affected the shoe's cachet, both in the States and abroad. In fact, while it was a hit in the U.S., it was the Japanese market that really gravitated toward it at first, with the model reportedly turning wearers into targets for thieves. It was also among the catalysts for the secondary market, with resellers pulling in more than $1,000 per pair on account of overwhelming demand for it in cities like Tokyo.

Over the years, the 95 has been the focus of high-profile collaborations with the likes of Supreme, Atmos, and Stüssy, while other models—like the Air Jordan IV—have adopted its most recognizable colorway. Its rereleases, meanwhile, also remain a draw. The shoe arrived during a period when Nike would more plainly label models from its line as simply "Air Max," so it's actually only come to be known as the Air Max 95 in its retro form. The addition of its year of release was inevitable, but in spite of it, the model is timeless.

1996 Reebok Question

In the mid-'90s, Nike dominated the basketball category and American sports footwear as a whole. The big names and the best shoes all existed under the Swoosh umbrella. To stay competitive in a crowded marketplace, Reebok wanted a player as electrifying as Allen Iverson. "He was 6-foot-1 and could jump through the gym, could do everything, and he was also a good-looking kid," said Todd Krinsky, a longtime Reebok executive. "He had the swagger. If you write down the ten things that need to work in our industry, you could check off all ten."

by John Gotty

In the wake of the sneaker wars of the '80s, which saw it cede its top spot to Nike, Reebok faced the difficult task of rekindling excitement around the brand. How could it harness the growing popularity of basketball to regain its spot in the industry? Its response came in the form of the Question—Iverson's signature debut.

The model, now almost a quarter-century old, sits near the top of the pantheon of basketball footwear. Reebok began crafting it for Iverson while he was still a sophomore at Georgetown University, well before he set foot on an NBA court, and before he signed with the company. Krinsky steered the project in its early stages. He and his co-workers watched the point guard wreak havoc on opponents throughout the college season and the NCAA tournament. Iverson's fast-paced play informed the initial design. "When we designed it, it was really all about performance," Krinsky shared in a 2015 interview with Nice Kicks. "We wanted it to be about speed, and we wanted it to have elements of speed to it." Led by designer Scott Hewett, Reebok created an initial prototype meant to embody the quickness and flash Iverson showed on the court.

But Iverson was still far from a lock for the brand. By the time he declared his intentions to go pro, he was still debating between shoe companies he wanted to represent him. All signs pointed to a deal with Nike. He'd worn its shoes throughout high school and college. Georgetown's coach, John Thompson, held a position on Nike's board of directors and served as a mentor for a young Iverson. David Falk, Iverson's agent, delivered a rookie Michael Jordan, Iverson's idol, and many other standout athletes to Nike in years prior.

Reebok knew that Nike was creating a shoe for Iverson. It also knew it desperately needed a jolt to its roster, which at the time included Shawn Kemp, Glenn Robinson, and Shaquille O'Neal as the company's biggest names. They were all great players, but not as attractive as the guards who were beginning to dominate the nightly highlights.

Falk was part of the reason Reebok was able to secure Iverson. The agent knew the player was a special talent and that Nike's long list of clients meant the rookie might not get the full attention he deserved. And at the time, the *New York Times Magazine* reported in a profile on Falk, Nike aimed to control the number of endorsement deals its athletes could take on by signing them to overall management contracts.

Reebok wanted to make the ballplayer a star, and the company didn't leave anything to chance. When it was its turn to make Iverson an offer, it proposed a ten-year deal for $50 million, an unheard-of figure at the time and far more than other companies reportedly offered. Even Thompson told Iverson it would be foolish to pass up the enormous payday from Reebok. "I told him what Reebok offered me and what Nike offered me, and it was a no-brainer," Iverson said in an interview at ComplexCon in 2019. Iverson concluded that Nike didn't realize who he could one day become.

Now that Reebok had its man, the two sides immediately went to work. The brand met with Iverson to show him the sample it created for him. He approved the design with only a few changes between the early prototype and what would become the

Question. The shoe featured a leather upper, a suede or pearlized toecap, Hexalite cushioning with windows in the midsoles, and a blue-tinted translucent outsole to round off the look. "The emphasis was really on the toe," Hewett told *Slam Kicks* in 2002. "We just wanted to have some different materials, especially on the toe. Then there was the ice bottom, the ghilly lace loops—we just wanted to keep it nice for him … we used Hexalite to keep some weight out, as well as a full mesh tongue."

The shoe's focus on the toecap and the lacing system drew comparisons to the Air Jordan XI, a model originally released in 1995 and one Iverson famously wore at Georgetown. Reebok contended it never had any intentions of making Iverson's first shoe a replica of anything Jordan wore. "No, it wasn't, really—it was more we were trying to bring some familiarity to the shoe in general with different elements," Krinsky told Complex in 2012. "But there was no, like, look to something. We didn't say, 'OK, he likes Jordans; let's try to make him comfortable.' Our goal was to make things that were really going to stand out on the court."

Reebok readied the shoes to launch by the fall of 1996. It couldn't, however, get the production numbers where they needed to be in order to orchestrate a wide release. Instead of flooding the market, Reebok took a measured approach by releasing the shoe in a handful of stores in Philadelphia, New York, and Washington, DC. To its surprise, people snapped them up with quickness. The Question sold through in days, even minutes in some cases. Reebok even had reports of heatseekers driving hours in search of the Question. "Allen had great style on the court, and [the Question] looked cool with jeans, especially all the toe colors. We didn't anticipate it to be a big fashion play, but it quickly became adopted on the street as one of those must-have looks for kids," Krinsky recalled in a 2015 interview with Nice Kicks.

Reebok knew it had a hit on its hands. But as big as the moment was for the company, it meant even more for Iverson. "When you're twenty years old, man, you ain't giving a fuck about what the shoe look like," Iverson said. "It's your shoe. It's your dream come true. You got your own shoe. So that was just the icing on the cake that it looked good and everybody loved me."

Iverson, who in 1996 was drafted first overall by Philadelphia (ahead of future MVPs Kobe Bryant and Steve Nash, and others like Ray Allen and Stephon Marbury), wore the blue-toe version of his shoe during his first NBA game, on November 1, 1996. "I think, for the most part, the fraternity was proud of me," he said. Not all rookies are blessed to start their careers decked out in a shoe named for them, but Iverson was. And he put up 30 points and 6 assists against the Milwaukee Bucks that night.

Iverson experienced his share of highs and lows during the first half of the season, but filled the box score each night with crazy stats. His play earned him a roster spot in the Rising Stars Game as part of All-Star Weekend in February 1997. In a matchup filled with future stars, two of the brightest and youngest—Iverson and fellow rookie Bryant—went head-to-head in a battle for the ages. Both players scored their fair share of points, Iverson notching 19, Bryant finishing with 31, a then-game record. Iverson's East squad won the game, and he earned Most Valuable Player honors, along with a cascade of boos from fans in Cleveland's Gund Arena.

To many, what transpired during the game was symbolic of the changing face of the league. Young players were leaving college early or skipping it completely for professional riches. Teamwork gave way to ego-driven, me-first play that frustrated a lot of people. "Perhaps people have been listening to the legends of the league talking about rookies like Iverson this week, grumbling about how selfish they are, and how they have an image before they have a game," read a report published the next day in the *New York Times*. "So what did Iverson do? He showed up with eye-catching cornrows, flashy passes behind his back, and greedy shot-taking in the second half. All of which only furthered the perception that he is a me-me-me rookie." For his part, Iverson soaked up the boos and barked back by reminding those same fans they would see him and his Sixers team the following week. "We play Cleveland Tuesday and I can't wait to play the Cavaliers," he told the paper. "I've never had people boo me for playing hard."

For everything polished players like Jordan, Larry Bird, and Magic Johnson represented, Iverson stood as the polar opposite, with his aforementioned cornrows, baggy uniform, black ankle braces, and colorful headband. He looked like a potential headache for a league attempting to wash away its less-than-stellar image from the early '80s due to drug use among players. But what he represented to a younger generation of basketball fans was an average-size athlete who was a scoring machine on the court.

As the Sixers guard made a name for himself, a cultural shift was occurring in the music world. Rap was experiencing a boom of its own. By 1996, hip-hop had moved beyond the park jams and underground scene with which it had been synonymous in previous decades. Artists like LL Cool J, Busta Rhymes, and Outkast worked their way onto the charts, while seminal albums like 2Pac's *All Eyez on Me* cemented hip-hop's crossover. But for all its good fortune, rap was still stigmatized, in part because of the coastal beef between the Bad Boy and Death Row record labels, which led to the killings of 2Pac and the Notorious B.I.G. Iverson represented the energy of hip-hop, which in the eyes of some eclipsed everything else about him. His attitude was hip-hop in every sense of the word. But, much like it did the music, the mainstream loathed him, since he came up before middle America was ready to embrace certain elements of Blackness. Players of previous generations called him selfish, and he represented regression for a league that had finally managed to scrub its image clean. Many considered Iverson a thug who skirted the law just because he could dribble a basketball well.

Despite the critics, A.I. grew to be beloved by younger audiences, who recognized that the twenty-one-year-old looked like them, spoke like them, and listened to the same music as them. He embodied the "stereotypes of a Black male misunderstood" the Notorious B.I.G. rapped about. Teens loved how Iverson comfortably straddled the line, with a foot planted in each culture's—the NBA and hip-hop's— rise to prominence. His clothing mirrored what rappers of the day wore: oversize tees,

excessively baggy jeans, flashy diamonds, expensive chains, and a fitted baseball cap with the braids and durag poking out underneath. How influential was his style? In 2005, the NBA instituted a dress code mandating that players wear business casual attire when on official business partly because of Iverson's sartorial choices. The same code also barred them from wearing chains and jewelry. Iverson was immediately critical of the new rules. "Just because you put a guy in a tuxedo, it doesn't mean he's a good guy," he told the *Philadelphia Daily News*.

Unlike the league, Reebok never asked Iverson to shift his image. Neither did his agent, Falk. Both parties knew times were changing for society and understood what

was expected of athletes as pitchmen. "With him, I have a penchant to do it differently," Falk told the *New York Times*. "It doesn't work to do the same stuff that Jordan did in 1984. It would be as if Allen Iverson wore Michael Jordan's custom-made clothes from 1984. They wouldn't fit and they'd be out of style." They saw the shift in the audience and anticipated Iverson being one of the key faces for the future.

Sports' relationship with sneakers had evolved in the wake of Jordan, and by the time Iverson arrived in the league with his own model, the landscape was crowded with players who either had a shoe bearing their name or a sneaker endorsement deal in place. "Today, the marketing of an athlete sometimes exceeds the potential of that athlete. Back then, the potential of the athlete built the marketing," Jordan told the *New York Times Magazine* in 1996, in Falk's profile. "Now, it isn't as important." He didn't single out Iverson, although the comments could certainly fit.

What happened on March 12, 1997, in Philadelphia changed how Iverson would forever be seen. A 16-45 Sixers team faced the defending champion Chicago Bulls, who were marching along to another title. Iverson and Jordan matched up against one another in the frontcourt. Wearing "Blue Toe" Questions, the scrappy guard hit Jordan with a low, quick crossover dribble that baited Jordan to reach for the ball.

Then Iverson rocked Jordan with another cross even quicker than the one before it. Jordan reached helplessly, leaving himself exposed in the process. "The only reason I did it the second time is because I seen how hard he bit when I wasn't even doing a move. I was setting a move up. I said, 'Oh, he's biting hard,'" Iverson told Complex in 2012. Iverson skirted past him, rose up and flicked a jump shot off his fingertips over Jordan's outstretched hand.

The shot only counted for two points in the box score. But it showed that the Sixers rookie had the potential Jordan spoke about, and it put the rest of the league on notice—if the greatest player ever couldn't check Iverson, every other player needed to worry. If there were ever any questions about whether he could play, Iverson answered with a highlight that certified his arrival.

Iverson went on to have a legendary career that spanned fourteen seasons. While he never won an NBA Championship, he earned nearly every other award in the NBA imaginable—one Most Valuable Player award, two All-Star MVP awards in his eleven appearances—and led his team to the NBA Finals in 2001 and ultimately entered the Hall of Fame his first time on the ballot in 2016.

But the accolades don't completely define what he meant to the culture of basketball and sports as a whole. His fingerprints show up every time a player enters the arena hallways wearing streetwear instead of a suit or hits the court with an armful of tattoos.

And even after more than twenty years, the Question remains one of Reebok's strongest models, and the Iverson franchise as a whole holds the distinction of being one of the longest-running signature series in basketball footwear. While Reebok has experienced ups and downs in recent years, shoe sales never falter when reissues of the Question hit store shelves. The model has been released in over one hundred different styles and colorways in its lifespan. In 2016, the brand commemorated the model's twentieth anniversary by releasing twenty different versions of the Question Mid. Those collabs with the likes of streetwear staple Bape, graffiti writer Stash, artists like Jadakiss and Teyana Taylor, and a slew of other partners introduced the shoe to a new generation of consumers. Much like Jordan's, Iverson's first signature sneaker will always be considered one of the greatest basketball shoes to find a life away from the court. Through the stunning performances of its namesake and its cultural staying power, the Question has made its mark.

Honorable Mention
Nike Air Penny 2

Nike owned basketball in 1996. Michael Jordan had stepped away from the game for what would be a brief hiatus, but the brand still had the coolest shoes and the best players, perhaps none greater than Anfernee "Penny" Hardaway and his Air Penny 2. The 6'7" point guard found success early in his professional career with the Orlando Magic after going third overall in the 1994 NBA Draft. Hardaway earned All-Rookie First Team in 1994, consecutive All-NBA First Teams in 1995 and 1996, and, along with Shaquille O'Neal, led his team to the 1995 NBA Finals and 1996 Eastern Conference Finals.

  With the Penny 2, Eric Avar designed a shoe that represented an evolution from Hardaway's first model, released in 1995, without abandoning what about it had worked. It sported clean, fluid lines mirroring Hardaway's style of play and disposi-

by John Gotty

tion. Elements like the reflective 3M on the piping, the Swoosh adorning the ankle, and Hardaway's One Cent logo stitched on the tongue distinguished it from other models. The combo of Zoom Air in the forefoot and Max Air near the rear created a responsive shoe built for Hardaway's quick, explosive play.

"The 2 was my favorite one to wear, because it was more comfortable to me, and it was just a tighter, snug fit," Hardaway told Sole Collector in 2008. "The [Penny] 1 was a little bit wider, and it was still a great shoe, but the [Penny] 2 is a bit more narrow and becomes more snug around my arches and were probably my favorites."

Hardaway wore the Penny 2 at the beginning of the 1996–97 NBA season, before buyers could get their hands on it for Holiday 1996. The model originally released in three colorways: a white-based "home" pair, a predominantly black "away" pair, and the "Atlantic Blue" version. Those sound tame by today's standards, but they synced perfectly with the Orlando Magic's team colors and pin-striped uniforms. Truthfully, though, the shoes didn't need to be loud, and neither did Hardaway. Nike left all the boasting to Lil' Penny, the player's puppet alter ego, voiced by Chris Rock, who sent the marketing into another stratosphere.

Nike continues to reissue the Air Penny 2 in an endless array of color schemes. They still sell, too, thanks to the nostalgia for their namesake and those commercials. But it all dates back to 1996, when a powerful mix of talents—Avar, Hardaway, and Rock among them—created the design and marketing alchemy responsible for one of the best models of Nike's 1990s basketball run.

1997 Nike Air Foamposite One

It looked like a shoe from space, or an alien vessel constructed from an otherworldly material that landed on the hardwood, something that might leave a crater behind. The Foamposite was wild—so wild it got kids jumping off their couches and squinting at their pre-HD TV sets extra hard to see what Mike Bibby had on his feet. What are those weird-looking blue shoes? Nikes? Is Bibby wearing another brand? Where's the Swoosh?

by Drew Hammell

The Foamposite One first appeared on the feet of Bibby and several other Arizona Wildcats players during the 1997 NCAA Tournament. During the 1996–97 college basketball season, Nike invited the Arizona Wildcats up to its World Headquarters in Beaverton, Oregon, to try out footwear that hadn't released to the public yet. The players were basically guinea pigs for Nike, as they were routinely sent prototypes to test out. Hence everyone's eyes locking onto that strange blue shoe Bibby donned during the '97 tournament.

Arizona was not favored to make it to the Final Four that year, so the Foamposites could have disappeared as early as the Sweet Sixteen, when the Wildcats faced Kansas. But Arizona kept winning, and those Foamposites kept showing up on the big stage—including the championship game against Kentucky, which Arizona won. All of a sudden, everyone was well aware of, albeit still somewhat confused by, those strange blue shoes.

By '97, every college team had adopted Michigan's Fab 5 mentality—baggy shorts and flashy sneakers were all the rage. But Arizona took things a step further, wearing the newest Nikes—some that hadn't even released yet. Bibby wasn't alone in wearing Foamposites against Kentucky. Several other players also donned them for that game. In fact, some of the team members had the Foams on their feet as far back as the Sweet Sixteen game against Kansas. A total of three Arizona Wildcats wore the never-before-seen sneaker during that game versus the Jayhawks: Bibby, forward Donnell Harris, and redshirt freshman Quynn Tebbs.

Nike Air Foamposite One

A few days after Arizona won, the main spokesman of the Foamposite One wore them on the NBA hardwood. Anfernee "Penny" Hardaway, the 6'7" point guard for the Orlando Magic, sported the Foamposites starting in April 1997. He would rock a white/black pair, an all-black pair, and, of course, the royal blue colorway, which went perfectly with the Orlando jerseys. After Shaquille O'Neal left Orlando in 1996, Hardaway was the main man for the Magic during the 1996–97 season. Though he battled through injuries that year, he was still named a starter for the NBA All-Star game for the third-straight time. And even though Michael Jordan was back in the league, Hardaway was still a marketing force for Nike and the NBA.

Nike, as always, enjoyed pushing the limits of what was deemed acceptable on the basketball court, and the Foamposite caught the eye of league officials, an echo of Jordan wearing his black and red Nike Air Ship that the league infamously banned thirteen years earlier. After Hardaway wore the Foamposites on court, the NBA ruled that Hardaway's all-blue kicks had to be at least 50 percent black to match Orlando's jerseys. So the Magic's equipment manager cleverly filled in the ridges of the upper with a Sharpie marker so that Hardaway could keep wearing them. The Magic fell to the Heat in the first round of the playoffs that year, so Hardaway wouldn't have another opportunity to wear them that season.

Incredibly, Nike wasn't originally planning on using Hardaway as the main ambassador for the Foamposite line. As the story goes, Nike met with Hardaway to show him samples of his newest model. He wasn't satisfied with any of them, until he saw a bag with the Foamposite One prototype inside. He immediately fell in love with the model, and so Nike proceeded to turn it into Penny's own—even sacrificing the Swoosh for a more prominent One Cent logo. According to sources, he was not happy when Arizona players got to wear them publicly on the court before him. After all, the sneaker was meant for him, not some college team.

Part of what made the Foamposite One appealing was its lack of Nike branding. With just a tiny white Swoosh on the lateral forefoot side, it was hard to tell that it was even a Nike sneaker. What stood out more than the Swoosh was Hardaway's logo on the tongue, heel, and outsole. First seen on Hardaway's Air Penny 1 and Air Penny 2 models, the logo strangely appeared on the Foamposite One, as well. This certainly wasn't the first time Nike limited its Swoosh presence on the exterior of a shoe—the Huarache line had moved units with minimal branding five years earlier.

Designed by Eric Avar and Jeff Johnson, the beetle-like Foamposite One was packed with new technology. Labeled "the shoe of the future," it featured a full-length low-to-the-ground Zoom Air unit. The incredibly light polyurethane upper and midsole surrounded the foot for protection and comfort. A carbon fiber plate provided stability and flexibility in the midsole. Nike partnered with Daewoo (the car company) to provide the proper synthetic materials. A synthetic liquid was poured into a $750,000 mold, which fused the upper, midsole, and outsole into one piece.

"It was basically just an envelope of material that we were pouring polyurethane into. And that was creating the form and the structure," Avar said in a post published on Nike.com. "The center core of the mold was a last, and then the outer walls of the mold was all this outer detail, and then you pressed everything together."

Nike has shared several prototypes over the years, including an all-white model similar to what Hardaway wore, as well as a Foamposite upper with a heel Air Max unit.

The brand ultimately released the Foamposite with Zoom Air cushioning and that translucent outsole. Bibby reportedly complained he was sliding all over the court when he wore them during March Madness.

For all this technology, the Foamposite One didn't come cheap; it retailed for a staggering $180—more than Air Jordans at the time. A new generation of sneakers had arrived. Nike successfully raised the bar for technology, fashion, and price point with the popularity of the model.

Nike promoted the Foamposite through a series of print ads. Right around the time Bibby and Hardaway revealed the Foams on TV, the brand produced a mysterious postcard featuring the Foamposite One on a wet basketball court. There was also a "phone ad" of the Foamposite—part of the two-year series from 1995 to 1997 of more than sixty different Nike sneakers that were featured on a simple white background with a red Swoosh logo and telephone number on the bottom.

As far as TV commercials for the Foamposite went, there were no ads featuring Hardaway or his sidekick, Lil' Penny. Instead, there were just two short clips of the Foamposite—one with the sneaker sitting on a subway seat and another with the shoe on a basketball court. There were anonymous voices in the background talking about Hardaway and his new "space basketball shoes." Considering the relative lack of marketing Nike put into the bold new design makes the fact that it was a phenomenon even more impressive.

In the fall of '97, a new Foamposite released: the Foamposite Pro. The Pro featured a jeweled Swoosh on the side and no Hardaway logo. It was originally designed for Chicago Bull Scottie Pippen, but he was not a fan of the model and never wore it in an NBA game. San Antonio Spurs star forward Tim Duncan famously wore it during the '98 All-Star Game that season.

Since Nike never planned on retroing the Foamposite, the original molds were destroyed. The next generation of Foams looked slightly different. That didn't deter sneakerheads from buying them, though. The Foamposite Pro retroed for the first time in 2001, and seven colorways would release over the next five years. The Foamposite One returned for the first time in four colorways in 2007.

Since 1997, Nike has released almost a hundred different colorways of the Foamposite, and countless other models have been inspired by the original design.

Nike turned up Foamposite frenzy to a fever pitch with the much-hyped Galaxy, from 2012. With a glow-in-the-dark outsole and printed upper (a first on a Foamposite), it inspired sneakerheads to camp out for days. It also drew police presence at its launch in Orlando at that year's NBA All-Star festivities. Thanks in part to platforms like Twitter and Instagram, where the pandemonium surrounding the model played out in real time, and the growing sneaker resale market, the Galaxy helped set off the current sneaker craze.

But the Galaxy isn't the only Foam to have met such a fervored response. Its success was followed by a sustained campaign of graphic pairs that were nearly unattainable. The *ParaNorman* and Doernbecher models, from 2012 and 2013, still remain highly sought after. And in 2014, the NYPD shut down the New York City in-store launch of Supreme's Foamposite. Videos from the event showed Lafayette Street closed as mobs of people flooded SoHo, hoping to walk away with the sneaker. Supreme stopped selling its Nike projects in store for years as a result. The Foamposite is beloved for its outrageous design, its once-futuristic tech, and the lore behind its introduction. As the years went by and sneakers grew lighter and more breathable, the Foamposite became increasingly known as a bulky, heavy "brick" of a shoe. Very few professional players break out the Foams on the court anymore, but the line continues to retro in new and OG colorways both in the Foamposite One and Pro models. When it first dropped, nobody on this planet had ever seen a shoe like the Foam. Footwear here on Earth hasn't been the same since.

1997

Honorable Mention
Nike Air Max 97

It's a flashing symbol of status on the street outside a Milan nightclub. It's a bullet train speeding through the countryside in sleek silver. It's a drop of water in a pond, the ripples drawing concentric circles. All of these storylines of varying veracity contribute to the mythology of the Nike Air Max 97, a model that went from cult favorite to mainstream smash over the long tail of its retro life.

The Air Max 97 debuted in the fall of 1997, an era when Nike could still reasonably bill its Air-bubbled shoes as legitimate runners. Track stars Michael Johnson and Carl Lewis endorsed it. The 97 had legitimate innovations, too, like that striking full-length bag on the bottom. Its metallic and reflective sheen (inspired, despite popular lore, by mountain bike finishes rather than Japanese bullet trains) cast it as a cutting-edge machine for athletes. But it was the shoe's impact outside the world of sports performance that made it legendary.

by Brendan Dunne

"It became the shoe for kids," Italian fashion designer Riccardo Tisci recalled in *Le Silver*, a 2017 monograph on how much Italy cherished the model. "You'd go to a rave and you'd see it on the feet of everybody."

Tisci traced the shoe's influence in Italy back to dangerous nightlife figures who picked up on its futuristic look early. In the year after its debut, the Air Max 97 moved from that world to runways, appearing in shows for Giorgio Armani and Dolce & Gabbana, back when sneakers were non-existent in fashion houses. Per *Le Silver*, one Foot Locker manager in Milan hoarded the 97s, refusing to put them on sale despite company orders and later feeling vindicated when people flocked to his store to pick up pairs as they gained momentum.

That energy around the Nike Air Max 97 didn't resonate globally until the shoe was resurrected for its twentieth anniversary. In the interim decades, it was very much a sneakerhead shoe—Nike wasn't making a significant amount of pairs, and a stroll through the fashionable sectors of any given city wouldn't necessarily yield many sightings. But a shrewd Nike marketing plan that saw pairs trickle out starting in late 2016 and went full force in 2017 turned the sneaker from cult classic to ubiquitous.

Christian Tresser, who designed the shoe, intended the wavy lines of the upper to represent a drop's reverberations in a pond. Look from the top down and you'll see the translation, the circles that start smaller and widen with the passing of time.

The design turned out to be prophetic; more than twenty years later, the imprint of the Air Max 97 is only getting bigger.

1998 Nike Air Max Plus

Over the decade that followed the introduction of visible Air on the Air Max 1 in 1987, Nike incrementally improved the technology on a near-yearly basis. Time after time, the Air-filled chambers would get bigger and bigger, more refined, and more spectacular from both an aesthetic and performance standpoint—see the Air Max 180, Air Max 93, and Air Max 95 as examples. Then, in the late '90s, following the introduction of its first full-length Air unit with the Air Max 97, things came to a bit of a standstill. The technology, for the time being, had reached its ceiling, maxing out—no pun intended—until the even more expansive Air Max 360 was introduced in 2006. But while the evolution of Air Max technology had slowed, a whole new contender would enter the fray.

by Riley Jones

In 1998, Nike introduced the Air Max Plus (known in some regions as the Air TN or Tuned 1, as a reference to its first-of-its-kind Tuned Air technology). Tuned Air itself was a pivot from the full-length Air Max 97 cushioning seen just a year prior. Instead of using a singular Air unit, Tuned Air combined what Nike describes as molded polymer "hemispheres" in the heel chambers for added stability. Notable for being the debut Nike running shoe to use Tuned Air, the Air Max Plus was designed by then-newcomer Sean McDowell, who created the sneaker as his first major project with the company.

In fact, McDowell's work on the iconic design began before he was even employed by Nike. In a retrospective for the sneaker's twentieth anniversary, McDowell recalled relaxing on Florida beaches, sketching the palm-tree-laden landscape that would later serve as the inspiration for the Air Max Plus's cage-like gradient upper. In theory, the upper's palm tree-like exoskeleton would cradle the foot, while the beach sunset would eventually lead to color inspiration for the sneaker.

McDowell joined the brand in 1997 and was soon tasked with delivering a special shoe for Foot Locker featuring Tuned Air cushioning. Foot Locker had already passed on more than 15 sketches submitted by other designers, putting the pressure on McDowell to come up with something radical enough to satisfy the retailer. With the sneaker's tentative name of "Sky Air," the designer was reminded of his pre-employment sketches on the Florida coast. He pulled out the drafts and got back to work, settling on three distinct color options in orange, blue, and purple. The former two would wind up becoming the Air Max Plus's definitive colorways, while the third purple style remained a sketch until it was brought to life for a twentieth anniversary release in 2018.

While the Air Max Plus may be best known for its Tuned Air cushioning, the research and development that went into finalizing the rest of the shoe was nothing short of impressive. Despite having sketched detailed renditions of what the upper would look like, its production presented a handful of challenges. McDowell recalls co-workers warning him the upper's gradient fades simply weren't feasible. "You'll never be able to do that; you can't find a material like that," someone told him, according to a post published on Nike.com in 2018. He was determined, though, and suggested Nike employ the sublimation printing it had previously used on apparel in hopes of achieving a look reminiscent of 1983's Omega Flame runner. The experiment paid off, but there was more work to be done. The upper's palm-tree-inspired caging would require a type of welding Nike hadn't used before. With just two weeks to go before a formal pitch to Foot Locker, McDowell flew to Asia to oversee the process first-hand. He was told the weld was still unachievable and that it either wouldn't bond properly or would risk melting the fabric. The designer suggested layering the TPU in three separate welds rather than one large piece—yet another experiment that paid off.

"The heel is separate from the midfoot, [which] is separate from the forefoot," McDowell said in a 2018 interview with Champs Sports. "So we welded three times and that sort of gave us the strength to bond and weld everything together."

1998

With a finalized sample in hand, McDowell was joined by Mark Parker, who would go on to become Nike's CEO in 2006, at meetings with Foot Locker executives. These meetings resulted in another risk, this time in the form of the sneaker's marketing. The retailer decided to place the shoe on its shelves with no warning, timing it right around when teenagers would be getting out of school. "Five or ten minutes later, there were like ten kids flocking to the shoe asking, 'What is this? How do I get it?" McDowell said. "The associates were looking around like, 'I've never seen that thing before, I don't know how much it costs; I don't know where it came from,' while the kids were running around like, 'I want to buy this thing.' They were almost frantic. I was beaming."

With Foot Locker's stamp of approval, the Air Max Plus would remain exclusive to the retail chain for years to come. The Air Max Plus is one of the rare examples of a shoe that hardly takes a hiatus from the marketplace—similar to other iconic models such as the Air Force 1 and Air Max 90. Its global success is also noteworthy, with legions of fans beyond the States, specifically in Australia, Paris, and London. Australia in particular has a striking fascination with the shoe, which has resulted in more regional exclusive styles than any other area. It's also got somewhat of a nefarious connotation Down Under, where it's often associated with some of the less favorable elements of street culture.

"It goes back to the sort of characters that wore TNs before it became a trend," said Raymond Ray, a Sydney native and Air Max Plus enthusiast who was once a member of the Facebook group TN Talk. "Can't pinpoint why lads, searchers, or whatever you want to call them chose TNs amongst other sneakers to represent what they're about. Could have been because at the time it was one of the most expensive Nike sneakers on shelves, [and] boosted with the aggressive look of the veins and multiple bubbles, it made an ultimate accessory for people who used to participate in [criminal] activities." These days, Ray theorizes that the shoe's popularity Down Under is more about image than lifestyle. "Now that they are a trend, it's mostly normal civilians wearing them. The TN scene recently has just been kids going to raves and wearing the shoes because they're popular. There's a new market for these kids wanting to look like they're criminals," he said.

More than twenty years after Nike introduced it, the Plus has become a staple of the brand's Air Max line despite its once-rebellious connotations. Following the initial design in 1998, the Air Max Plus franchise would continue with multiple sequels throughout the 2000s, wrapping up with a tenth anniversary Air Max Tuned 10 model in 2008, but none of them have held quite the same staying power as the OG. McDowell's unique design and willingness to push the envelope paid off handsomely, resulting in a shoe that's withstood the test of time and still manages to have some futuristic flair to this day. And from the beaches of Florida to the underbelly of Australia, the Air Max Plus has quite literally gone global.

Honorable Mention
Nike Air Zoom Flight ("The Glove")

In 1998, perhaps the most exciting Nike signature line outside of Michael Jordan's belonged to Gary Payton, the All-Star point guard famous for his lockdown defense. While the following year's Zoom GP would be the first sneaker to bear his initials officially, the Air Zoom Flight—better known as "The Glove," a name by which Payton also happened to be known—is his most famous model.

Despite its relatively short run, Payton's line saw no shortage of design risks, including interchangeable uppers on 2001's Air Zoom GP 3 and ski boot–style buckles on 1999's Zoom GP. It was Nike designer Eric Avar's "The Glove," however, that set the precedent for these later models. The shoe featured a

by Zac Dubasik

full-shrouded upper fastened via zipper, which housed a TPU monkey paw–shaped support structure along its sides. Combined with Zoom Air cushioning, it was about as high tech as a sneaker got in 1998.

"We did not originally plan on shrouding the shoe," Avar told Sole Collector in 2013. "We were working with the [Nike] Advanced Group, and we were working closely with [developer] Tom Foxen. He had done a lot of the original performance design of the monkey paw."

The team believed the tech was becoming too visually complex and wanted more balance. "We had the science behind it covered, but, aesthetically, we just couldn't get to a point where we felt comfortable with the monkey paw being a simple and modern and very wearable solution. So we collectively decided to wonder, 'What if we just put this skin over the top of the shoe?'"

Once Payton's signature line had run its course, he had a stint with Jordan Brand. Late in his career, though, he went back to "The Glove" and wore the model in the 2006 NBA Finals, playing for the Miami Heat, when he won his only championship. Despite the shoe's return in new Heat–themed colorways that year, it never actually retroed until 2013.

"I wouldn't say the design at the time was busy, but there was definitely a lot of technology and a lot going on with shoes," Avar told Sole Collector. "The Glove was interesting and almost a complete departure toward utter simplicity at the time. I think that was one of the more unique things about that shoe and about that time. And, of course, it was perfect for Gary Payton's nickname."

1999 Air Jordan XIV

Six. Fourteen. Forty-five. For Michael Jordan, a man who cares deeply about numbers, the stars have always had a tendency of aligning. Take that fateful evening in Utah—on June 14, the sixth month of the year. That night, Michael Jordan of the Chicago Bulls scored 45 points in Game 6 of the NBA Finals versus John Stockton, Karl Malone, and the Utah Jazz. With the Bulls trailing, 86–85, and Bryon Russell draped all over him, Jordan penetrated to the right, crossed over, stopped on a dime, and pulled up for a long jumper with six seconds left on the clock to give the Bulls the lead and their sixth title. Talk about destiny. And on MJ's feet that fourteenth day of the month was a brand-new sneaker that had sneakerheads glued to the TV set, trying to get a good look at it.

by Drew Hammell

What was Mike wearing? Whatever he broke out during the 1998 NBA Finals for two out of the six games, they sure weren't the Air Jordan XIIIs. Throughout the playoffs that year, Jordan sported all-black AJ XIIIs, just as he had traditionally rocked black sneakers in the past. But during that Finals series, MJ started alternating between the XIIIs and something new. Was it an updated XIII? It was tough to tell on those blurry TV screens. The red shank plate and yellow circle of the new logo didn't look like the XIII, so it had to be a new model. Whatever they were, those shoes were sleek, and MJ seemed to like them.

It turns out the sneaker Jordan was wearing while hitting his last shot on June 14 was the fourteenth Air Jordan model—a sneaker that Jordan was not ready to unveil. But, obviously, that didn't stop him from wearing them. Just as he had with previous models that looked and felt too good not to try out (like the AJ XI), Jordan laced up the all-black XIV prototype several times in the NBA Finals against the Jazz. That particular colorway became an instant classic because of the technology and legacy behind it.

By this point, Nike designer Tinker Hatfield had crafted eleven-straight Air Jordan sneakers. Teaming up with Mark Smith, Hatfield's goal for the XIV was to evoke the feeling of extreme speed on the basketball court. Touted as a "high-performance, luxury ride," the XIV featured full-grain leather with an internal lacing system, a Phylon midsole with articulated heel, and forefoot Zoom Air units.

The XIV was clearly inspired by Jordan's favorite Ferrari—the 550 Maranello.

Air Jordan XIV

Its aggressive lines and luxurious styling gave nods to the car with a new Jumpman shield logo, which echoed the prancing horse fender badge. Additionally, the XIV resembled the 550, with a tire-tread-like sole that rode up the heel in the back, along with red jewel taillights. On the front of the sole were shark teeth that resembled headlights. There was also a state-of-the-art ventilation system that resembled an exhaust cutout on the medial side of the outsole. There was a unique bar at the top of the tongue that almost looked like a steering wheel. And there was memory foam in the ankle padding that felt like custom bucket seats. Numbers played a key role on the shoe as well—each sneaker featured seven Jumpman logos, for a total of fourteen.

Several months after Jordan debuted the XIV, *Slam* magazine dropped its first annual "Kicks" issue, with clear pictures of the black/red version. In the era before social media, this was the public's first opportunity to see the sneaker up close and personal, aside from photos of MJ wearing it in the Finals.

Jordan Brand dropped a cryptic print ad featuring a simple image of the black/red version with a small message tucked away in the bottom right-hand corner of the page. It read simply and fittingly: "We apologize for the flashbacks this may trigger among Utah fans."

Officially releasing on Halloween in 1998, the "Black Toe" Air Jordan XIV in white/black/red was the first colorway to drop. Due in part to several factors, including the NBA lockout and that Jordan didn't wear the white model in an NBA game, the release was less hyped than those of previous Jordan sneakers. Several months later, on March 27, 1999, the black/red "Last Shots" released to the public.

After that "Last Shot," MJ stepped away from the game of basketball for a second time early in 1999. Rumors were swirling for months, and everyone assumed that he would be retiring again soon. In the wake of that final season, the entire Chicago Bulls squad was dismantled after their sixth and last championship run in '98. Phil Jackson stepped down as coach. Without Coach Jackson, MJ wasn't coming back, either. Jordan's sidekick, Scottie Pippen, was then traded to the Houston Rockets. The charismatic Dennis Rodman was released and joined the Los Angeles Lakers. It was the end of one of the greatest eras in sports history.

Though Jordan never wore the "Black Toe" colorway on the court, he did sport it in CGI form in the IMAX documentary *Michael Jordan to the Max* in 2000. Jordan is shown wearing a white Bulls uniform, running down the court in black socks and the AJ XIV. He leaps into the air to take off for his patented free-throw-line dunk as the camera circles around him 360-style.

There were nine original colorways of the XIV—both in mid-cut and low-cut models. Some versions featured smooth full-grain leather on the upper, and others had ribbed perforated panels. As with the Air Jordan XI mid and low, Hatfield mixed it up with the design of the Air Jordan XIV mid and low. There were plenty of similarities between the two, but the cut of the sneaker and the heels were noticably different. Additionally, the low came in non-Bulls colorways like royal blue, Columbia blue, and ginger. During the summer of 2000, Eastbay dropped an exclusive UNC mid-cut

version, which took people by surprise. The mids also came out in non-Bulls colorways—an effort for the brand to demonstrate that Air Jordans were for everyone and were stylish both on and off the court.

For the first time in Air Jordan history, the Jordan XIV came in a cleat version as well. The New York Yankees phenom shortstop Derek Jeter, at the time the newest member of the Jordan team, rocked it on the diamond.

Like every Jordan before it, the XIV has seen its share of retro models, both in OG form and new colors. It didn't take long for the XIV to return, as it came back in 2005 in a slew of new colorways, along with a rerelease of the "Last Shot" black/red model.

In 2005, before the "Last Shot" XIVs returned as a retro for the first time, samples of a pair featuring a red tongue surfaced. This somewhat subtle yet perceptible difference caused a ruckus on the early internet sneaker forums. True-school sneakerheads typically wanted to see their cherished models return true to their original form, down to the smallest detail. There was immediate backlash from sneaker purists who flooded message boards, venting about the new red tongue. How could a shoe so symbolic as the black/red XIV be changed like that? Fortunately, Jordan Brand heard the feedback loud and clear and restored the shoe's original look. Ironically, to this day, the sample XIVs are extremely sought after.

The white/red and white/black versions returned in 2006, although the "Black Toe" swapped out the smooth leather upper for the perforated upper. More colorways have released over the years, including an all-red suede "Ferrari" model in 2014. Supreme gave the XIV a reworking in 2019—inspired by a studded jacket MJ once wore. The XIV also received the Doernbecher treatment in 2019. Hospital patient Ethan Ellis's design paid homage to his favorite team, the TCU Horned Frogs, along with people and places that were part of his health journey.

Style-wise, many argue that the XIV was the last great Air Jordan model. Beginning with the Air Jordan XV, Jordan sneaker designs got a little too wild, and the sneaker community was not impressed. It also didn't help that the main spokesman—MJ himself—was out of the league until 2002, when he returned to play for the Washington Wizards.

Performance-wise, the XIV will always be known as one of the best. It was the perfect court shoe for college players and pros alike. For Jordan, it was the last sneaker he'd wear as part of the Chicago Bulls organization—a sneaker no one else had. Just like when MJ debuted the Air Jordan XI in the '95 playoffs, the XIV was a model that stood out more than any other on the court. The shoe generated its own hype by the sheer shock and surprise it created in the sneaker community, because no one had seen anything like it. Had Jordan missed that shot, the Jazz might have won the game, and who knows what he would have donned for Game 7? But the fact that he was wearing the XIV and hit one of the most clutch shots ever locked the sneaker in history as one of the most memorable he wore.

Honorable Mention
AND1 Tai Chi

When Vince Carter dunks, the world pays attention. That's the way things were in 2000, a year that had him throwing down no small number of the most vicious slams ever recorded. There was his performance in the Slam Dunk Contest over the 2000 NBA All-Star Weekend, which featured reverses, heroic spins, an elbow in the rim, and some very reasonable braggadocio. Hopefully you've seen the GIF evidence of Shaquille O'Neal reacting with pure awe and excitement, era-appropriate camcorder in hand. These were feats of otherworldly athleticism. The bending of the laws of physics that made them possible just didn't seem feasible for the average ballplayer. Although maybe getting the same sneakers as Carter could help matters.

by Brendan Dunne

It was the Slam Dunk Contest that exploded the popularity of the AND1 Tai Chi, a relatively plain basketball sneaker that arrived in 1999. Carter wore the original red and white colorway from the upstart brand and soared fiercely toward the rim time and time again that weekend. The moment was huge for AND1, which had begun in 1993 as a grad school project dreamed up by a trio of students at the University of Pennsylvania. At first, the company sold only apparel, finding significant success doing so with its "trash talk" line of tees and shorts. Eventually, it parlayed that success into partnerships with some of the NBA's brightest stars of the decade. In 1996, Stephon Marbury became the first pro player to align himself with the brand. Kevin Garnett and Latrell Sprewell followed, getting their own signature shoes with AND1.

Ultimately, none of these held the same cultural weight as the Tai Chi. It wasn't a signature shoe for Carter, who went on to wear Nike at the Olympics just months later, but it was forever connected to him thanks to his dazzling performance at the Slam Dunk Contest. The sneaker helped turn AND1 into a serious contender in the category in under ten years—before the new millennium, when Nike bulldozed the competition in the space. AND1 couldn't sustain its momentum and petered out as the Swoosh poured more money and resources into serious signings of rookies and footwear innovations.

While the AND1 Tai Chi may not mean a lot to today's younger consumers—it would be an exaggeration to say that its rerelease amid major drops at ComplexCon 2018, one of several times it's retroed, was more than a blip on their radar—its spot in sneaker and Slam Dunk history is unquestionable.

At the turn of the century, Michael Jordan left the game of basketball, his fade to black turning him from superhero to Jumpman silhouette. His sneakers remained, but their power had diminished. Where did the industry turn? To lines from new signature shoe superstars who would forever be measured against him. Beyond shoes anchored to players, brands flaunted technology that would change the way we think about sneakers.

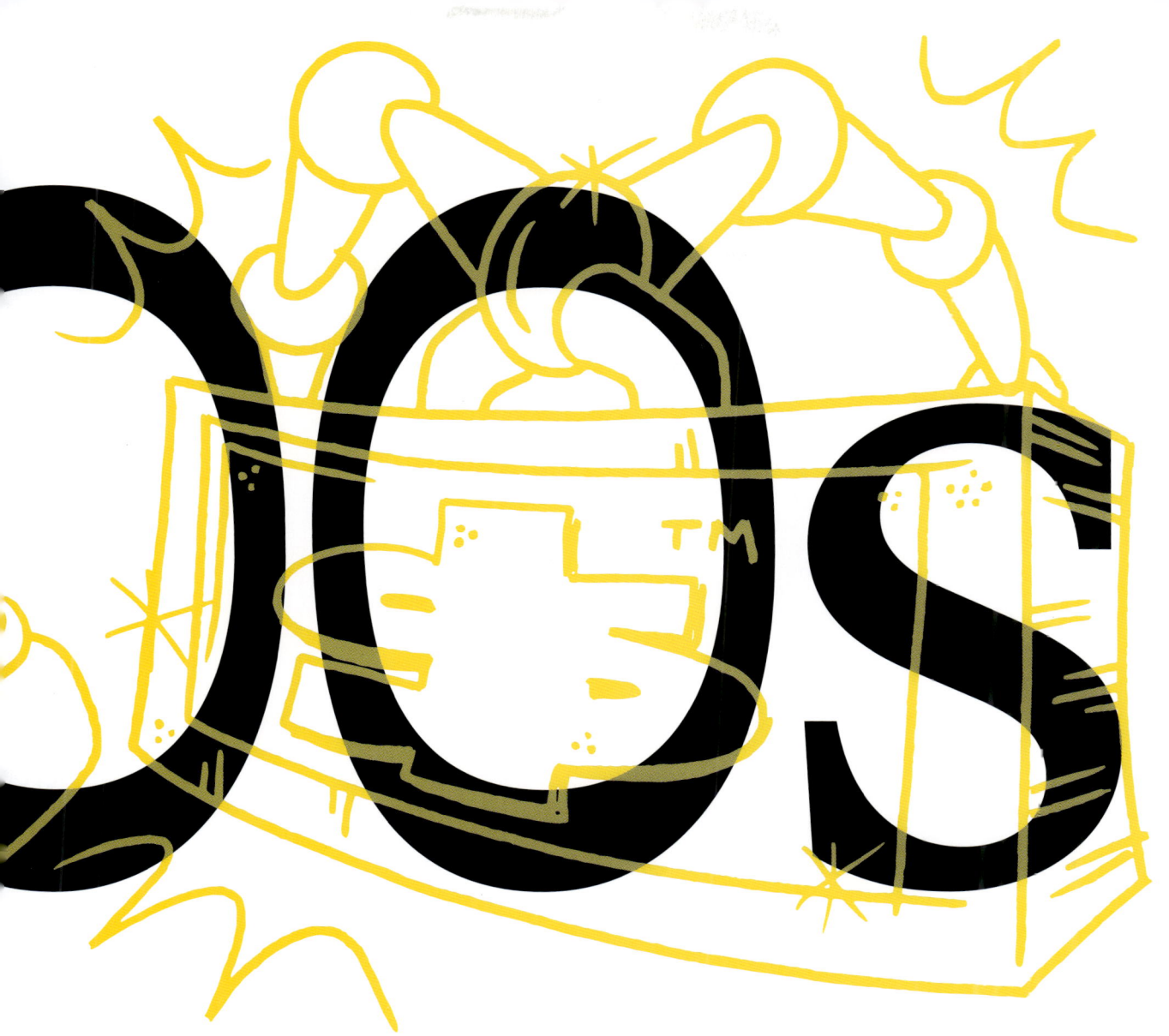

The kids who saved up their allowances to buy the original Air Maxes and Adidas now had salaries. Brands seized upon their purchasing power, cranking out retro editions that in some ways overshadowed their new designs. It was these, often produced in limited numbers and with the help of collaborators, that put hype on steroids and created the resale market, which ushered a subculture into the mainstream. This is when sneaker culture grew up.

2000 Nike Air Presto

It's a shoe that would have been called the Air Comfy if a slipper brand in New England hadn't already owned the rights to the name. "What is it going to take to get that mark?" future Nike CEO Mark Parker asked the sneaker's designer, Tobie Hatfield, in the late '90s, when he found out the company's legal department was nixing the original name of the model.

"We'd have to talk to the company," Hatfield replied. "Well, how big is the company?" Parker said, determined to secure the moniker for this upcoming shoe. "Maybe we entertain buying the company so we can get that name."

by Gerald Flores

Fortunately for sneaker enthusiasts, and for that unnamed New England company, Nike chose to go with Air Presto. Although it's not as self-explanatory as Air Comfy, *comfy* was the word the first testers of the prototype used to describe the sensation of wearing the shoe, which is what inspired the original name in the first place.

"Ninety percent of the time, that's the word that came out of their mouth when they tried it on," Hatfield recalled. He knew it was a hit when they showed it off at a Rock 'n' Roll Marathon expo and sold out of all 120 promotional pairs. Six people even took the shoes and ran the marathon in them the next day.

Hatfield came up with the concept for the shoe while opening Nike's first research-and-development facility in Taiwan. Unlike most of Nike's products, there was no product brief or athlete asking for it. Hatfield simply came up with the idea after walking by a yet-to-be-used sample room full of fresh materials and components. He wanted to be the first to play with what was in there. "The room was just for innovation and for starting new things," Hatfield said. "Nothing was going in it. And I had this, like, real, I guess you could say, an epiphany."

He was wearing one of the company's Air Max sneakers at the time. While he liked the model, he and others to whom he spoke were concerned about fit and comfort. After taking stock of the materials in the room, he cobbled together a shoe that would address those issues, using an existing model as a base and stripping it down to its essentials.

"Nobody was necessarily telling me what to do," Hatfield said. "I decided to go ahead and just do something on my own."

The result was a running sneaker with a stretchy sock-like upper. He decided to put it to the test by giving it to somebody who was going for a run. It just so happened that the runner was a size 11, two full sizes bigger than the size 9 sample.

Hatfield didn't tell him the shoe was two sizes too small, though he expected to hear it was too tight. The feedback he received an hour later mystified him. The runner didn't mention the size discrepancy, instead reporting a mostly smooth ride.

"Why was he not able to detect that it was too small? The only thing I could think of is that, when we build a shoe normally, you have areas all along the shoe that [have] tension in [them]," Hatfield said, referring to the parts of the sneaker he stripped from the prototype. "When you do this, essentially, you're elongating the shoe, and so it essentially grew with his foot because that tension wasn't there to hold it up."

Presto. Hatfield inadvertently created sneaker magic. He knew he had to develop this concept further and put it in front of Parker.

As he built on the idea, Hatfield actually looked to one of his brother Tinker's designs from the '90s for inspiration: the Air Huarache. The form-fitting silhouette on that running sneaker used a scuba-like material called neoprene. There was only one problem with it.

"The one thing that people didn't necessarily like about it was that it was too hot," Hatfield said. "We did poke some holes in [it] and tried to ventilate it as much as possible. But it still was pretty toasty."

So the designer looked to the medical industry. There, he found a vendor that provided a mesh material that was replacing neoprene in hospitals. The material came in a variety of thicknesses and could stabilize, for instance, wraps for tennis elbow but still allow a little bit of movement. The Presto marked the first time the material was used in a shoe.

The next part of the puzzle was figuring out its sizing. How could Nike put true sizes on something that could fit a range of feet?

"Every foot is very different, morphologically, and then, on top of that, everybody's perception is different. Some like it tight; some like it loose. It's all over the board," Hatfield said. "Then [I] took a step back and thought when I buy a shirt or whatever, the fact is that it's labeled a small, medium, large. I already know what's going on, that it's a range."

The Nike Presto came in a T-shirt-like assortment of sizes, hence the tagline "T-Shirts for Your Feet." The designer even envisioned the sneakers hanging on vertical racks in stores next to packs of socks instead of in traditional shoeboxes.

When the Presto rolled out—in boxes—it released in an astonishing thirteen colorways, an anomaly for a totally new product, which would normally be available in three to four, at most. Twelve of the thirteen colorways also had their own cartoon characters that were featured in a series of TV spots—a marketing effort devised by agency Wieden+Kennedy. The sneaker was an instant success.

"The buys were starting to be very, very strong," Hatfield said. "We'd hear from the Foot Lockers and the big-box stores how much they wanted to buy into this because it was different. It wasn't like anything else on their wall."

The shoes, released close to the 2000 Summer Olympics in Sydney, were an immediate success. In addition to athletes, special editions of the sneakers also made their way to pop culture icons. In 2001, Nike gave Eric Clapton an exclusive run of Prestos while he was on his world tour. A special checkerboard-print version of the sneaker was specifically made for Rick Nielsen of the band Cheap Trick. An extremely limited Hello Kitty collaboration was made in 2004 to mark the character's thirtieth anniversary. Friends-and-family pairs were even produced for the cast and crew of the *Sex and the City* movie in 2008.

Unlike the Air Jordan or other sneakers in Nike's lineage, the Presto was seldom retroed. It has, however, seen a few iterations over the years, including a slip-on version of the silhouette without the plastic cage, the Air Presto Chanjo. In the early 2000s, the sneaker was reconfigured by Mark Parker, Tinker Hatfield, and Hiroshi Fujiwara's design team, known as HTM, to function more like a boot, with only about 1,500 pairs made. A reinforced version of the shoe, which could be used as a cross-trainer, also released at mass retail.

Collaborations helped bring the Presto back to the fore in the '10s. German brand Acronym, led by designer Errolson Hugh, who was also working on the Nike ACG line at the time, retooled the Presto to be a zip-up mid-cut sneaker with updated fabrics in the fall of 2016. The silhouette was also included in Virgil Abloh's "The Ten," a collection of deconstructed sneakers by the designer meant to represent the ten models that changed Nike's trajectory.

The Presto helped pave the way for other products inside the brand, too. If it weren't for the model, Hatfield wouldn't have gone on to create the Nike Free line, the cornerstone of Nike's natural-motion footwear. Not only is the Presto an important part of the company's genealogy of sneakers, but it also holds a special place in the hearts of aficionados. More than twenty years later, Hatfield is still in awe of its success.

"In 2000, I just felt we were on to something," Hatfield said. "It wasn't supposed to be our highest-performing running shoe that year. It wasn't intended to be that. But it was supposed to be our most comfortable and maybe provocative, unexpected kind of thing that we could have also have fun with."

Honorable Mention
Nike Shox R4

With its mechanical cushioning units, the Nike Shox R4 is one of the most distinctive athletic footwear designs of the early 2000s. Some have fond memories of the model; others deride it as the ultimate bro shoe, a perfect complement to cargo shorts, a watery beer, and a frisbee in hand. But any way you slice it, it's an important model from the era, and one of the most influential sneakers of its time.

Air Max is the technology that Nike has built most of its cushioning legacy around. That design, which exposed the Air units in Nike midsoles, was created by Tinker Hatfield in 1987. But three years earlier, in 1984, Bruce Kilgore, the designer of the Air Force 1, flirted with mechanical cushioning. His first prototype looked nothing like the final product; a Nike waffle sneaker was suspended with a massive spring. The idea would never work in retail footwear.

by Matt Welty

Nike was finally able to nail down the modern Shox concept in 1997, three years before it released the inaugural models. The sneaker's midsole featured four rubber columns that could absorb impact and return energy, in theory to better the athlete's performance. Shox appeared on Nike basketball, training, tennis, and running shoes. But the model for the last of these sports is what turned the system into an icon of techy fashion.

The first Shox running shoe, the Shox R4, looked as technical as it sounded. The upper had a metallic fabric, white accents, and bright red Shox along the heel. In its wake, visible tech, something the Air Max series popularized, spread quickly across the industry in more outrageous ways. Adidas, Reebok, and Puma tried it to varying degrees of success. But the Shox was still the gold standard. The R4 had street cred, too. The runner was a staple of Harlem in the age of True Religion jeans, and it's seen a reemergence uptown with retro versions over the past few years.

The biggest moment for the Shox, however, didn't come with the R4, but rather its basketball counterpart, the BB4. In the 2000 Summer Olympics, Vince Carter dunked over Frédéric Weis, a 7'2" center from France. Weis, who was drafted by the Knicks, never played in the NBA. He battled alcoholism and depression before moving home. Carter's feat was labeled the "dunk of death," and it signaled the beginning of the end of Weis's career. And it took place in a pair of Nike Shox. It was the colossal "boing" the brand was looking for at the time. Twenty years later, it's hard to find someone who hasn't owned a pair of the sneakers.

2000

2001 Reebok Answer 4

To fully grasp the significance of Allen Iverson's Reebok Answer IV, context matters. Perhaps as much as it does for any other sneaker ever produced. It's not a shoe that transcended its time because of a futuristic design or catchy slogans. It matters today because Iverson wore the shoe during a moment many describe as the very peak of his Hall of Fame career, a moment that stands as one of the greatest underdog stories in NBA history. Before diving into the shoe itself—a model best known for its zip-up upper and on-court moments—the stage must be set to explain why it resonates with so many people.

by Brandon Richard

Some say championships define legacies in sports, and, for the most part, they're correct. Beyond championships, MVP awards, retired jerseys, Hall of Fame inductions, and impact on culture have a unique way of separating legendary athletes from true icons. Iverson never won an NBA championship. His Georgetown teams never advanced past the Elite Eight in the NCAA tournament, and his version of Team USA famously stumbled into a bronze medal at the 2004 Summer Olympics. But nobody would dare say that he's not a champion—particularly a champion of the culture. Street culture. Hip-hop culture. His culture.

At the time, Iverson embodied everything hip-hop had become, style-wise. Fur coats, throwback jerseys, oversize jeans, fitted hats, durags, and diamond chains in the tunnel. Cornrows, head-to-toe tattoos, and accessories like his famous shooting sleeve were front and center on the court. In fact, he even dabbled in music himself, releasing the controversial and profanity-laden single "40 Bars" under the moniker Jewels. Iverson wasn't the first NBA player to represent hip-hop culture in the league, but he was the first whose appearance was an in-your-face reminder of the lifestyle he was about.

What he was about didn't appeal to everyone, particularly out-of-touch critics threatened by his refusal to conform to the false social standards imposed on athletes, especially athletes of his background. He never claimed perfection—in fact, his willingness to be openly flawed was part of his charm. Iverson never wavered. He stayed true to who he was and where he was from, despite constant pressure to change. He was unapologetically himself.

The best way to shut your critics up is to be the best at what you do, and, in 2000–01, Iverson was the world's best basketball player. He dominated the season, claiming All-Star MVP; his second scoring and steals titles; nabbed First Team All NBA honors; and was named the league's Most Valuable Player. Most important, he led the Philadelphia 76ers through a grueling playoff run to reach the NBA Finals, setting the stage for a showdown against the defending champion Los Angeles Lakers.

While led by the superstar tandem of Shaquille O'Neal and Kobe Bryant, the Lakers turned to little-known reserve guard Tyronn Lue as their surprise weapon for the Finals. Lue was tasked with imitating Iverson's style of play during practice and guarding him in the series, despite having only played sixty-one games total through his first three seasons. The Lue-Iverson matchup would lead to a moment that would go on to largely define both players' careers.

With the Sixers leading by two, and with less than a minute to play in overtime of Game 1 of the Finals, Iverson had the ball and an opportunity to give his team some much-needed extra cushioning. Hounded by his unlikely nemesis, Iverson sized Lue up and hit him with the essential AI package: jab step, crossover, and a sixteen-foot fadeaway over his outstretched arms. The ball found the bottom of the net without making contact with the rim. As the shot went through, Lue lost his footing and fell to the ground. What happened next has become one of the most iconic moments in the sport's history: Iverson stepped over Lue, his eyes staring him down. It was a message. Ruthless. Calculated. The Lakers went on to win the Championship, but the series would be remembered for Iverson's game-clincher and stepover in Game 1 and, of course, the Answer IV—the sneaker he wore.

As Iverson faced growing scrutiny over his persona, the Answer IV was almost Reebok's way of standing in solidarity with its superstar. Making it his most personal model yet, the shoe featured a portrait of Iverson on the outsole, prominently displaying his trademark braids and headband. Above it was the phrase "Only the Strong Survive," which was inspired by the tattoo on his left arm and styled in the exact same script. The Answer IV wasn't merely a sneaker—it was part of Iverson and the culmination of everything he had worked for.

Leather sneakers were fairly standard when the Answer IV hit shelves, but its leather-on-leather build, down to the inner lining, gave the model an extra-premium feel. While the retail version was released with an exposed zipper, the league issued a mandate requiring him to cover the zipper on his game shoes, hence the addition of a cross-strap to his player-edition versions and future rereleases. Still, Iverson wore his Answer IVs unzipped and unstrapped throughout the season. DMX I-Pak cushioning and split traction aided Iverson's unique ability to accelerate past defenders and made the model a speedy guard shoe by default.

"These are special to me because this is the one and only time I went to the Finals," Iverson said in a 2017 episode of Complex's *Sneaker Shopping*. "And all season long, I did these in so many different flavors. It was

crazy. I had, like, twenty-something different styles."

Ironically, the colorway of the Answer IV that Iverson wore in Game 1 of the Finals wasn't available to the public. Dubbed "Playoffs" or "Step Over" and eventually released as a retro in 2017, the simple black-and-white makeup was personally requested by Iverson, who wanted to mix up his colorways as much as possible during seasons.

"Basically, he was like, 'Yo, we got to flip it,'" Todd Krinsky, senior vice president of Reebok, told Complex in 2012. "And sometimes we do it with the foam, so it was like, 'What do you mean, flip it?' He was like, 'The white goes where the black goes, the black goes where the white goes [on the general release version].' I was trying to visualize it—like, that's not going to look right. He goes, 'Make it.' So we made it, had it for Game 1."

The Answer IV was primarily marketed by way of a commercial in which the instrumental to "40 Bars" served as the backing track. Shot in the vein of an early 2000s rap video, the clip featured scenes of Iverson playing pickup, driving his car, and going to the club. In each segment, an alternate version of himself confronted him. The clip concluded with the tagline "Defy Convention," two words that perfectly encapsulated everything that Iverson stood for and what his signature sneaker represented on the court.

Later in the year, on the heels of his MVP season and the global success of the Answer IV, Iverson signed his much-talked-about "lifetime deal" with Reebok. An extension of the original ten-year agreement Iverson signed with the brand in 1996, the deal reportedly pays him $800,000 annually and includes a $32 million trust that he can access in 2030—ensuring that he's taken care of well beyond his basketball career.

"After he went to the Finals and had an amazing run in those Answer IVs, we started thinking more about the future and his family's future," Iverson's longtime manager Gary Moore told Nice Kicks in 2015. "We just felt like Reebok would always be there for him and he would always be there for them."

Today, the Answer IV is viewed as one of basketball's most memorable shoes, and for that to happen, a lot of things had to fall into place. Iverson had to be a generational talent. He had to be uniquely competitive. He had to sign with the sneaker company that may not have been the obvious choice. He had to be defiant. He had to take on Shaq and Kobe. He had to be resilient. He had to step over the competition. But most important, he had to be Allen Iverson, unapologetically.

Honorable Mention
Visvim FBT

Raymond Loewy, the visionary behind designs like the US Air Force logo and the Coca-Cola bottle, developed an approach dubbed the MAYA principle: "Most Advanced, Yet Acceptable." Loewy recognized that "the adult public's taste is not necessarily ready to accept the logical solutions to their requirements if the solution implies too vast a departure from what they have been conditioned into accepting as the norm." In other words, people want that new new, but not if it's too new.

It's unknown if Hiroki Nakamura, the founder of Visvim, knows who Loewy is, but the two share a similar ethos. Visvim, a Japanese clothing brand, is known for pieces that feel at once familiar and futuristic. No item in the brand's oeuvre speaks to that mission more than the FBT.

by Damien Scott

Inspired by a boot Nakamura discovered at age fourteen, the FBT fuses a fringed moccasin upper with EVA Phylon and Vibram midsoles commonly found on sneakers and performance boots. Early in Visvim's existence, Hiroshi Fujiwara, streetwear icon and founder of Fragment Design, showed Nakamura the cover of Fun Boy Three's 1984 greatest-hits album, *The Best of Fun Boy Three*. Both designers were interested in the dark brown suede mocs band member Terry Hall was wearing. Fujiwara convinced Nakamura to make his own version of the shoe. Nakamura's take appeared for the first time in Visvim's second collection in 2001.

"The basic concept was fairly simple: to keep the raw appearance of Native American moccasins, but with the added functionality of being wearable in the city," Nakamura explained in his 2014 dissertation on the FBT. "Being suitable for city life entailed more than just adding a sneaker sole; I was also concerned with the styling of the shoe, and the ability to mix and match with different outfits. This is where the idea of a removable fringe was born."

Celebrities including Kanye West, John Mayer, Drake, and Eric Clapton have all sworn by FBTs. They were exclusive, expensive, versatile, and comfortable. They felt at once like something you had never seen and something you always had. And, per Nakamura, that was the goal all along. In a 2004 interview with Beinghunted, he explained, "One of life's daily tools is a pair of shoes. We rely on them every day, so they should perform comfortably, be made of the nicest and high-tech materials available today, and still look great."

Raymond Loewy would be proud.

2002 Nike SB Dunk

Nike SB may have started in 2002, but it wasn't Nike's first foray into skateboarding. In 1996, the brand came out with a collection of skate shoes that's remembered most for an infamous model named, wait for it, the Choad. We'll leave it to you to look up the definition on Urban Dictionary. Let's just say the name probably wouldn't pass muster in Beaverton today.

by Justin Tejada

That mid-'90s collection of Nike skate shoes included other groaners such as the Snak, the Trog, and the Schimp. Nike did enlist Bam Margera—pre-*Jackass* fame—to ride for the brand. But Margera found the shoes so awful to skate in that he would wear éS Accels and affix a Nike sticker to them with Shoe Goo so it looked like he was still repping his sponsor's product.

It wasn't all bad. Nike produced some clever campaigns during this time. With the tagline "What if we treated all athletes the way we treat skateboarders?" the ads showed tennis players and golfers getting kicked off the court and the links by police and security guards in the way that skaters are booted from skate spots.

But even those ads had a tone-deaf quality to them. When Margera filmed a kickflip for the closing sequence of the campaign, the producers made him wear new shoes (at least he was wearing real Nikes) that had makeup applied to them so they looked worn-in. He wasn't permitted to wear actual broken-in shoes that would have allowed him to land the trick much faster.

While Nike's first attempt to break into skating was brief, the effects were long-lasting. In the insular world of skateboarding, where the worst thing you can call someone is a "poser," Nike earned a reputation of not getting it. It was the eight-hundred-pound gorilla that loudly came into the room trying to earn some cool points without actually paying any dues. All take, no give.

So when Nike tried to re-enter the skate market at the turn of the millennium with the SB line, there was a fair amount of trepidation and skepticism. "I had concerns, and I was somewhat vocal about them," said Reese Forbes, one of the original skaters on the SB team. "I was nervous about a couple of things. One is how Nike could come back into skating and screw it up again. Then I was nervous about everybody's reputation. What would it mean to Richard [Mulder] and myself and Gino [Iannucci] if we went and rode for Nike and it was a flop?"

But Nike had a few things going for it this time around. For starters, the brand paid heed to the maxim "Those who do not learn from history are doomed to repeat it." More important, Nike had a basketball shoe ripe for reinvention that would change sneaker culture forever: the Dunk.

The Dunk was not even the most famous shoe that Peter Moore helped design in 1985. That honor went to the debut signature shoe for a 6' 6" guard from the University of North Carolina who was drafted behind Sam Bowie. But the Dunk still made an impression.

Originally named the College Color High, the Dunk was a mash-up of other Nike basketball styles at the time, borrowing the outsole pattern from Moore's "other" creation, the Air Jordan 1, and featuring an upper inspired by the first Jordan and the Nike Terminator.

From the outset, one of the distinguishing features of the Dunk was how well it lent itself to storytelling. "You can do a lot with those panels," said Forbes. "The shoe itself is somewhat easy to manipulate with different textures and colors."

Nike's "Be True to Your School" campaign accompanied the release of the Dunk in the mid-'80s and showed styles designed for top college basketball programs, including Syracuse, Iowa, and Kentucky. It was the first time Nike used a bold array of color

ways on a basketball shoe and foreshadowed how much bolder the Dunk silhouette could become.

Skaters gravitated to those early Nike basketball shoes because they had a relatively slim profile and the high-top styling offered good ankle support. Powell-Peralta's iconic skate video *The Search for Animal Chin* came out in 1987, and, in one of the most famous scenes, four members of the Bones Brigade do handplants on the spine of a ramp. Three are wearing Air Jordan 1s.

Though less documented, the Dunk was also worn by skaters in the 1980s. In the '90s, though, as skate footwear grew more specialized, the model was all but forgotten.

This was the era of "bigger is better" skate shoes (think the Osiris D3), when skate companies, in a misguided attempt to ape athletic brands, added as many layers as possible to a) show that they could and b) ensure the shoes could stand up to the rigorous demands of skaters. The downside of that approach was that skate shoes of the time looked clunky and barely had any board feel.

The Dunk was not that, and that was part of its appeal. For skaters who were used to wearing one pair of shoes for skating and packing another pair for after the session, it could do double duty. "They were the exact opposite of the bread loaf skate shoe," said Richard Mulder, the first skater on the Nike SB roster.

They also looked right for skaters when they looked down at their feet on a board, which may sound trivial but is incredibly important.

"Back then, it was like, if I don't like what I'm wearing or riding, then I'd probably go home," said Forbes.

"Everything needs to be right," Mulder added. "You have to feel it from your sneakers to the shirt you're wearing. Everything needs to be aligned for you to have this good energy when you're skating."

While he wasn't a skater, Sandy Bodecker—who passed away in 2018—understood concerns like those. Bodecker was a runner who started off as a wear-tester for Nike. Even though his feet were a size and a half too big for the samples he was wearing, he would write incredibly detailed reports, which landed on the desk of eventual Nike CEO Mark Parker. Bodecker joined the company officially in 1982 and made his name at Nike by growing the company's soccer business into a juggernaut, starting in the mid-'90s.

The artist C. R. Stecyk III, who designed numerous iconic skate graphics, including the "Skate and Destroy" motto and typography, described Bodecker in a Nike SB video as "always ahead of the curve" and "always over it by the time everyone else got there."

So perhaps it should have come as no surprise when, for his next act at Nike, Bodecker went from the world's most popular sports to one of its most niche, and became general manager of Nike SB in 2001.

While Bodecker didn't have a background in skateboarding, he understood athletes and did everything he could to get up to speed quickly. "He became a skate fan first, and then built from there," said Paul Rodriguez, the first skateboarder to have a Nike signature shoe.

"He read every skate magazine cover to cover," said Forbes.

What Bodecker gleaned from those magazines went beyond an academic understanding of the difference between a Smith grind and a feeble grind. He developed a nuanced understanding of skate culture.

"[Nike] brought a lot of firepower to a relatively small industry. And he was sensitive to that," said Forbes. "Everyone knows everyone here. [Skateboarding] is a really small place. I think he had a really good understanding of what he was doing and how Nike could help. It was really about how he could serve the community."

Bodecker saw that skateboarding wasn't like other sports and, therefore, Nike couldn't approach it like other sports. Rather than going mainstream, Nike SB went grassroots. Rather than signing household names, Nike SB signed lesser-known but highly respected skaters. Rather than selling in big-box stores, Nike SB sold at core skate shops. Rather than releasing the most innovative, teched-out shoe, Nike SB brought back the Dunk.

"It only makes sense to bring back a shoe that is classic and timeless and reintroduce yourself into the culture with something that was already there in the first place," Mulder said.

The first Nike SB Dunk had no lenticular panels, no faux bear fur, no Supreme cosigns. Before the official launch of Nike SB, Bodecker and Forbes went on a trip from Washington, DC, to New York City, visiting skate shops along the way in an attempt to drum up interest in the new iteration of the Dunk.

The shoe they had in hand was relatively simple. It had a navy base with gray overlays. The silhouette had been modified for skating with a Zoom-cushioned insole, to protect against dreaded heel bruises, and a padded tongue.

The trip itself was a signal of Nike SB's unorthodox approach.

The skate industry has historically been centered around Southern California. But many cultural trends begin in cities on the East Coast, particularly New York, and East Coast skaters have a style that's shaped by their urban environment and is unmistakably cool. This is where Bodecker wanted to do a temperature check on his new shoe.

"We visited a variety of core shops in every city—we wanted to hit shops that were open to Nike, ones that were on the fence, and ones that were anti-Nike," Bodecker told Nike News in 2017. "It was important to get a complete read on how the core shops and the core community were really reacting and feeling on the ground face-to-face."

"In general, we got some support from most of the shops at some level," he said. "But many of them were up front and said they wanted to see if we would come proper or just jump in and jump out again."

Even Forbes, who had already signed on with Nike, had reservations. But the trip helped assuage them. "I knew that this was not, like, fly by night. They were invested in this for the long haul. I didn't have any doubts once I saw the intent and the purpose of what the mission was."

Today the original SB Dunks are prized and revered. When they were created, it was a different scenario.

Each of the original Nike SB skaters—Mulder, Forbes, Gino Iannucci, and Danny Supa—was given the opportunity to design his own Dunk as part of the "Colors By" series. "It wasn't a big deal back then. They're like, 'Hey, we're all going to do a Dunk colorway.' And we're like, 'Cool,'" Mulder remembered. "It wasn't serious. I didn't even spend more than ten minutes on [it] because I didn't know it was going to be this historic thing."

While Mulder may not have spent a long time on his colorway, his shoe accomplished the most important goal for any Nike SB model. It told a story. In 1994, Mulder had been in Chicago on a tour with his board sponsor, Chocolate Skateboards, and the crew stopped into a Nike outlet.

"I got these Tennis Classics. They were exactly what my [Dunk] colorway was," he recalled. "They were all white and had an Orion blue Swoosh. I remember when I got home from tour, I put them on and skated them. So when the time came to do a shoe, I was like, 'Oh, I want to do that one shoe.' It was seriously a no-brainer."

Forbes's "Wheat" colorway was inspired by Timberland work boots; Supa's reflected the colors of his hometown New York Knicks. Nike SB also tapped some of its riders' board sponsors to put their spin on the Dunk. Chocolate, which sponsored Mulder, did a version, as did Zoo York, which sponsored Supa.

Nike SB also worked with a skate shop on Lafayette Street that, at the time, wasn't really known outside of the skate and downtown New York City community. Supreme took the elephant print detailing from the Air Jordan III and added it to the Dunk in both a black and white version. It was an instant classic. What distinguished these stories of the early SB Dunks is how intimate they were. Not everyone needed to get it. In fact, if everyone did get it, it probably wasn't that good of an idea. But if you did get it, you felt like you were in on something special. And if you were in on it, then you were all in.

That didn't mean it was easy to get your hands on a pair. From the start, Nike SB Dunks were released in limited quantities. This, as much as the SB design ethos, helped make the shoes a full-blown cultural phenomenon.

These were not shoes that you could walk into your neighborhood Foot Locker and buy. SB Dunks were sold through skate shops. And not just any skate shops. Slinging trucks and bearings wasn't enough. It had to be the right skate shop. Nike SB was becoming an arbiter of cool.

So while Forbes recalled that "it wasn't like applause and confetti coming from the ceiling," when his "Wheat" colorway came out, the limited supply was creating widespread demand. The effect of these factors—the aesthetics of the silhouette, the distribution strategy, the credibility of the skaters and collaborators—was compounded by the rise of the internet. The age of hype had dawned.

After releasing city editions of the SB Dunk Low Pro in Paris, Tokyo, and London, Nike tapped Jeff Ng, aka Jeff Staple, and his Staple Design to create a Dunk that paid homage to New York City. Thinking about what would best represent New York, Staple landed on the pigeon and designed his Dunk around that. "It's something very innate to New Yorkers. And something you wouldn't necessarily relate to the city if you didn't in fact live here," Staple told *Sneaker Freaker*.

The "Pigeon" Dunks released on February 22 at Reed Space, Staple's gallery and

store. But a couple dozen sneakerheads began camping out days in advance. By the morning of release day, those numbers had swollen to triple digits, and Reed Space only had thirty pairs on hand. When late arrivers tried to cut the line, the "ruckus" was sparked. There were police on the scene, and while no arrests were made, one person was put in handcuffs, and a knife and a baseball bat were found afterward.

The headlines on the front page of the *New York Post* on February 23, 2005, were pretty grim. "Lost Souls," led a story about the struggle to identify more than one thousand victims of the 9/11 attacks. "Co-ed Dies in Ex-Con's Drug Lair," declared another. Atop all of them was a photo of the Nike SB Dunk "Pigeon" alongside the blaring headline "Sneaker Frenzy–Hot Shoe Sparks Ruckus."

"There were thugs on all four corners waiting to grab kicks from kids who were waiting in the line," Staple told *Sneaker Freaker*. "The cops saw this. So they called a fleet of cabs to our back door. Kids would come in through the front, buy their pair, and then be escorted through the back right into a cab and off they went."

While there had been important moments in sneaker history prior to this, the overwhelming majority of them were tied to sporting events, such as Michael Jordan winning the Slam Dunk Contest in 1988 in the "White/Cement" Air Jordan III. The "Pigeon" Dunk was different. This was a moment that was purely about the sneaker itself, and it represented a major turning point in sneakerhead culture.

It had little to do with the actual aesthetics of the shoe, and a lot to do with that *New York Post* cover. For years, sneakerheads had their own version of "this thing of ours," something to be chatted about and obsessed over in tiny corners of the internet, such as the NikeTalk message boards. Now it was literally front-page news in the media capital of the world. The word was out.

In addition, the *Post* story revealed that there was money to be made from these things people put on their feet. An infographic showed that, while Nike's suggested retail price was $69, Reed Space sold them for $300, and the highest eBay price was $1,000. This wasn't just shining a light on sneaker culture but on resale culture, too.

That "Pink Box" era—a name derived from the design of the SB boxes at the time—was a high-water mark for the Dunk.

(It's further testament to the power of Nike SB that even the shoe boxes are a topic of discussion.) In addition to the "Pigeon" Dunk, a number of seminal editions were released between September 2004 and December 2005: the first Dunk with renowned Japanese vinyl toy manufacturer Medicom; the collaboration with the band U.N.K.L.E., using art by Futura 2000; the De La Soul pack; and the "Diamond" Dunk, which propelled a little-known company that made actual nuts and bolts for skateboards into the streetwear stratosphere.

As disparate as those collaborators might seem, they all tied back to skateboarding in some way. If you were in the scene, it made sense. Skateboarders who went on tour in Japan would return with Medicom Bearbricks. Mike Carroll skated to De La Soul's "Oodles of O's" in the first Girl Skateboards video, *Goldfish*.

This was an important part of what set Nike SB apart. The brand stayed true to its roots, even as it exploded in popularity. Nike had cracked the code to enter the secret society that is skateboarding, but it wasn't trying to leave the door open for everyone to flood in.

"They didn't bend their own rules on what they originally intended for all of these shoes," Forbes said. "It wasn't like, 'Oh, now that we see the popularity with this, let's just go ahead and make more of them.' They stayed true to their word. It's contributed to the fact that we're even talking about it [today]."

For folks who remember being able to actually go into Supreme without having to pass by a burly security guard, Nike SB became like the indie band that you saw in the small club that blew up and was now selling out arenas. And the Dunk was the frontman.

The Nike SB team, which had begun with names that wouldn't ring out if you weren't a regular *Thrasher* reader, grew to include some of the most famous faces in skateboarding, like Eric Koston and Paul Rodriguez. The shoes also became more accessible. With that came the criticism that's inevitable whenever something transitions from subculture to pop culture.

But while the Dunk moved on from being the "it shoe," the things that made it great in the first place—the stories, the designs, the nods and winks—remained. The Black Box era brought collabs with Dinosaur Jr. and MF Doom. The first Concepts "Lobster" Dunk arrived in the Gold Box. A "Space Jam" Dunk arrived in 2011 in the Blue Box. Supreme celebrated the tenth anniversary of its first Dunk with a "Red Cement" version that came in the Taped Box. The Teal Box has seen more flips on the greatest hits, such as revamped "Diamond" and "Pigeon" collaborations. But it has also breathed new life into the silhouette with projects with Parra and Soulland.

While many moved on from the Dunk in the 2010s, Nike SB stayed true to its original game plan. And when people like Travis Scott began shining a new light on the silhouette at the end of the decade, the core DNA that made Nike SB so special in the first place remained unchanged.

In short, the SB Dunk got big, but it never sold out. In skateboarding, that's all you can hope for.

Honorable Mention
BAPE Bapesta

The Nike Air Force 1 is among the most iconic sneakers of all time. Plenty of brands have produced their take on the clean, simple low-top version of the shoe over the years, but none have been nearly as popular and respected as A Bathing Ape's Bapesta, Nigo's love letter to the original.

The Bapesta's design was nearly identical to the AF1's, but instead of Swooshes, it had star logos, and in place of "Nike Air" branding was a "BAPESTA" tongue tag. It also came in vibrant colorways that used patent leather or exotic materials like snakeskin that Nike—until that point—hadn't employed. (Interestingly, Nike never sued Bape or Nigo.)

When the first Bapesta dropped in 2002, Bape was still a few years from the height of its popularity in both Japan and the United States. Nigo has famously said that it wasn't until the US (with help from the cosigns of Pharrell Williams, Clipse,

by Mike DeStefano

and Kanye West) got behind the brand that Japan did, too. But the Japanese took to the Bapestas—essentially a remake of a familiar shoe from the '80s in bright, glossy colors—instantly. Launched just as Japan's sneaker boom went into overdrive, the Bapesta, with its old-school feel, set itself apart from what was happening in sneakers elsewhere and became a local hit.

Stateside, the shoe was initially met with some resistance from sneakerheads who saw it as a knockoff more than an homage to the American culture that Nigo was so obsessed with. Bape fans, though, became enamored of the flashy and extremely limited sneakers. Still almost impossible to get if you lived anywhere but Japan, Bape was becoming a status symbol, a head-to-toe uniform for those in the know, and the Bapesta was part of the equation.

"In a way, Bapesta sneakers happened by accident, so I did not expect them to have such a strong following in and outside Japan," Nigo said in *A Bathing Ape*, the book published by Rizzoli. "Let's just say the line was a product of last resort that made a good turn for the better. We are not a proper sportswear manufacturer but a fashion brand, so the sneakers are merely a component of the seasonal collections, but they definitely set the trend for colorful sneakers."

Since their initial release, there have been several Bapesta collaborations, including versions by N*E*R*D, Kaws, Marvel, and, perhaps the most coveted, a pair designed by West. Today, Bape (without Nigo, who left the brand in 2013) continues to release Bapestas. While the appetite for them has diminished over the years, they represent a very specific time in streetwear, when all-over-print hoodies dominated people's closets.

2003 Nike Air Zoom Generation

LeBron James signed a lifetime deal with Nike in 2015 for a reported $1 billion. That's a lot of money, no doubt, but perhaps fair compensation for a generational athlete who's not only exceeded expectations on all fronts for the entirety of his professional career but also become a fixture in the "greatest of all time" debate. But before that could happen, Nike had to get him to the party.

by Zac Dubasik

By the night of the 2003 NBA lottery, when James learned he would land with the Cleveland Cavaliers (playing a short drive from his hometown of Akron, Ohio), he'd been featured on the cover of *Sports Illustrated*, the magazine dubbing him "The Chosen One." He would still have to prove himself and deliver on an NBA level, but the eighteen-year-old was able to sign the endorsement contract of his choosing before he knew which team would draft him.

Along with Nike, Reebok and Adidas desperately wanted to ink James. His then-agent, Aaron Goodwin, set up meetings with all three brands and planned to secure the deal before the lottery even happened. "We felt like LeBron's market was not going to be predicated by where he played, but by how he played," Goodwin told The Undefeated in 2018.

Having already received and played in player-exclusive sneakers from all three brands in high school and All-American games, James was familiar with each company. But despite spirited pitches, including the offer of a $10 million cashier's check from Reebok if James agreed to eventually sign with the brand and not hear any other proposals (Reebok was the first of the three brands to meet with James's team), he followed his heart and ultimately signed with Nike on the day of the 2003 lottery—for significantly less money than Reebok had been offering.

In a statement that day, James reasoned that "Nike is the right fit and has the right product for me at the right time," and that the brand had "committed to supporting me throughout my professional career, on and off the court." The first glimpse of that product would come in the form of the Nike Air Zoom Generation—James's inaugural signature model.

The Air Zoom Generation arrived at a time when Nike's signature sneaker landscape was all but barren. Michael Jordan had played his last NBA game in the spring of 2003, and there were questions as to how long the Air Jordan series would even continue. Kobe Bryant signed with Nike that summer but became wrapped up in a sexual assault case, leaving his future signature line in doubt. Vince Carter's Shox series was a few models in, but it never took off the way Nike had hoped. In other words, the sneaker world needed its next hero, and so did the NBA. So the Air Zoom Generation wasn't a new sneaker for a player with the potential to become the next big thing—it was the foundation for the next generation of basketball footwear.

"Growing up, I did not think I would have my own shoe," James told Sole Collector in 2004. "But once I saw that I could make basketball a career, I started thinking about it and it started wearing on me, and I knew I could do it."

Nike showed no shortage of support, trotting out an all-star team of designers for James's first model that included Tinker Hatfield of Air Jordan fame; Eric Avar, who'd worked on Penny Hardaway's (and, later, Kobe Bryant's) signature line; and Aaron Cooper, whose résumé included models for Kevin Garnett and Scottie Pippen. Then–Nike Basketball global category leader Kris Aman told Sole Collector in a 2004 interview that they'd "spent a lot of time with [James] from a relationship standpoint, trying to get to know him, trying to understand him, figuring out what he might want in a product we can deliver on."

With such a high-profile product in the works, it should come as no surprise that, for Aman's team, the design process was politically fraught, with the biggest issue being the Swoosh itself. "Some people wanted a smaller Swoosh in the corner, some wanted a bigger one in the forefoot, and we were sort of divided on it," Aman told Sole Collector. "Once we finally got to working with LeBron, he liked it better on the quarter panel, and that was that, so that worked out better all the way around."

Being a part of the process, and then getting that final version, was a big moment for James. "When I first saw the Air Zoom Generation, I couldn't believe I was holding a Nike sneaker with my name on it," he told Complex in 2017.

James played his first regular-season NBA game in the Air Zoom Generation against the Sacramento Kings on October 29, 2003, wearing a low-key white-and-black colorway of the shoe (not to be confused with the white and red "First Game" colorway that he didn't wear until his first home game in Cleveland). The Cavs lost the game, but James put up 25 points, 6 rebounds, 9 assists, and 4 steals in forty-two minutes, offering just a glimpse of what was to come. "The first game in Sacramento was the most prized moment in my life," he told Sole Collector in 2004. "Just to come out with high expectations from everybody—I mean everybody, including Nike, including the NBA—and then to come out and perform the way I did, you know it was a little relief."

Still, a segment of the conversation at the time centered around the Air Zoom Generation's design, which was partly indebted to the Hummer H2, a vehicle James drove during his season as a high school senior, prompting investigations into his amateur

status. The shoe's eyelets mimicked the truck's wheel locks, while the logo on the tongue used a typeface similar to that of the SUV's logo. According to Aman, though, this was a relatively small piece of the puzzle. "We didn't even get into the Hummer side of things until deep in the process," he told Sole Collector.

Where the H2 most significantly inspired the Air Zoom Generation was through carrying the original Hummer's utilitarian design over to a more civilian-friendly vehicle. "That was a thing that LeBron was big on: He wanted his shoe to be sophisticated," Aman said to Sole Collector. "We used the H2 to get a little more of a rugged profile."

Another point of differentiation came with the shoe's naming. While every other model in James's signature line has carried his own moniker, the Air Zoom Generation stands alone in its naming convention. Aman said this name came about because the brand felt that he was "the athlete that will define the next generation." He explained that James, despite all the hype and his obvious talent, was aware that he still had much to prove at the time. "He's a very thoughtful young person, and to his credit, he was like, 'Yeah, I'm with the Zoom Generation.' Everyone knows it's his shoe—we'll get to the LeBron 5 down the road."

The short-term goal was making a great shoe that would help James play better, but Nike had a bigger strategy at work, knowing the caliber of athlete James could become. "LeBron has one of those things that very few athletes have," Aman said to Sole Collector. "That is to [be able to] take a shoe and, when it's just sitting there, have a reaction of, 'Eh, don't need it.' The minute he puts it on, he has the ability to make it something that you *have* to have." That ability was something Nike planned to take advantage of.

The Air Zoom Generation is seen as a classic these days, but the initial response to it wasn't 100 percent positive. That was deliberate. Aman said the shoe was "not made to be universally loved. Some products are not for you. We are in great shape when people love or hate our shoes... The minute we start getting comfortable, then we're just like everyone else. That's what we're *not* looking to do—certainly not with LeBron."

What was positive from the jump were the shoe's performance attributes and its relative value. At a time when the Air Jordan line was ringing up at a $175 price point, the AZG's $110 sticker was much more palatable. It didn't skimp on the features, either, packing in heel Air and forefoot Zoom cushioning, a full-length carbon-fiber shank plate, and Nike Sphere lining. It may not have provided any groundbreaking innovation, but it was an amalgamation of Nike's tried-and-true tech that resulted in a versatile performer.

Almost fourteen years after its initial launch, the Air Zoom Generation finally came back in retro form in early 2017—fittingly, while James was back with the Cleveland Cavaliers. James confirmed the long-rumored return on social media, summing up just how important the model was to him after all those years. "This shoe changed my life, my family's life, and we've been lucky enough to change the lives of people around us," he said. "This shoe is for every single person with a dream and a passion. No matter what your situation is. From the projects to the palace, this shoe is a symbol that you can do anything."

Honorable Mention
Reebok S. Carter

It took a long time from Run-DMC's '80s cosign of Adidas for a footwear brand to fully capitalize on the potential value of a rapper endorsement. It didn't happen until 2002, in fact, the year Reebok signed Jay-Z—and he didn't even have to make a song called "My Reeboks" to secure the bag.

Hov's multiyear Reebok deal was the first nonathlete sneaker contract of its kind, and it certainly wouldn't be the last. On April 18, 2003, with Jay seven months away from releasing *The Black Album* and embarking on a short-lived retirement, Reebok, via its RBK line, dropped the S. Carter, his first signature shoe. The low-top white sneaker was a nod to—if not a direct bite of—the Gucci Tennis '84, famous for its soft leather and red-and-green shoelaces. ("Got the sole of the old Guccis," rapped Jay in a Reebok ad. "If you upset, sue me.") Crucially, the Gucci '84 was a pricey status symbol for neighborhood hustlers, thus providing the inspiration

by Donnie Kwak

for Jay's remake. The 2003 RBK version, however, sold for an affordable retail price of $100. It'd be like if Jay remade the Lexus GS 300, only with Nissan.

Beforehand, the brand was uncertain of Jay's ability to move footwear. "As big as Jay was, and he had Rocawear and all that, we were not really sure if the guy [could] sell sneakers," said Reebok senior vice president Todd Krinsky. According to reports following its release, though, upward of ten thousand pairs of Jay's S. Carter were sold within hours, making it the fastest-selling shoe in Reebok's history—even faster than Allen Iverson's Question.

Unsurprisingly, Reebok already had its next rap signee on deck: 50 Cent, who inked a five-year deal to release G-Unit footwear. Together, Jay and 50 helped Reebok to an 11 percent jump in footwear sales in 2003. Later that same year, Reebok signed Pharrell Williams and his Billionaire Boys Club line.

Reebok's rap bubble didn't last long. The company shipped five hundred thousand pairs of S. Carters, oversaturating the market; subsequent models failed to ignite the same flame. Meanwhile, 50 Cent's next G-Unit sneakers came and went without much fanfare, and Williams ended up suing Reebok for breach of contract before he and the company agreed to part ways in January 2005. The brand ended up signing the likes of Lupe Fiasco, Mike Jones, Daddy Yankee, and Nelly, never recapturing the energy of G-Unit and S. Carter.

Still, Jay's first shoe lives on as both a disruptive moment in sneaker history and a turning point in the way footwear brands engage with hip-hop culture. The S. Carters walked so the Yeezys could run.

2004 Nike Free 5.0

In the year 2000, a pack of track athletes train on the searing emerald greens of Stanford University's golf course, their precious feet stamping carelessly through the grounds. They are free. In 1980, seven-year-old Tegla Loroupe runs—no shoes on her feet—through the west end of Kenya on her daily path of over six miles from her home to school. She is free. Well before there are dates to write down, a group of hunter-gatherers in the cradle of civilization bound after their prey, the bare anatomy supporting their newly upright bodies kicking up clouds of dust. They are free.

by Brendan Dunne

The men's team at Stanford would go on to win the NCAA Outdoor Track & Field Championships in 2000. Loroupe would go on to win the New York City Marathon back-to-back in 1994 and '95. If our prehistoric ancestors got any award for bringing the meat back to their dens, the accolade is sketched onto a cave wall in some primitive script. The idea here is not that the shod are shackled, but that barefoot running offers a distinct advantage, one that hadn't been fully explained to casual runners in the Western world until Nike introduced its Free 5.0 running shoe in 2004.

That shoe, and the huge number of Free models that followed, owes its existence to the drills that played out on that collegiate course in Stanford. Around 2001, Tobie Hatfield, brother of legendary sneaker designer Tinker Hatfield and a Nike employee since 1990, observed the team training barefoot. Tobie had already built up an impressive résumé of his own through his work on impactful models like the Air Presto from 2000.

Stanford's shoeless practices were implemented by Coach Vin Lananna, who believed that his athletes could strengthen their feet and avoid injuries by training in a freer fashion. "I felt that as shoes became more elaborate and intricate, the feet were getting weaker," he told the *New York Times* in 2005. This feeling was supported by research—a 1987 study from Concordia University cited data that showed barefoot runners generally suffered fewer injuries across many different populations. But not everybody has the privilege of running on the crisply kempt grounds of a prestigious college. People running in New York, in Paris, in Tokyo cannot do so on bare feet.

Hatfield's challenge, then, was to design

a shoe that harnessed the physiological benefits of barefoot running while keeping its wearer safe from the detritus and underfoot hazards common in the twenty-first century. He had to trust that feet were perhaps a more elegantly functional design than footwear could ever be. "We had to take that control away," Hatfield realized, "meaning the shoe is less in control, the foot is more in control." This relinquishing of control came at the urging of Coach Lananna, who went hard at Nike for forgetting the foot. The input from Lananna, who cofounded the Nike Farm Team running program in 1994, gave the sportswear company its design brief. How would he feel if they could create a product that provided a protected environment while letting the foot be free? "How many can I get?" was his response to the prospective shoe.

The sneaker still had to have a sole, of course, but its movements were to be guided by the wearer's foot. In the same way that Hatfield had to dissect the tendency for control that a sportswear supplier has over its customer's body, he had to literally cut through the platform his new design would ride on to create the Nike Free cushioning system. The result was a shoe whose hero was its outsole, a siped foam platform that looked something like a set of sci-fi piano keys or a Cheshire Cat grin. Hatfield's design team at Nike iterated through the process, figuring out exactly how many flex grooves they needed along the bottom to truly liberate the runner. The upper, which is far less discussed in all the literature around its genesis, was built on an inner bootie not unlike that of the aforementioned Air Presto. The number in each Free model's name describes its level of cushioning, placing it on a scale from 0.0 (true barefoot running) to 10.0 (running in a traditional sneaker). Hatfield called the Free 5.0 "the most researched and the most peer-reviewed, white-papered product that we've ever done."

Where was this sneaker research happening? Much of it came from the Nike Sport Research Lab, the group at the brand's Oregon headquarters that establishes the science that turns into product innovation. Crucially, it also came from outside sources less inclined to be biased. A 2005 study funded by Nike and published by the German Sport University Cologne concluded that the new minimal approach of the Free increased significantly the muscle strength capacity of the parts of the foot the shoe helped activate. The control group in the study didn't enjoy the same benefits. (Yes, despite battling Adidas for decades at that point, Nike was not averse to turning to Germans to legitimize its product.)

While this kind of sneaker science may not be first in mind for the average consumer, it is vital to the obsessive's relationship with the world of sports footwear. These kinds of studies, these precious points of data, make real the dreams sold by brands in a way that even the sexiest of marketing materials and most colossal of athlete endorsements cannot. They prove that—under the right conditions, when used properly—these things can actually make us stronger or faster. Recent decades have heightened the cultural potential of the average sneaker. Yes, more often they are used to make us look cooler, but these items at their core are still tied to a notion of making us somehow perform better.

As Nike found success with its Free line, it carried its foot-first footwear ethos and tech into other sports. It created basketball sneakers with Nike Free cushioning on the bottom. It has put Nike Free cushioning on skate sneakers. Tiger Woods's golf shoes, designed with the help of Tobie Hatfield, used articulated Nike Free nubs along their bottoms. Even certain beloved silhouettes born way before the advent of Nike Free returned with that contemporary treatment in an effort to earn more converts. Hatfield recalls that the shoe's central aim of listening to the demands and guidance of the body and reacting to them was influential on more than just shoes across Nike. "That included not just footwear," he said of the affected product, "but, like, I remember backpacks, when the backpack designer is looking at the straps and how the straps could articulate better with the shoulders."

Although Nike Free and the principles behind it spread wide, the man most responsible for that wave points out that the shoes are meant for a specific purpose. "It was always intended to be another tool in the toolbox," Hatfield said, explaining that the Nike Free 5.0 and its successors were never supposed to replace the other shoes athletes had access to. This narrow vision of its implementation is ironically opposite to the intent of the Nike Air Trainer, a 1987 shoe created by his brother, Tinker, that was designed as a cross-sport trainer that could do it all. The view of the Free shoe as one of many an athlete could take advantage of also came with the upside of helping Nike convince people that one pair of shoes was not sufficient for the modern athlete. The underlying logic of the toolbox metaphor is that without the proper set, your exercise regimen might still be in the Stone Age. Then again, the original studies supporting the idea of the Nike Free as a performance-tested piece of footwear were also specific about its use. "It should be an effective approach for injury prevention and performance enhancement to use minimal footwear in well-defined training regimes," one of the papers from the German Sport University Cologne concluded.

This sort of science-backed design married with easily recognizable visual cues is what made the Nike Free line so successful. While of little concern to researchers in labs and universities, the visual aspect of the sneaker is essential. Hallmark Nike designs, like its Air Max bubble or Flyknit uppers, have relied heavily on communicating their functionality to consumers via their unique look. Were the brand not so adept at these kinds of visual design transmissions, its footwear would be nowhere near as popular. The barefoot-running trend in the 2000s has produced shoes with similar intentions, like Vibram's FiveFingers silhouette, which launched in 2005 with barely any cushioning and a foot glove shape, but none have enjoyed the sustained popularity of Nike Free. Maybe the design lesson here is that nobody wants to see your toes.

The design insights from the Free 5.0 continue to be relevant for Nike, which still produces Free shoes regularly and will occasionally bring back the original 2004 model for a retro treatment. In some ways, the heavily researched runners were a precursor to the brand's controversial Vaporfly line of long-distance sneakers that launched in 2017, spurring conversations around what exactly a shoe should be allowed to do for its wearer. Like the Free 5.0, the Vaporfly shoes captured public attention by promising real performance benefits that could

be confirmed by science and, for the Vaporfly and related models, a whole lot of broken records. Still, the two designs are nearly antithetical in their relationship to the user. The Free 5.0 sought to let the foot be its guide and muse, minimizing how much influence the actual shoe had. The Vaporfly sought to enhance it with stiff carbon-fiber plates embedded in the soles that would spring the wearer forward during marathon runs. This difference underlines the extent to which the philosophy behind the Free line at its onset ran counter to the standard of progression-sportswear brands, which are very much invested in the idea of upgrading your foot rather than listening to it.

The very idea that barefoot running is so beneficial is in some ways a threat to the existence of a sneaker company. Rather than framing it as such, Tobie Hatfield took it as a challenge. He pushed back against what had been marked as technological advancements, questioning whether the tendency to upgrade and continually add more to our footwear actually pushed it forward. In a way, he plucked that purest form of running from thousands of years ago and placed it delicately into the twenty-first century, atop a more period-appropriate platform. "Sometimes we do lose our way, and sometimes we get enamored with just design," Hatfield said, recalling the path of Nike when the Free 5.0 arrived in 2004. "And design tends to overtake what is actually needed for the athlete." It turns out, all we needed was to be Free.

Honorable Mention
Nike Air Zoom Huarache 2K4

Simply put, the Nike Air Zoom Huarache 2K4 was the late Kobe Bryant's unofficial first signature sneaker with the brand. On a deeper level, it was the return of a staple Nike design concept from the '90s, one that had been mostly abandoned until it came back here. By using a neoprene inner bootie, the shoe stayed true to previous Huarache incarnations, but it was its combination of Phylon foam and responsive Zoom Air cushioning that took it over the top from a performance perspective.

    Designed by Eric Avar—the man responsible for many of Nike Basketball's most memorable creations, including the Air Foamposite One and several of Bryant's groundbreaking signature models—the Air Zoom Huarache 2K4 ended up a favorite of basketball enthusiasts. The sneaker was commonplace on the college hardwood; in fact, part of its rollout included lacing players up for March Madness. It was Bryant, though, who ended up becoming synonymous with the model.

by Riley Jones

"From a functional standpoint, thinking forward to the emergence of players like Kobe and his versatility—that was the driving functional inspiration behind the product," Avar said in a 2012 Nike.com post, during the sneaker's first retro run. Despite not being officially considered part of Bryant's signature line, the Air Zoom Huarache 2K4 was included in Nike's 2016 "Fade to Black" collection to commemorate his final season in the league.

Avar remembers the creation of the Zoom Huarache 2K4 as a reaction to the loud footwear design language of the decade prior. "It was very good for the athletes and for the marketplace, but we questioned whether we were being bold and crazy for the sake of it," Avar said in the same post. "How could we return to more purposeful and 'grounded' product?"

With that in mind, the brand looked back to 1992's Air Flight Huarache, redesigning the original sneaker from the ground up but maintaining its signature exoskeleton fit. The overall shape, ankle cutouts, and inner bootie remained, but the entire model had been overhauled for modern play through the use of Zoom Air and other advancements.

Off the court, the updated Huarache lineage would eventually etch its name into modern sneaker culture. In 2008, the similar Air Huarache '08 model was used for one of Kanye West's earliest collaborations with Nike for his Glow in the Dark Tour. Produced only in sample form, the sneaker preceded the rapper's Air Yeezy line.

Today, the Air Zoom Huarache 2K4 is respected for being both classic and contemporary. The model reintroduced the discontinued franchise and left a lasting imprint on the world of basketball footwear.

2005 Nike Zoom LeBron 3

In 2005, LeBron James symbolized the future of basketball, and Nike knew he could carry its basketball footwear into the future with him. The company bet heavily on the Chosen One with a reported $90 million endorsement deal before he ever set foot on an NBA court. By his third season in the league, James's impact on the game continued to grow, as many predicted it would when he was a high school player in Akron, Ohio. And as his game developed, so did his signature sneaker line when he laced up a new model, the Zoom LeBron 3.

by John Gotty

Nike Zoom LeBron 3

The 2005–06 season represented a pivotal one for Nike Basketball. As James came into his own and his sneaker line expanded right in step, the company also relaunched its business with Kobe Bryant by releasing the Zoom Kobe 1. Both players filled the stat sheet and dominated highlight reels on any given night. The tandem created a formidable one-two punch on the marketing side for Nike, setting the stage for a remarkable run that extended for several years and across multiple models for each star.

James averaged 31.4 points per game, which made him the youngest player in league history to average over 30 points. He led his team to the playoffs for the first time in seven years. He was also selected for his first All-Star Game, in which he won MVP honors. He finished second in MVP honors for the season.

By round three, James, then only twenty-one, possessed more awareness of what he wanted out of his signature model, following his involvement with his two previous sneakers. "The 3 was when I really started to open up, knowing more about the shoe game and how they were created and things like that. I wanted them to be light, I wanted them to look good, and I also wanted them to feel good," he explained in an interview for *Laced*, Nike's 2007 self-produced shoe documentary.

Designer Ken Link was tasked with finding a way to build a shoe strong and agile enough to support a 6'8", 240-pound force like James, whose explosive first step and powerful dunks made him unique in the league. His physique and style of play required a shoe that would keep him cinched down while also allowing a range of movement. The Zoom LeBron 3 built off the success of its well-received predecessor. James liked the LeBron 2, so Link was able to retain certain elements of its design. But the designer wanted James's signature line to continue to grow as the player progressed. In 2007, in *Laced*, Link shared that "The [LeBron] 2 was more raw. [The LeBron 3] is a little more dialed up and [predicated on] the idea of dressing him and getting him ready for the game."

The shoe resembled a boot, with its leather upper, high ankle cut, and metal eyelets. Where the LeBron 2 used a velcro ankle strap, the LeBron 3 worked with a series of thin, unstitched straps, connected only at the base of each strap and at the eyestays, which created a better lockdown fit without compromising movement.

The double Air Zoom unit came in a Pebax casing slightly thinner than that of the LeBron 2 to help reduce weight. The Pebax shell supported the Zoom Air against all the quick, lateral shifts and hard landings to which James might subject the cushioning system. A carbon-fiber shank plate further boosted the responsiveness. The foot bucket shell stretched from the midfoot to high up the ankle and heel to stabilize the foot. "The [LeBron] 3 actually encompasses a whole new way of looking at this whole heel chassis," Link explained in *Laced*. "It locks the heel back into the footbed and still allows the forefoot to move and make that first quick step."

The initial "Home" colorway released on November 12, 2005. The pair sported a majority-black leather upper, while the toebox, heel, and midsole were dressed in white. Crimson red accented the Swoosh, the full-length Zoom Air unit, and a portion of the outsole. It was the first in a slew of in-line releases that followed—black and gold, navy and white, black and red—in what seemed like an endless array of options.

In fact, colorways make up a major reason why the LeBron 3 has been beloved by footwear fans over the years. Throughout the 2005–06 season, James donned countless looks, each as uniquely colorful as the next. The shoe appeared in close to twenty colorways, which was more than the Air Zoom Generation and Zoom LeBron 2 had seen combined. The number sounds normal by current standards, when player sigs pop up in new iterations regularly. But in 2005, such a vast number of makeups represented a shift for Nike.

Most signature shoes released in "Home" and "Away" editions to match team uniforms. An additional playoff colorway might be thrown in if the namesake player were on a contending team. Ramping up the number of LeBron 3 colorways made every game must-see TV to witness what he wore on his feet just as much as what feat he might perform. And when he did wear a new colorway, it instantly dominated the comments sections of sneaker blogs and forums.

James and Nike took the storytelling to a new level. The young star's on-court exploits established everything the brand needed to work its magic in design and marketing. "It's very easy to design a shoe around an athlete because they bring so much more than just the way they play," Link explained in *Laced*. "It's the way they think, it's their family, it's where they're from, it's where they're going. It all just gets blended into the shoe, and you can start to see personality."

The storytelling expanded beyond the court as Nike sought ways to showcase the multiple sides of James's personality in an early effort to prove he was more than an athlete. Part of the push birthed the LeBrons, a group of four characters—"Kid," "Athlete," "Business," and "Wise" LeBron—reflecting the different sides of King James. Each character scored a special colorway of the LeBron 3, and, once again, Nike only released an extremely limited number of the shoes, along with an accompanying action figure, to the public for $200 a pair.

James wore a white and red pair bearing his name in gold block lettering for the 2006 NBA All-Star Game. That colorway dropped at retail, but there was another pair that surfaced the same weekend, causing a frenzy. Dipped in light blue, white, and red, an Oilers-inspired version, a nod to the host city of Houston's former football franchise, was given exclusively to James's friends and family, along with other celebrities. Sure, no one outside those circles could get it immediately, but the hype made it an instant hit and turned it into a grail for collectors.

The exclusive releases created excitement around the LeBron 3, drawing in a new set of collectors who sought out the player exclusives and special editions attached to James by any means necessary. The demand created skyrocketing prices, which in turn elevated the sneakers.

2019 saw the model return in retro form. Nike dropped six different colorways. Never-before-released exclusives like the "Oilers" and "SuperBron" finally found their way to retail. James wore purple and gold color-ups to match his Los Angeles Lakers uniform and made appearances rocking

assorted exclusives, like a cool grey suede, a tonal navy low-top, and more that could only be added to the wish list for collectors.

Even before his first NBA game, James was fated to be a signature-sneaker-level player. What was not predetermined was whether his shoes would have any sort of impact or longevity. The Nike LeBron 3 was one of the first inklings that, in the world of footwear, his star would be one to look up to for years to come.

Honorable Mention
Air Jordan XX

With an eye toward the future and the past, Tinker Hatfield introduced the world to the Air Jordan XX—a model that reflected the Jordan Brand legacy he'd helped establish—in 2005. Being that this was the twentieth anniversary of the Air Jordan line's proper debut, Hatfield aimed to include elements of the prior nineteen Jordan sneakers, as well as key moments from Michael Jordan's career, in its design to mark the milestone.

    The Jordan XX is most recognizable for the laser-etched pattern that first appeared on the midfoot shroud on its original colorways. In an effort to communicate Jordan's long history by way of a single sneaker, Hatfield returned to work on the mainline Jordan model for the first time since the Air Jordan XV. The laser-etched pattern consisted of two hundred symbols that helped tell Jordan's story, and the shoe had sixty-nine dimples on its side as a nod to his highest-scoring game. Those symbols would become an important part of the Jump-

by Ben Felderstein

man's legacy, materializing on icons like the Air Jordan 1, the Air Jordan IV, and the Air Jordan V.

While Hatfield created the symbols, the method by which they arrived on the shoe owed to an unlikely inspiration: custom trumpet designer David Monette. Monette frequently lasered designs onto the instrument, giving Hatfield the idea to work with Nike's Mark Smith to bring the process to the sneaker world. The XX's overall shape was inspired by racing boots, a nod to Jordan's love for motor-sports.

Among the most significant releases of the XX was the three-piece "Regional Pack," which included different makeups for the East Coast, the West, and the Midwest—with the laser pattern covering the majority of their uppers, rather than just the midfoot shroud. Notable Jumpman athletes from the early 2000s like Ray Allen, Richard Hamilton, and Carmelo Anthony had their own player-exclusive versions, keeping Jordan's sneaker legacy on the court.

If those eye-catching symbols weren't enough to distinguish the XX, Hatfield created an ankle support system that was not fully connected to the sneaker, which gave the model a futuristic look.

There's no question that the Air Jordan line lost a lot of its appeal when its namesake quit basketball for good—the source material of his achievements just wasn't there anymore. Rather than look forward to new models each year, consumers have since become obsessed with retros. But while the post-Bulls Jordan models will likely never carry the same cultural weight as the originals, the XX proved that, with Hatfield on his side, Jordan could still make magic.

2006 Nike Zoom Kobe 1

The basketball footwear category owes more to Kobe Bryant than any other athlete not named Michael Jordan. Bryant was considered an exacting player whose attention to detail went unmatched, and that focus carried over to the shoes he wore on the court. The five-time NBA champion worked with Nike Basketball on a signature series defined by a performance-first approach. The first entry, the Zoom Kobe 1, laid the groundwork for what grew into one of the Swoosh's most important and innovative lines. From the outset, Bryant worked closely with designers—setting the ultimate standard for athlete-designer rapport—to communicate his needs when it came to his sneakers.

by John Gotty

Nike Zoom Kobe 1

Kobe's tenure at Nike began in the summer of 2003. In the NBA seasons that followed, he sported what would become unofficial signature models: the Air Zoom Huarache 2K4 and 2K5. Designed by Eric Avar, the two models were Bryant's starting point with Nike after he paid a reported $8 million to break free from his previous contract with Adidas. The Huaraches were unofficial in the sense that, while the shoes were made to Bryant's specifications, they weren't promoted as true signature models. At the time, Bryant's 2003 Colorado sexual assault case cast a dark shadow over his public image. Fans turned against him, and most of his sponsors dropped him as it unfolded; Nike remained one of the only companies that didn't cut ties with him.

Once his legal issues were resolved, in March 2005, the time arrived for Bryant and Nike to craft the Zoom Kobe 1. But with Avar on leave, Nike Basketball design director Ken Link stepped in to help bring Bryant's first official shoe to life. It didn't stray far from the blueprint laid by the Huaraches, since both models were known to perform. The Huarache carryovers to the Zoom Kobe 1 included the pronounced outrigger for lateral stability, the high ankle collar, and Free movement, used for the soles. The model adopted Zoom Air in its forefoot and heel for the cushioning system and a large carbon-fiber plate that extended the length of the shoe for support.

Removing a section of the collar in the heel represented a noticeable shift from the ankle strap featured on the Huarache 2K4 and 2K5. The change allowed the foot to bend and flex naturally, and the emphasis on range of motion emerged as a staple of later entries in the series. According to Link, Bryant asked to do away with the strap. "He said he didn't want one," the designer told Sole Collector in 2013. "We wanted to focus on the collar, and you'll start to see it in other shoes [later in his line], because a lot of times, he was already thinking about, 'Could I get to a low?' Getting to a low is not necessarily the easiest thing to do, but he felt like his game and where he was headed was getting to that low thought process."

The Black Mamba's increased workload in the wake of Shaquille O'Neal's departure from the Lakers in 2004 necessitated all of the shoe's tweaks and changes. After missing the 2005 playoffs, the franchise entered rebuild mode, and the roster lacked the firepower of previous seasons. Bryant knew he would be carrying the bulk of the load on both ends of the court, with opposing teams keyed in on him. But he prepared for the challenge by training relentlessly during the off-season. He also put in time with designers to articulate his performance needs for his footwear. "I think the best thing about Kobe is when he looks at a shoe, he wants to see himself and his game in his shoe," Link told Sole Collector. "I think that's one of the things about Kobe, is that he gives so much information that it truly drives the process." Bryant entered the 2005–06 campaign with a newfound warrior mentality, and his new shoes would soon be part of his arsenal.

Bryant wouldn't begin wearing the Zoom Kobe 1 until the Lakers' Christmas Day game, donning a black and maize colorway for the nationally televised matchup against the Miami Heat. The Lakers lost, but it didn't matter. Sneaker enthusiasts tuned into the game just to get a glimpse of the Mamba's new Nike model.

In the aftermath of a disappointing season, Bryant willed the Lakers to win by scorching opponents nightly. He notched twenty-seven 40-point games, and even crossed the 50-point barrier six times. But the most memorable scoring output of them all came on January 22, 2006, against the Toronto Raptors.

On that night, despite the Raptors' best efforts to slow his assault, the Black Mamba poured in bucket after bucket. Bryant ended the game with 81 points, including 55 in the second half. The Lakers needed every one of those points to pull out the come-from-behind victory of 122–104. The performance placed him in the history books, second only to Wilt Chamberlain, who put up a 100-point game in 1962. The night of his own feat, Bryant laced up a player-exclusive pair of the Zoom Kobe 1 dressed in predominantly white, with black and varsity purple accents. The makeup never received a wide release, much to the dismay of enthusiasts and collectors, but Nike did celebrate Bryant's performance through later releases with commemorative nods to the 81-point outpouring. The PEs Bryant wore stand as a collector's item, the memories of that night at the Staples Center attached to them.

Bryant went on a tear the whole month of January 2006, averaging 43.4 points per game. At the time, it once again put him behind Chamberlain for the highest-scoring month. Over the course of the season, Bryant scored over 2,800 total points, a number eclipsed only by Chamberlain and Michael Jordan, cementing his status as a member of the league's upper echelon.

Seasons of that caliber don't require a heavy marketing push or embellished stories to sell sneakers; Bryant created enough moments on a nightly basis for fans to connect their own memories to any of the many ZK1 colorways he wore.

Nike continued to revisit the original Zoom Kobe 1 over the years, most notably with a black-based "81 Points" pair for 2013's "Prelude Pack" and another sail-colored version for the "Fade to Black" collection in 2016. But the most significant return of the model arrived in 2018, when the Zoom Kobe 1 received new life as the first remake in Nike Basketball's Protro series. Bryant shunned the idea of rolling out retros of his old shoes. "Kobe was like, 'I want to take the best of ten years, give or take, later. The best of materials or technologies or processes that we have, knowing what we know now—how could we make some of the earlier Kobes better?'" said Avar, Nike's vice president and creative director of innovation.

Bryant wanted any footwear bearing his name to symbolize performance above anything else and stayed involved in the process to make sure of it. "Hopefully the consumer knows by now that if you're buying a Kobe product, you're buying something that's been thought through," he emphasized in a 2016 interview with Sole Collector as his playing days were winding down. "We pay attention to detail all the way through. You're buying something that's going to help you perform better."

To achieve those goals, Nike shaved off foam and did away with any excess materials, lightening the sneaker. Designers added full-length Zoom Air and trimmed the carbon fiber shank for a better feel. The final product bore a leaner, meaner physique better fit for modern athletes—but the fact that so few alterations were necessary testifies to the original version's greatness.

Link would remain involved with the Zoom Kobe line throughout the early years before handing the reins back to Avar. It's part of the reason why the first two entries in the series carry a decidedly different look and approach than later ones. Link's works could be characterized as overbuilt, while Avar, under Bryant's direction, took a more minimalist path in creating the Lakers star's shoes. Avar started removing layers, weight, and height, pushing for the greatest range of movement possible as Bryant's playing style evolved.

The ZK1 highlights the relationship between athlete and designer, born from Bryant's tenure with Nike, and how the two forces push each other toward higher-performing footwear. The player's sneakers redefined how signature models come to life and pushed the boundaries of design and innovation. Bryant knew his needs and was able to communicate them in ways other players could not.

"Kobe, he's so far along the spectrum of what he expects out of a shoe and what he wants to put into it, and so he's been there every step of the way," Link told Sole Collector. "He really is ahead of his time, the way that he thinks about his game, the way he thinks about training for his game, the way he thinks about how his game interacts with the rest of his world and the world around it—he really gets that on a level that most people don't get."

Bryant understood that his shoes played a pivotal role in his quest to win championships and cement himself as one of the game's greats, and the Zoom Kobe 1 laid the foundation for what became one of Nike's most groundbreaking series to date, opening the door for the industry-shifting Zoom Kobe 4, the wildly popular Zoom Kobe 6, and the still-evolving Protro series.

"The shoes are part of the journey," Bryant told Sole Collector in 2016. "They go hand in hand with the ring. I can't get no ring without the sneakers that I'm wearing. They really helped me get there."

Honorable Mention
Air Jordan "Defining Moments Pack"

To some, the only thing better than one pair of Air Jordans is two. It's common now for Jordan to package two pairs of sneakers and sell them as a collector's edition. The first time this happened, though, it featured two of the most anticipated Air Jordan sneakers of all time—a black/gold Air Jordan VI and a "Concord" Air Jordan XI with a gold Jumpman—and was called the "Defining Moments Pack," or "DMP."

Both models in the pack were especially popular in 2006, before the Air Jordan 1 retro craze began. The Air Jordan VI is significant to Michael Jordan because it was the first sneaker he won a championship in. The Air Jordan XI matters because it's the sneaker he wore with the infamous 72-10 Chicago Bulls (and in *Space Jam*). Jordan also wore the models at the beginning of his two three-peat campaigns in

by Matt Welty

the NBA. Pretty simple to get Jordan fans amped up over this idea: make the shoes limited, then double down.

Bobbito Garcia got his pairs early on his ESPN show *It's the Shoes*. Rob Heppler boasted on *The Weekly Drop* podcast that he'd be able to get them on sale after release (that didn't happen). There are stories of madness breaking out at malls over these shoes; naturally, their resale value skyrocketed. Sneaker Politics owner Derek Curry has described securing a bunch of pairs, and the craziness that ensued, at a mall in a post-Katrina Louisiana.

"It was like the zombie apocalypse," Curry said in an interview with Complex in 2020. "Kids came barreling in, pushing, tripping, running, and banging on the gates at the store. There was no hype like this."

The pack became a coveted buy-or-trade item on forums like NikeTalk, with many searching out a set for a decent price in a pre-StockX era.

"Back then, $800 for a pair of shoes was insane, and they were going for $1,000 on eBay. It was the most money I'd ever made off shoes," Curry said.

The DMP set a blueprint for Jordan Brand. The next year saw it release the majority of its retro product strictly in "Countdown Packs," collections that included two Jordans that would add up to the number 23 (the 1 and XXII, the III and XX). Some were good, some were bad. Some sold out, some went on sale. In the ensuing years, Jordan would release Air Jordan 1 packs, packs with retros and performance shoes, and other combinations of sneakers. The DMP Air Jordan VI even received a retro in 2020, proving the colorway's lasting impact.

2007 Supra Skytop

In 2007, the skate shoe industry was in the midst of a dramatic shift, even if the major brands of the day didn't recognize it. The designs of the late '90s and early 2000s—puffy and wide, crafted around largely ornamental technologies—were giving way to minimalist silhouettes offering more subtle and significant advances. After a series of false starts, athletic brands had gained traction in the market and were slowly suffocating endemic competitors like éS, DC, and Lakai. And while skate shoe manufacturers had long seen crossover success, Nike had turned its sneakers into collectibles sought out by a niche that seemed to grow each year.

by Lucas Wisenthal

Chad Muska, a longtime pro skater whose first signature sneakers embodied the era of bloated silhouettes, saw skate shoes changing. Muska was the architect of an éS model best remembered for its hidden stash spot and the Circa brand as a whole, and his style—cargo pants, sleeveless undershirts, visor beanies—influenced a generation of skaters.

But by the middle of the 2000s, Muska's first act was seemingly up. As his skate coverage waned, his appearances in tabloids rose, owing to friendships with Paris Hilton, Nicole Richie, and their circle of socialites. His fashion influences seemed to grow in tandem; Muska had abandoned his signature look for runway attire. But despite his distance from the skate industry, when Supra Footwear launched in 2005, he was among the first riders it introduced.

"Right before Supra started, I had about a year or so where I wasn't working in footwear," Muska said.

He also wasn't skating as much. "I was in Paris for fashion week during that time," Muska said. "I was going to London Fashion Week and seeing Balenciaga shows, and Dior, and all these different high-end things."

So when he returned to skate shoe and clothing design, it was with a broader perspective.

"I was really becoming influenced by what was happening in high fashion, and I was super hyped on the idea of bridging those worlds and bringing some of those elements into skateboarding. I felt that at that time, especially, it became kind of stagnant, where it was just a lot of T-shirts, and just really plain, kind of normal stuff."

With that in mind, Muska created the Skytop, a Supra model that ran counter to almost everything happening in skateboarding in 2007. The exaggerated high-top dwarfed—in the most literal sense of the word—the lows and mids that dominated skate shop walls. So did its price point, which started at $120. And the premium materials on certain colorways were equally at odds with the product the industry at large was pushing—so much so that some Supra reps refused to show it during its initial seasons. But as its momentum built, the Skytop transcended skating, with celebrities including Jay-Z, Kanye West, and Justin Bieber wearing the shoe and turning it into, in retrospect, the last blockbuster sneaker released by a traditional skate label.

Supra, however, didn't see itself as a conventional skate shoemaker. At the time, brands were usually one-dimensional, churning out sneakers and supporting content that channeled hip-hop or punk rock exclusively. Alongside the hip-hop-influenced Muska, Supra's original team included Jim Greco and Erik Ellington, pros who had ushered in a sort of punk renaissance in skating a few years earlier. And, from its beginnings, Supra had looked beyond skating, both for design cues and an overall market.

"Nothing was good to me at that moment in skateboarding," said Angel Cabada, Supra's founder. "I mean, I hated skate shoes at the time. That's the reason why I made shoes."

Prior to launching the footwear company, Cabada had built KR3W into one of the biggest skate clothing brands of the 2000s, as with Supra, fusing punk- and hip-hop-inspired imagery and ethos. And before that, he took TSA—Team Santa Ana—from a minor Orange County name to a clothing label that counted Muska among its flagship riders.

Supra's creative leeway helped draw designer Josh Brubaker from Sole Technology, the company behind Etnies, Emerica, and éS. "They weren't ready to go to the fashion world and try to do this, maybe because they knew they couldn't. I don't know," said Brubaker. "But that's just really what I was into at the time."

Muska was moving in a similar direction. So when the two met to discuss his inaugural Supra shoe, Muska showed up with a bag of sneakers that included models from Dior Homme (now Dior Men) and Marc Jacobs, along with throwback basketball silhouettes.

"I started to see this vision in high fashion where I definitely was super inspired by Hedi Slimane," Muska said. "He was designing for Dior at the time, and he was really doing some high-top shoes like that. They were elongated toes with a slimmer fit and a really high structure."

That notion was key to the sneaker Muska wanted to produce. In the ten years that preceded the Skytop's release, skate fashion had gone from baggy cargos and carpenter jeans to a more narrow silhouette that ranged from bootcut to skintight denim. Sneakers, however, hadn't evolved in lockstep, so it was not at all uncommon for skaters to pair tight jeans with wide shoes, a combo immortalized in the best-loved videos of the early 2000s.

"I had designed skinny jeans for KR3W Apparel at the time," said Muska, "and I just saw this skinny leg. And so, all of a sudden, I saw this cool skinny, long-leg jean sitting inside, tucked in this ultra-high-top shoe. And I just thought that seemed like such a

cool look and a way to adapt that high-top shoe into that style."

In Muska's eyes, the design amounted to a subcultural Venn diagram illustrating the overlap between '80s rappers and metal musicians, many of whom favored higher silhouettes.

"I was really infatuated by the idea, or really interested in the idea, that these two completely different cultures could adapt and wear a similar type of sneaker," Muska said. "I thought that there was really something powerful to that, because if the gap that bridges those two cultures is so huge, but they could wear something similar, then that idea could apply well to a mainstream product, too."

Though Cabada and Brubaker were immediately on board with the concept, it polarized others at Supra.

"Every single person in the company looked at me, and they go, 'You're fucking crazy,'" Muska said. "And our shoe developer, he was like, 'I don't know what the hell you're thinking, but I'll make it if that's what you want to make.'"

Brubaker, said Muska, "just happened to be on the same tip around that time, and he instantly saw what my vision was, what my initial sketches were, and perfected it."

The team went through roughly three samples before they arrived at the silhouette they'd imagined.

"There was a lot of tweaking of the toe length," Brubaker said. "We were being, I guess, cautious of how far out we could take it, so trying to key in on key opponents of it being somewhat digestible." The tongue was also cut by "five or six millimeters from the original sample." At the same time, the sole was a departure from Muska's catalog. Prior to the Skytop, his signature shoes had been emblems of their era, with thick cupsoles and visible airbags complementing their bulky uppers. In 2007, though, skate shoes had begun to shed their layers, and classic silhouettes like Vans's Half Cab and Era—models built atop vulcanized soles—were on the cusp of a resurgence. So, unlike any shoe tied to Muska, the Skytop bore a vulc sole.

"The times had changed, and I wanted to go against everything possible that was traditional skate at that time," Muska said. "And everything was chunky, cupsole, airbags, all of this different stuff. And I wanted to create something that was more of, like, a sleek, slim, and a flexible product, I think."

Cabada recognized that such flexibility could come at the expense of the shoe's comfort. "Something Angel did want—he's like, 'They've got to be comfortable,'" said Ashley Nichols, former global marketing director of One Distribution, Supra's parent company. To that end, Supra spent in the neighborhood of one dollar per insole for the shoes.

"I loved it instantly," Muska said. The sneakers suited all aspects of his life. "You could slip them on and off, but when I would skate, I would tighten them up," he said. "It was, for me, the best ankle support and protection as well." With its higher profile, the Skytop guarded the metal plate in his right ankle. "It just protected the whole area, and it was vulcanized, so it was very flexible."

But Supra didn't position the Skytop solely as a high-end skate model, something its colorways made abundantly clear. While the first makeup of the sneaker was white, it subsequently arrived in black crocodile suede, as well as gold and silver. Skaters are notoriously guarded, and the silhouette, combined with the color palette, was met with skepticism.

"I think the initial reaction for any skateboarder to see something that comes from within our industry be applied outside of it anywhere is usually an instant negative backlash," Muska said.

Even internally, at Supra, the Skytop left many wary. "People were afraid of it," Brubaker said. Literally, people laughed in our face. 'What is this, a moon boot? What the hell is that?'" The company's sales reps didn't know how to sell the model. "After it went into production, it actually became part of the line, it was still, that first season—I heard multiple sales reps say they weren't even taking it out of the bag. They weren't going to bother to show it to people."

But it almost didn't matter. Muska was still a fixture of Hollywood nightlife, and he was photographed in the sneaker. As the image circulated around the internet, interest in the sneaker increased. "Well, the first couple of seasons were slower, and then, I think in, like, 2008, it really started going," Brubaker said.

That bump owed, at least in part, to Jay-Z. In 2007, the Roc-A-Fella Records cofounder wore the gold Skytop in Rihanna's "Umbrella" video. While Jay wasn't the first to be documented wearing the shoe—Will Smith wore brown Skytops on *TRL* during the *I Am Legend* press run—"Umbrella" peaked at number one on the Billboard Hot 100, and he was one of the most recognizable entertainers alive. Nichols—an alumnus of Roc-A-Fella—was responsible for the placement. He was also instrumental in putting the Skytop on Lil Wayne, who wore the sneakers throughout his *Tha Carter III* campaign. "From his videos to his award appearances, he was wearing nothing but Supras," Nichols said. That included the video for "A Milli." "He's in the red patent leathers," Nichols said. "He was the first to wear those."

Sales spiked, and two hundred units of the gold and silver makeups "would turn into fucking millions," Cabada said.

"It took about three years for it to really take a nice rollout, and then eventually every color was thirty, forty, sometimes a hundred thousand. We're doing ten, twenty colorways, and you're talking to us about, that's a lot of shoes."

By the early 2010s, following the last iteration of the Skytop, skate shoes had once again begun to change, and the appetite for exaggerated high-tops had faded. But for Muska, Cabada, Brubaker, and Nichols—and, really, for Supra as a whole—the impact of the model can't be overstated.

At the time of this writing, Supra's future appeared uncertain, with rumors of its collapse circulating. But no matter the brand's circumstances, Muska credits the Skytop with rejuvenating his career. "I think it came back as complete positive feedback and encouragement to not only continue as a designer, but to continue as a skater, too, and keep putting out more video parts and skate content as well. So it kind of breathed life into me in many different ways."

"We left something in the history of skateboarding, and footwear as well," Brubaker said. "A lot of people knew, I think, what the Skytop name was before they even knew what Supra was."

Honorable Mention
Nike Zoom Soldier

LeBron James was the first overall pick in the 2003 NBA Draft at only eighteen years old. By 2007, he was already on his fourth signature shoe. The Cleveland Cavaliers had completed back-to-back fifty-win seasons, and James had led the team to their second playoff berth of his career. Before the start of the 2005–06 season, Nike decided to double down on the annual offerings from his signature line, adding to it the 20-5-5, named for his season averages from his rookie year, for outdoor use. While that would be the first pair he laced up in the post-season, the performance-driven Zoom Soldier he debuted the following year would become more memorable, thanks to its link to one of James's most iconic performances.

by Mike DeStefano

The silhouette featured a leather and nubuck upper, a large Velcro strap across the midfoot, and an ankle wrap system that provided additional lockdown on the court. It was a far cry from the boot-like Foamposite upper of the Nike LeBron 4 he wore throughout the regular season.

The Soldier elicited some questions. Would anyone remember a takedown model from James's line? And was it even a "real" LeBron sneaker? It had his name and logo on it. But, at $110, it cost $40 less than the 4. It also didn't have the full-length Zoom Air unit, with its cushioning system limited to the heel. The sneakers were geared up for the Cleveland Cavaliers' 2006–07 playoff run, which saw a young James take his team to his first NBA Finals.

James wore multiple Soldier colorways through that playoff campaign, none more memorable than the navy blue, white, and gold pair that he laced up for Game 5 of the Eastern Conference Finals against the Detroit Pistons. He scored 29 of the Cavs' final 30 points—including the last 25 straight and a game-winning layup—on his way to an overtime victory in one of the best individual playoff performances in NBA history. That singular superhuman performance was enough to make the sneaker important. The display against the Pistons made the Soldier more than a model—Nike went on to produce yearly Soldier editions in its wake.

It was such a memorable moment that Nike even brought that Zoom Soldier colorway back in 2018 as part of its "Art of a Champion" collection, which remains the only time that the model has received a retro release. Whether it's a "real" LeBron shoe or not, James has done remarkable things in this sneaker.

2008 Nike Zoom Kobe 4

There was a general consensus around low-top basketball sneakers in 2008: they were dangerous. For two decades prior, the majority of sneakers spotted on court were high- or mid-cut, with players living with the fear of an ankle sprain or something even worse. There were a handful of NBA players who braved the court in low-tops, such as Steve Nash and Gilbert Arenas. But there was one name that was a true catalyst for changing how every basketball player looked at hooping in lower-cut sneakers: Kobe Bryant.

by Gerald Flores

Bryant's fourth Nike signature sneaker was, by his own admission, his bravest. If you look at the first three signature sneakers in the line, you can see each model evolving from a bulky leather upper to more form-fitting and closer-to-the-ground silhouettes. From the Zoom Kobe 1, which was an all-leather shoe, to the Zoom Kobe 3, which had an upper made from a web of injected mold, you can trace its development. In this next iteration, Bryant pushed his sneaker designer, Eric Avar, vice president and creative director of innovation at Nike, for a low, a move inspired by Bryant watching soccer players perform footwork that mimicked the movements of basketball players without suffering ankle sprains.

"The real insight was Kobe challenging us that he wanted a true low-top, like a running shoe or a football cleat," Avar said. "My personal design approach has always been a minimal approach of just what you need and allow the functionality of your body to provide as much performance as possible."

The advent of Nike's Flywire technology made this minimalism possible. It was first seen in the Nike Hyperdunk, a basketball sneaker Bryant wore during the 2008 Summer Olympics in Beijing. A lot like how cables on a suspension bridge work, wires positioned strategically along the shoe kept the foot protected while making the model more lightweight and flexible.

Although Bryant and Avar agreed on the direction of the player's fourth signature sneaker, it was tougher to convince everyone else. Inside the company, people were concerned about how consumers would perceive it and how it would sell. The player himself helped pitch the shoe to retailers.

"I remember having to go speak to buyers and having to explain to them why I'm going low, from an innovation standpoint, from an athlete performance standpoint, and the things we put into the shoe, like heel lock, that actually make the shoe safer than a high-top," Bryant recalled in a 2016 interview with Sole Collector. "That was one of the more courageous leaps. It was one of those things where, if it succeeds, it's going to be industry-changing, and if it fails, we're going to be up shit creek."

Avar also remembers the internal battles to make the shoe. "At that time, that was a radical notion, but Kobe was adamant that this is the type of performance and the type of shoe that he wanted," he said. Bryant wasn't just thinking about what he was going to play in during the next NBA season. He was also thinking about the future of basketball sneakers. "I remember he's like, 'I want to prove to everyone and to

Nike Zoom Kobe 4

kids coming up that you don't need all this extra bulk around your ankle.'"

Although the sneaker seemed risky, Bryant and Avar were able to get it done. The Nike Zoom Kobe 4 was about to debut on the NBA's best player during the 2008–09 season.

Bryant was cemented as an all-time great but continued to add accolades to an ever-growing résumé. He was league MVP for the 2008 NBA season and made a strong run to the NBA Finals. Although his team lost to the Boston Celtics in the championship round, he represented the US on the "Redeem Team" during the Beijing Summer Olympics and won a gold medal shortly afterward. Going into the 2008–09 season, Bryant and the Lakers were poised to light up the league again and were early favorites to return to the Finals.

"Through my experience, I've developed a little bit of a philosophy that good design is always a balance between science and art—the functionality and its form of expression," Avar said. "But I've come to add the notion of story, and I think story is so important. So it's really kind of the balance between science, art, and story."

Unlike the decade before, during which ads lived primarily on television, marketing for basketball sneakers in this era started to roll over to the internet. In addition to Nike-sponsored videos that showed him in Hyperdunks, jumping a car and performing with the cast of *Jackass*, Bryant appeared in a series of shorts promoting the Kobe 4, aptly titled, "Ankle Insurance." The vignettes featured Bryant playing an ankle insurance salesman, pushing the "unorthodox low-cut shoes" to keep basketball players' ankles from being broken. There was also a TV ad that premiered during the NBA All-Star Game that featured comedian Mike Epps and the late DJ AM in a pair of original Air Yeezys, with Bryant handing them some "ankle insurance."

Bryant had some career moments on the court in the Kobe 4 as well, which helped fuel the legacy behind the man and the shoe. On February 2, 2009, he scored a then–Madison Square Garden record against the Knicks with 61 points, breaking a record held by Michael Jordan. As predicted, the Lakers went on to the NBA Finals again, but this time secured Bryant's fourth NBA Championship and first NBA Finals MVP.

Houston Rockets forward P.J. Tucker— among the foremost sneakerheads in the NBA—called the Zoom Kobe 4 one of the most memorable models he's ever played in. "It's a perfect basketball shoe, but also a shoe you can wear hanging out," he said. Through his line, the low-top basketball sneaker became more popular and even started diffusing into other lines. Currently, over 60 percent of basketball players in the NBA wear low-tops on the court.

"The Kobe 4 was a fight, but that's one of my probably more indelible memories of working with Kobe, and because it was so different and the voice of the athlete was so important with that," Avar said. "That gave us great confidence and really helped push this idea and this concept through."

Honorable Mention
Nike Hyperdunk

In 2008, the perfect storm of the Hyperdunk's futuristic style, massive worldwide introduction, and revolutionary viral-marketing campaign established the era's blueprint for sneaker launches. Its design team, led by Eric Avar, set out to make the lightest, best-performing basketball sneaker on the market. The model marked the category debut of Flywire, a Vectran cable support system, and Lunarlon foam cushioning. Together, Flywire and Lunarlon helped Nike achieve its goal of shedding weight without compromising performance—the Hyperdunk weighed in at thirteen ounces, 18 percent lighter than the brand's average basketball shoe at the time.

    Despite having his own signature line, Kobe Bryant was tapped to help with the Hyperdunk's rollout. Bryant had a reputation for pushing new tech and was set to make his Olympic debut in Beijing, where Nike planned to introduce the shoe officially.

by Brandon Richard

"The thing that sold me on [the Hyperdunk] was the technology," Bryant told Sole Collector in 2009. "I'm a real big technology guy, and there's not a lot of people who would push that boundary or hop in a shoe that's so new. It was pretty easy for me to jump into a shoe that fit everything that I had been talking about for years."

Bryant actually gave the public its first look at the Hyperdunk months earlier, playing a few regular-season games in Lakers-inspired colorways. Nike even released an ultra-limited run of twenty-four pairs in those Lakers colors in May 2008. Most, however, became aware of the shoe via a guerilla-style marketing campaign. Two online-exclusive videos featured Bryant jumping over a speeding Aston Martin and then over a pool of snakes with the *Jackass* crew while wearing Hyperdunks. The stunts were staged, but they added a layer of mystique to the sneakers, creating the industry's first viral moment.

The stage was set for Beijing, host of arguably the most anticipated Olympic basketball tournament to date, following Team USA's shocking loss in 2004. Half of the '08 "Redeem Team" roster, including Bryant, played in the "United We Rise" Hyperdunk en route to winning the gold medal, giving the shoe its defining on-court moment to go along with the viral appeal. Members of the Women's National Team and players from rival countries wore the model as well.

The original Hyperdunk kicked off a highly touted performance line that continues to produce new models annually. Its legacy, though, lies in how far it propelled basketball footwear, both with its design and distinctly twenty-first-century marketing campaign.

2009 Nike Air Yeezy 1

By 2008, Kanye West had reached the pinnacle of global influence in pop culture. He'd delivered four exceptional, genre-bending studio albums (*The College Dropout*, *Late Registration*, *Graduation*, and *808s & Heartbreak*) that yielded over ten Grammy wins and changed the look and feel of hip-hop. But West, who was well on his way to solidifying himself as a generational talent in music, wanted to focus more on design and product. Since he'd come onto the scene in 2003, every outfit, every accessory, and every sneaker he wore was fodder for the blogs, almost a decade before Instagram's Explore page arrived. He was the kid in fourth grade who drew sneakers in class and the man in 2007 who shaved a Fendi logo into his hair. Now was his time to make his claim as a designer. And it would only be a matter of time until the most influential artist of the day linked with the most dominant sneaker brand in the world.

by Joe La Puma

There's an infamous photo of West on a private jet, pencil in hand, dripped in a vintage patchwork Nike jacket, drawing sneakers on a fateful trip from Miami to New York. West has said that he'd become inspired following Nike's "One Night Only" Air Force 1 event in NYC, which celebrated twenty-five years of the iconic Bruce Kilgore design. The drawings he was putting together were heavily influenced by the '80s classic *Back to the Future*, the Nike Mag, and his love for anime. Those sketches from 35,000 feet in the air would eventually be brought to Nike's creative director of special projects, Mark Smith.

From the start, West and Smith tried to marry a design that satisfied the rapper's out-of-this-world appetite for a futuristic, moonboot-esque sneaker and Smith's focus on making something that could still seamlessly exist in Nike's catalog. They worked with former Nike developer Tiffany Beers at the brand's infamous and ultra-exclusive cook-up center, the Innovative Kitchen, and created tons of prototypes, samples, and designs.

"The original shoes were battery-operated, and they lit up. I have a version of the first shoe that has a push-button on the side, and it lights up and stays lit," West told Complex in 2009 about an early iteration of the Yeezy 1.

In the end, they revamped a sole from the Air Assault, put their twist on the classic elephant print tooling from the Jordan III (dubbed the "Ylephant patent pattern"), and capped off the design with glow-in-the-dark outsoles. But the centerpiece of the upper was a forefoot strap that added support and reimagined the DNA of Bo Jackson's Air Trainer 1 from the late '80s, bringing it into the 2000s. "It felt like a true collaboration," said Ronnie Fieg, footwear designer and founder and CEO of Kith. "There were key elements of Nike's history you could see, like the Jordan III/Air Assault midsole, but fused with details that you could feel stemmed from Ye's signature aesthetic."

Around 2006 to 2009, the sneaker space was still heavily dominated by classic Air Jordans and the signature sneakers of top-tier NBA athletes. The West/Nike partnership marked the first full nonathlete sneaker collaboration under the Nike umbrella. Although the sneaker wasn't made for an athlete per se, its function was still crucial. "I always try to look at things through an athlete's eyes—if you look at a basketball player, his or her performance is on court, in the middle of a game. The equivalent for Kanye would be

to get onstage and rock it for a couple of hours," Smith told Complex in 2009.

With rumors of a West x Nike collaboration reaching fever pitch, the rapper finally debuted the Nike Air Yeezy 1 onstage at the fiftieth annual Grammy Awards in 2008. That night, West paid tribute to his mother, Donda, who had recently passed, and performed "Hey Mama." The performance hit its apex around a minute and a half in, when West emotionally bent down. This document meant a lot more in the grand scheme of things, but it's the photo clamoring sneakerheads still pass around over a decade later: West, mic to his side and his eyes closed, in an unreleased sample of a black-on-black Nike Air Yeezy 1, the first clear look at his signature shoe. Just how special is that Grammy pair? As recently as 2017, the never-released makeup was fetching over $100,000 at consignment shop Flight Club.

Even after West debuted the Nike collaboration on the biggest stage, it took the brand two months to officially confirm it. Nike finally sent out a press release on April 6, 2009, that read: "Nike and Kanye West Present the Nike Air Yeezy Sneaker." At the end of the statement, it was announced that the Nike Air Yeezy would come out in the spring of 2009 in three different colorways: zen grey/LT charcoal in April; black/black in May; and the final net/net in June. "I wanted to give the Yeezys their own colorway. You wouldn't have a whole fuchsia wall in your house, but you might have a little Jeff Koons piece of art that's fuchsia and small. So I do it small, on the inside of the tongue," West said about the subtle pop of color featured on the tongue of the sneakers in his 2009 Complex cover story. In the months leading up to the releases, he wore the three-pack of sneakers courtside, onstage, and in music videos (now's a good time to revisit Keri Hilson's 2009 classic "Knock You Down" clip). But as West was continuing to build hype for the sneakers, the rest of the world was strategizing on how it would get them.

Information about how many pairs were created for retail is murky, but West mentioned in the 2009 Complex cover story that there were nine thousand hitting the market. The sneakers were only released at high-end stores around the country, rumored to be less than forty shops nationwide. In Detroit, the boutique Burn Rubber received less than forty pairs. "I think that the Yeezy 1 was historic," Burn Rubber co-owner Rick Williams remembered. "I can't speak for anyone else, but we learned a lot from that drop. It definitely ushered in a new era of hype. The Yeezy 1 helped further what we were doing in the boutique world."

While West's partnership with Nike was successful from execution, mindshare, and legacy standpoints, it eventually frayed. Shortly after the Nike Air Yeezy 2 was released in 2012, West became vocal about the limitations he felt the brand put on the collaboration. There were onstage rants; the notorious "Facts" diss track, where West rapped about Nike's treatment of employees; and the instant classic "Hold up, I ain't trying to stunt, man / But the Yeezys jumped over the Jumpman" bar from the song "New God Flow." The partnership officially ended in 2013, with West signing with Adidas. West's main point of contention was the royalties he believed he was owed for the sneakers, but also the constraints he felt from Nike in developing even more products with the brand. In an interview with Charlamagne Tha God in 2018, he got candid about how tough it was when the Nike relationship ended. "When I was young, I used to sketch the Swoosh and everything. It was heartbreaking for me to have to leave Nike, but they refused to allow me to get royalties on my shoe, and I knew I had the hottest shoe in the world," West said. Later in the same interview, he would apologize to then–Nike CEO Mark Parker for the times he lashed out at the exec and the brand.

Since signing with Adidas, West has gone on to create an absolute industry juggernaut. His Adidas Yeezy line reportedly raked in $1.5 billion in sales in 2019, an accelerated threat to Nike's biggest subsidiary, Jordan Brand, which generates $3 billion in annual sales. Ironically, Nike has found huge success in tapping West's longtime inner circle, including Virgil Abloh, Jerry Lorenzo, and Don C, all three of whom have been major drivers of its energy moments in the last five years. Abloh's design project "The Ten" and subsequent collaborations have been some of the most hyped Nike products of the 2010s.

Still, the Nike Air Yeezy 1 was a revolutionary piece of design that shifted the way brands thought about collaborations and heightened the freedom with which non-athlete pop culture figures could develop product. The substantial staying power of the silhouette that West created is easily measured to this day. Go to any major consignment store around the country and you'll see the Nike Air Yeezy 1 behind the glass in "trophy" cases and "grail" walls. What Nike and West designed together will forever be a part of sneaker history. And the fact that the Yeezy 1 could be released in 2030 and still seem forward is a testament to West's knack for pushing design to what he considers perfection.

"Kanye started really taking things to the next level of being influential," said P. J. Tucker, the NBA's undisputed sneaker king, who owns one of the world's most impressive sneaker collections. "Entertainers taking over basketball shoes and sportswear kind of stuff. I don't know if, in history, anyone has done it the way he has—that shoe, the hype behind it. At that time, Kanye was the hottest in the rap game. When it comes to really influencing people, when you look at the core of influencing people, he's it. That shoe, at the time, was so anticipated. It might still be one of the most anticipated ever. It's easily a top ten shoe of all time."

Honorable Mention
Nike SB Zoom Stefan Janoski

If Stefan Janoski's Nike SB signature model isn't one of the best-selling skate shoes of all time, it's one of the most ubiquitous. Since its launch, the design has appeared in hundreds of colorways and taken numerous forms, a slip-on, a mid, a high-top, and an Air Max–inspired lifestyle model among them. You'd be hard-pressed to find a skater under thirty-five who hasn't owned a pair. And most nonskaters who have likely weren't familiar with the pro—a Habitat Skateboards rider from Vacaville, California—prior to lacing up his namesake shoe.

But before the Janoski could reach that level, Nike had to okay the model. And it almost didn't.

"Everyone hated it," James Arizumi, senior global creative director of Nike SB and ACG, told Complex UK in 2019. "When we had the first sale presented to our VPs, they basically said to us, 'How are we supposed to go to Mark Parker and Phil Knight and say this is a signature model?'"

by Lucas Wisenthal

Skate shoes had shrunk to a point that even the Dunk—once an alternative to the overwrought tech of the late '90s and early 2000s—had begun to look outmoded. But by almost no one's estimation was skateboarding ready for what was essentially a skateable boat shoe.

As the site Jenkem wrote in 2019, Janoski was adamant that his model have a minimalist design and a flat toe. "It went through some crazy times of people having to deal with the fact that I was right and what they wanted to happen was not happening," Janoski said. "But if it's gonna have my name on it, it's gonna be the way I want."

The shoe sold so well that a rumor that Nike had bought Janoski's name for $4 million began to circulate. "What I can tell you," Janoski told RIDE Channel in 2015, "is that it is most definitely not true."

For Nike, the model was a win on several levels. While the Dunk had cemented the brand's spot in skating and drawn sneakerheads to skate shops for limited releases, the revamped '80s basketball silhouette was not a new product. The Janoski was an entirely new shoe that, though functional for skating, penetrated the mainstream. It did spawn a couple of hyped releases, including the coveted "Digi Camo Floral" makeup from 2013, but its wide appeal is why it remains an integral part of Nike's skate lineup. It's also why we'll probably never see a true successor to the model.

"No, there's not going to be a Janoski 2," Janoski told Transworld Skateboarding in 2019. "I always say, 'It's better to be right the first time.'"

Obsessing over sports footwear used to be a niche activity. This was before your family asked about the latest Jordans and the long line-ups for them around Christmas. Before the resale industry became a billion-dollar behemoth driven by global frenzy. That all changed in the last decade, when sneaker collecting became mainstream.

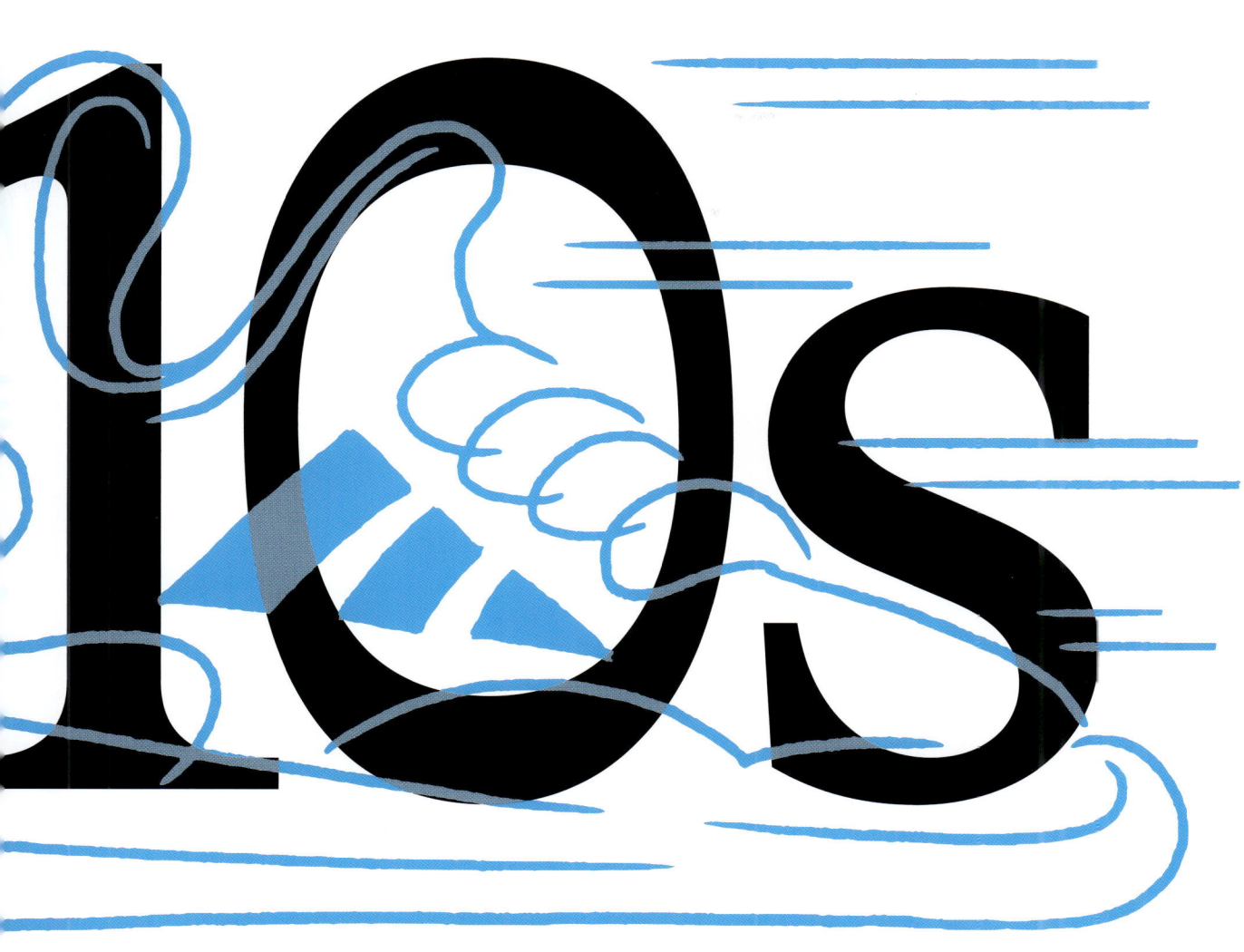

The sneaker wars returned, with Adidas threatening Nike's dominance. The shift in power owed largely to Kanye West, who went from checks to stripes as Adidas was hitting a serious stride. At the dawn of the decade, we were buying shoes from the past disguised as the future. By the end of it, we had really arrived in the future—NASA cushioning, automated manufacturing processes, and relentless robots snapping limited stock right out from under us.

2010 Nike LeBron 8

LeBron James was coming off of what many people consider to be the strongest model in his arsenal, the Nike LeBron 7. On top of that, he was fresh off the single-biggest free agency decision in the history of sports, when he chose to take his talents to South Beach and form what would be known as the "Big Three" with Chris Bosh and Dwyane Wade.

by Ben Felderstein

Pressure was mounting to follow up on the success of the LeBron 7, as well as live up to the hype of his infamous "Not one, not two, not three, not four, not five, not six, not seven..." championship-promising speech. Ultimately, in 2011, James delivered, making the All-NBA and All-Defensive first teams, leading the Miami Heat to the NBA Finals, and rolling out the LeBron 8.

The shoe, among the best of the models bearing James's name, changed basketball footwear forever.

"We just wanted to create a silhouette that, on the shelf, didn't look like anything else," designer Jason Petrie said. "You can notice it from one hundred yards away just because of that. You needed a silhouette and an outline that stood proud, above the rest of the stuff out there."

With the arrival of the 8 came the release of the very first of James's "South Beach" sneakers. It also marked the first "Pre-Heat" drop in Nike's history. "Pre-Heat," a launch method to bring out a bold colorway before the proper debut of a signature model in a tamer, usually team-based palette, was a new term to the sneaker world back then.

Released on October 16, 2010, the Nike LeBron 8 "South Beach" was a departure from the status quo. The Heat's uniforms were black, white, and red, but this new sneaker was teal and pink. It completely shifted the idea of what a basketball sneaker could look like. While James never actually wore this pair on the court, we now see wildly colored sneakers on a nightly basis.

"LeBron, to his credit, was like, 'Okay, man, let's roll,'" Petrie said. "And I do remember saying to LeBron, 'I feel like this is our opportunity. I've been waiting for this my whole life.' You're at this point in your career where everything's going nuts."

2010 was a perfect year for James and Petrie to release a teal and pink sneaker. Adding to the hype "The Decision" created, James and Nike filmed a ninety-second "Rise" commercial that further leaned into the "heel" character that he was becoming to the rest of the league.

"Overall, to the sneaker community globally, it's a huge sneaker," said Jaron Kanfer, now the CEO of UNKNWN, the Miami sneaker store James opened with Kanfer and Frankie Walker Jr., both high school friends. "All the Heat fans were excited to be in Miami. The city was on fire. This was the first [LeBron] colorway dedicated to the city of Miami, so I think it was special to the city."

Beyond changing the way that designers look at colorways, the "South Beach" 8s sent the industry into a brand-new era. On-court footwear became more of a focal point, the sneaker resale market began to rise, and sneaker culture in Miami was forever changed.

"The 'South Beach' was the shoe that really took [basketball sneakers] and ignited this, I don't know if you want to call it a 'culture 2.0 or 3.0'—it just started that next wave of stuff," Petrie said. "We knew we were onto something because you could just see it if you check the sneaker news and you just see kids in the street and you just hear people with these resale values and hear about these mob scenes at the malls."

James debuted the iconic sneaker at a Foot Locker launch event, wearing a teal Florida Marlins hat and a black "Witness" Nike T-shirt. It was the perfect introduction for James to Miami fans. He was repping

the hometown baseball team, and he was rolling out a sneaker that was a true tribute to his new city, paying homage to the TV series *Miami Vice*.

"You could just see there's going to be a ton of kids that are going to want to do exactly what he's doing with them," Petrie said of the outfit James wore to debut the "South Beach" 8s. "He sold it that day to me—that's where the pictures came from. Somebody wearing it. He had it before anybody. Fit was crazy."

Even today, the "South Beach" 8s have a measurable impact on the game. The league's defending sneaker king, P. J. Tucker, wore them on court during a 2018 game against James and the Lakers and claims that the shoes are one of the most memorable pairs of all time.

"It was a basketball shoe that was super limited and a dope colorway for LeBron being in Miami and going to the Heat at the time," Tucker said. "There was so much heat behind the sneaker, and that was during that crazy time where people were really starting to go crazy about sneakers. It was something outside of a Jordan, which was big during that time. It's one of the most iconic shoes ever."

While the "South Beach" colorway is certainly the most notable footprint in a long line of LeBron 8 memories, it's still only one part of the sneaker's impressive history. With the 7 having been such a success, abandoning the design entirely would not have been a wise decision. Petrie carried over a Flywire chassis for stability and lockdown, as well as another 360-degree Air Max bag for comfort and protection on the court.

Unlike the 7, though, the 8 featured a menacing lion head on its tongue with piercing eyes to represent James's "King" moniker. An "828" stamp denoting the 82 games in the NBA's regular season and the maximum of 28 it takes to win an NBA championship also appeared on the sneaker.

"I do think that that shift to Air Max had something to do with helping him stay on court a little longer," Petrie said. "We did that because of his insight. It's not like our genius led to the advance. 'Protect me from myself.' He was saying it from day one."

The transition period between the 7—Petrie's first sneaker with James—and the 8 was important for his and James's relationship, Petrie said, as he began to get closer to the player's inner circle, learning more about his preferences and predilections. He wanted to "craft something that was going to fit into his world" and develop a sneaker that was perfect for all aspects of James's life.

One of Petrie's most innovative design concepts was to adjust the sneaker as the year went on. While a sneaker has to sell, it also has to stand the test of time for one of the hardest-working athletes in the world.

"We realized that his body changes, his mindset changes, the game changes," Petrie said. "December games are not the same as they are in October or in March, right? So there's different levels of intensity, different climates. Teammates change, you know? Game plan changes. So we wanted to kind of have fun and iterate those changes in his shoe. So we figured, let's bring him these new benefits through changing the shoe with him as the season goes."

With that came the V1, V2, and V3 versions of the 8. The key differences between the first two versions of the sneaker included a more exposed set of Flywire in the second iteration, providing a slightly more breathable shoe. While the design alterations were made with function in mind, aesthetically, the V1 seems a bit more premium, done up in high-end leathers and even suede textiles. Finally, just in time for another deep playoff run, Petrie and Nike shaved off another ounce for the V3, or the P.S. (for postseason), to give James the lightest and smoothest on-court ride yet.

Now, some ten years later, James's impact on the world of basketball sneakers is that much clearer. His signature series changed it irrevocably, combining performance with style. In 2020, the basketball sneaker conversation begins with James, with Petrie at his side.

"I'm looking at it as, like, a young Tinker-and-Mike situation with the whole world here—everything's set for us," Petrie said. "And that's what I promised to do. I know you're going to do what you need to do, and he's always said, 'Don't worry about me. You guys do what you're supposed to do; I'll take care of things on the court.' Obviously he's done that. We're just trying to keep up ever since."

Honorable Mention
Nike Zoom Kobe 6

Before Nike debuted Kobe Bryant's sixth signature sneaker in 2010, the player's "Black Mamba" moniker was just a nickname. But with the Zoom Kobe 6, Nike Basketball and designer Eric Avar brought Bryant's alias to life, delivering an on-the-nose interpretation of the late NBA legend's defining qualities on the court. From a distance, the Kobe 6 wasn't a radical departure from the Kobe 4 and Kobe 5. The 6 used a similar lightweight low-top silhouette, as well as Zoom Air cushioning, both of which came to be staples of Bryant's signature line.

    A closer look, however, revealed that the model was unlike any that came before it. Its three-layer upper was covered on the outside by what Nike described as polyurethane "islands," resulting in a snakeskin-like texture all over the shoe. Beyond being striking, the scaly pattern provided a performance

by Riley Jones

advantage. According to Nike, the scales were strategically positioned across the upper, increasing and decreasing in size in areas where durability was most needed.

"The Kobe 6 is a very character-driven shoe, with the alter ego of the Black Mamba prominently featured," Bryant said in a press release during the shoe's 2010 rollout. "We continue to evolve the technology to make it a performance-based shoe, but aesthetically you haven't seen a shoe pop like this before. It brings to life what drives me."

The Kobe 6 stuck with the low-to-the-ground, responsive feel of Bryant's two preceding models, but carried the concept further by improving its fit through the use of a dual-layer memory foam sockliner. To drive the point home, the insole was literally printed with a request from Bryant: "I want a shoe that molds to my foot."

"The Black Mamba to Kobe means being one of the deadliest predators on the planet," Avar said in the same press release. "That's his approach to every game. He's very calculated, and he's very quick." With that in mind, Nike also coined the word "venomenon"—seen on the sneaker's toe—in further reference to Bryant's nickname.

The Kobe 6 was also notable for its range of memorable colorways, including Christmastime "Grinch" and soccer-inspired "Barcelona" makeups that have gone on to become some of Bryant's most coveted sneakers. Releases like these represented a new storytelling trend in sneakers that Nike Basketball capitalized on to great effect in the last decade. It was selling you shoes, sure, but it was also selling you the narratives around them.

2011 Nike Mag

When filming began on *Back to the Future Part II* in February 1989, the creators had spent more than two years working on the script and building sets for a movie. From that late-'80s vantage point, the filmmakers had to envisage a world more than two decades in the future, and they did an amazingly prescient job, imagining things that would eventually become reality, such as wearable technology, drones, and video conferencing.

by Justin Tejada

But director Robert Zemeckis and stars Michael J. Fox and Christopher Lloyd could not have imagined when *Back to the Future Part II* debuted in theaters on November 22, 1989, that one of the film's most enduring futuristic creations would be a pair of sneakers that is only directly referenced once—and with just four words—a few minutes into the movie's 105-minute run time.

When Lloyd's Doc Brown character presents Fox's Marty McFly with a large black tube adorned with the words "Nike Footwear" in volt lettering, the legend of the Nike Mag is born.

McFly unceremoniously puts them on and the shoes tighten around his foot, prompting him to remark, "Power laces, all right." That's it. When Doc meets up with Marty, he focuses on McFly's jeans, jacket, and hat to make sure they are period-correct for October 21, 2015, but he doesn't say a word about his footwear.

Nevertheless, the Nike Mag became a grail in the truest sense, its legend fanned by its unattainable nature. For twenty-two years, the Mag was a shoe that could not be had. While it was lusted after on forums like NikeTalk and rumors of a release would occasionally circulate, nothing ever materialized. Then, in 2011, that all changed.

That September, the word went out that the "greatest shoe never made" was actually going to become a reality. With a clever headline that worked on many levels—"It's About Time"—Nike announced that it was going to create 1,500 pairs of the Mag, with all net proceeds going to the Michael J. Fox Foundation. Fox had been diagnosed with Parkinson's disease in 1991 and revealed it to the public in 1998. The release of the shoe became an opportunity not only to give sneakerheads what they'd been pining over for so long, but also to raise funds to combat the devastating disease. The shoe would go on to generate millions for the foundation.

None of that was on the minds of the filmmakers. In the original *Back to the Future*, McFly wore a pair of Nike Bruins. The story goes that Fox showed up to set wearing the white Nikes with the red Swoosh and they became part of his character's wardrobe. For Nike, which wasn't the corporate behemoth it is today, the product placement was huge. So when it came time for the sequel, both the brand and the film's producers wanted to keep McFly in Nikes. "We went to Nike and we said, 'What would a shoe look like thirty years in the future?'" executive producer Frank Marshall said in a 2011 video from the brand.

Nike put Tinker Hatfield in charge of developing what would become the Mag. By this point, Hatfield had designed the Air Max 1 and the Air Jordan III, but conceiving a shoe that could be worn nearly three decades down the road wasn't a simple task, even for someone like him. "It wasn't a normal thing for me to think that far in the future," Hatfield said in an interview with *Colorblind*.

Hatfield wasn't the only rising star charged with working on the Mag. Future CEO Mark Parker, then a designer at Nike, also contributed to the design. One meeting between Hatfield, Parker, screenwriter Bob Gale, and Zemeckis produced an idea that the shoes might levitate, but Hatfield couldn't wrap his head around why someone would need to levitate and the idea was shelved. Instead, Hatfield reinvisioned the creative brief, looking at the project "like someone had asked me to reinvent footwear for actual performance reasons, in the real world, only I had thirty years to figure the technology out," he told *Wired* in 2016.

The result was a shoe that could essentially come alive. It would sense a wearer's feet and signal this awareness by lighting up and tightening its laces. Though never overtly mentioned, the Mag name comes from the shoe's ability to adhere to surfaces like the famous hoverboard that McFly zips around on in the movie. Six pairs of Nike Mags were made for the film, including the pair whose power-lacing system actually "worked." To make it believable during filming in 1989, holes were cut in the Mags, and a prop person was positioned under the street to manually tighten the laces.

Those six pairs were all that fanboys and -girls and sneakerheads had to dream about for more than two decades, until 2011, when Nike finally decided to release a version of the Nike Mag for consumers.

The aesthetics of the shoe matched the movie version to a tee, with each contour of the upper replicated faithfully. LED lights in the heel illuminated with a pinch of the collar on the ultra-high-top silhouette. But one crucial detail was missing: power laces. Remember that the only line that McFly utters about the shoes in the movie is "Power laces, all right," so it was a disappointment to some when the shoe was released without the key feature.

Still, it was a victory for most fans. Prior to release, there had been a petition signed by more than thirty thousand people, asking Nike to release the shoe. The petition eventually made its way to the desk of Hatfield, who started spearheading the project with the help of Parker and a rising new engineer in Beaverton named Tiffany

Beers. It was a rare example of a brand actually responding to direct input from sneaker fans and acting on it.

Fifteen hundred pairs were auctioned over ten days on eBay, ranging in price from $2,300 for a pair of size 7s to $9,959 for a pair of size 10s. The release raised more than $4.7 million for the Michael J. Fox Foundation. In a fortuitous turn of events, the foundation had announced a matching challenge with Google cofounder Sergey Brin and his wife at the time, Anne Wojcicki, a few months prior to the release of the Mag. With the match, the final amount donated to the foundation was over $9.4 million.

Despite the fervor the sneaker inspired, there was still that pesky issue of the power lacing. Then came NBA All-Star Weekend

in 2014. During an appearance at a Jordan Brand event in New Orleans, Hatfield was asked about a version of the Mag that could do what the movie shoe did. "Are we gonna see power laces in 2015? To that, I say, 'Yes!'" he replied.

Except Hatfield's pronouncement and timetable had not exactly been vetted by higher-ups at Nike. "It's not unheard of for me to get things moving in unexpected ways," he told the *New York Times*. The prediction was picked up widely in the press, so Hatfield used that as a moment to get the ball rolling. Now all he had to do was figure out how to get a shoe to lace itself.

That job fell primarily to Beers. She'd been poking around the project for a few years by that point, but there was nothing that led her to believe that anything was imminent. All-Star Weekend changed that. Beers put up makeshift walls inside Nike's renowned R&D studio, the Innovation Kitchen, and dubbed the area the "Black Hole." As far as things in Beaverton go, it didn't get much more top secret than that.

The large cutaway section in the bottom of the Air Jordan XX8, another Hatfield creation, gave Beers the idea of a place to house the motor required to tighten the laces. After years of little progress, "everything kind of came together all at once," Beers told *Wired*.

The primary recipient of Beers's innovation was the Nike HyperAdapt 1.0, but you can't create self-lacing technology and not put it in a Nike Mag. With that in mind, Beers told Complex in 2016, "I grabbed a couple of engineers and said, 'Today we gotta figure out how to put it in *here*.'"

The first tweet from the Michael J. Fox Foundation went out at 3:05 p.m. on—when else?—October 21, 2015, the date Doc and Marty travel to in *Back to the Future Part II*. It said simply, "This is real. This is today. Coming spring 2016. cc:@RealMikeFox @Nike," and showed a picture of Fox sitting on a chair in a pair of Mags as Emmy awards sat on a shelf behind him. In a subsequently tweeted video, Fox tries on a pair of Mags and you hear a whirring sound as the laces tighten automatically when he applies pressure on the heel. With the same sense of wonder that his character exhibited in the movie, Fox says, "That's insane. That's really great."

Hatfield also sent Fox a handwritten letter, accompanied by a drawing of McFly trying on the shoes in the movie, that started, "Almost thirty years ago we embarked on a journey to create a glimpse into 'The Future.' Although the project started as science fiction, we're now proud to turn that fiction into fact."

Though the 2015 Mag was originally intended to be available in spring 2016, its release was pushed to October 2016. Only eighty-nine pairs were made. As opposed to the 2011 release, the 2015 edition wasn't just open to the highest bidder. Fans were able to purchase $10 tickets to a draw, with winners receiving pairs. This approach helped raise $6.75 million for the Michael J. Fox Foundation, bringing the total for the two versions released to more than $16 million.

While the shoe's place in sneaker and pop culture lore is firmly cemented, it would be even more amazing if the enduring legacy of the Nike Mag was its role in helping to find a cure for Parkinson's disease. That may seem far-fetched, but, as Mark Parker said, "By imagining the future, we create it." And it doesn't even require a DeLorean.

Honorable Mention
Nike Zoom KD IV

Kevin Durant's long list of career achievements was considerably more concise back in 2011. He'd earned a couple of MVP designations—one at the McDonald's All-American Game in 2007 and one at the FIBA World Cup in 2010—but none in the NBA. He had a gold medal from his performance at the 2010 FIBA World Cup, but didn't yet have any Olympic hardware. And he had his own sneaker line with Nike, but hadn't released many truly memorable shoes. The turning point for Durant's footwear résumé came in 2011, with the arrival of his fourth model.

It was the Nike Zoom KD IV that really fulfilled the promise of a signature line, making his shoes more personal. The first two Nike KD models were unremarkable, both mid-

by Brendan Dunne

dling in their height and their ability to translate any of the greatness of the young Durant into footwear. His third, which released in 2010, was sleeker and sharper, but didn't feel distinct from other performance basketball designs of the era. The Nike Zoom KD IV broke from the expectations that trilogy created, shortening the silhouette and embracing the standard for low-top basketball shoes set by Kobe Bryant's fourth model, which came in 2008. It also moved the Swoosh, setting it aside and letting a cross-foot strap dominate the upper.

The Nike Zoom KD IV was one of those rare sneakers that made consumers feel like they were getting some extra value from the brand behind it. At just $95, this brand-new performance basketball offering was considerably cheaper than the retro Air Jordans and Air Maxes sneakerheads were consuming en masse at the time. This helped change how the scene spent its money, resulting in a renewed interest in actual new shoes.

The Nike KD IV also enjoyed a new and brief golden era of design for Nike Basketball, which focused on storytelling through unique and bold colorways. A weatherman-themed version of the KD IV proposed how Durant might have spent his time had that year's lockout kept him from professional basketball. A Nerf one came complete with a matching hoop and ball. While these early colorways released at the end of 2011 hinted at how great the KD IV could be, the shoe enjoyed an extended period of relevance throughout 2012, thanks to pairs like the "Galaxy" and "Aunt Pearl" editions. The Thunder star also got a gold medal at the Olympics that year, along with a matching colorway of his KD IV to go with it. Durant, and his sneakers, had truly arrived.

2012 Nike Flyknit Racer

Sneaker technologies come and go, with only a handful managing to have the power not only to stick around but to influence the marketplace for years to come. Nike has a particular knack for creating such tech—its ubiquitous Air technology has been ever-evolving and endlessly mimicked since its introduction in 1979. There's also the Flyknit, which has been cemented in the mercurial world of sneaker tech.

by Riley Jones

Flyknit was brought to the market in 2012, debuting on the Flyknit Racer runner and the more lifestyle-apropos Flyknit Trainer. Here, we'll focus mostly on the former, which managed to remain on shelves for five straight years after its debut, a rare feat in today's rapidly changing marketplace.

The Flyknit Racer was literally engineered for the world's top runners, making its grand debut at the 2012 Summer Olympics in London, where it could be seen everywhere from the tracks to the winners' podiums. Deviating from the leather, mesh, suede, and synthetics seen on performance shoes in the past, the Flyknit Racer was constructed with digitally knitted yarns, resulting in a sock-like feel and look. From a performance standpoint, this meant that the shoe was far lighter than comparable running models. At the time of release, Nike noted that a size 9 in the Flyknit Racer clocked in at 5.6 ounces, which was 19 percent lighter than the Zoom Streak 3, a model considered to be one of the brand's elite running shoes. Beyond its lighter weight, Flyknit also provided the advantage of a more dialed-in fit, wrapping the wearer's foot in what the brand touted as a "second skin."

After a limited release in February at Nike's 21 Mercer store in New York City, the Flyknit Racer hit retailers worldwide on July 27, 2012. Unlike the rainbow of ten Flyknit Trainer colorways that would drop from the gate, the Flyknit Racer was made available in just two variations: its signature "Volt" scheme, contrasted with a black medial panel, and a secondary "Total Orange" colorway, split with gray. Although it would be a relatively slow start for the model at retail, things would pick up steam quickly, with it eventually releasing in dozens of colorways over the following year, including the fan-favorite "Multicolor" and "Oreo" styles. It would remain relatively available in a wide range of men's and women's options through 2017, when it was quietly discontinued.

While the Flyknit Racer was intended for serious running use, the Flyknit Trainer was also a performance model, although it catered more to the everyday runner than marathoners. With a slightly bulkier profile and a wider range of colors to choose from early on, the Flyknit Trainer managed to catch on with the lifestyle crowd, too. Like most trends in footwear, it built up slowly, but by the time Kanye West adopted its monochromatic white- and black-based colorways, it had become one of the must-have models on the market. "The shoes were not so popular back in 2012," French Flyknit connoisseur Pierre-Emmanuel Zamane told Complex in 2017. "It was purely a demonstration of new Nike technology. The sneakers hit outlets here in France, but one day that guy named Kanye West decided to wear them, and the hype magic happened. I remember getting a pair for 50€ at a Nike outlet. That's insane."

What made the Flyknit Racer and Flyknit Trainer explosion especially noteworthy was that they were entirely new designs. In a market that's more often than not dominated by retro shoes, the fact that two radically new models were able to catch on was impressive—enough so to warrant an actual retro of the Flyknit Trainer in 2017. Flyknit's takeover touched nearly every aspect of sneaker culture, from hyper-limited Supreme collaborations to general releases at Foot Locker. And its

2012

minimalist, sock-like design DNA would eventually extend far beyond Nike, serving as a precursor to of-the-moment knits like West's Adidas Yeezy Boost 350 V2 and Balenciaga's Sock Runner.

Over the years, Flyknit would proliferate far beyond the Flyknit Racer and Flyknit Trainer, becoming a staple technology from Nike. It's been used for a variety of purposes, including everything from reimagining classic sneakers like the Air Force 1, Air Jordan 1, and Air Max 1 to meeting the needs of elite athletes such as Kobe Bryant and LeBron James, whose signature lines regularly featured the material.

Around the same time Nike was pumping marketing dollars into its newest innovation, one of its biggest competitors, Adidas, was preparing to unveil a strikingly similar technology. Adidas introduced its take on the technology, Primeknit, in July 2012, beginning with a staggered rollout in its home country of Germany. Nike was quick to act, filing a patent infringement lawsuit in Nuremberg, Germany, where it was successful, and the court forced Adidas to stop selling its Primeknit footwear.

Adidas denied the claims, and by November, German courts had overturned the initial ruling and allowed the brand to continue producing its knitted shoes. It ultimately decided that Nike's technology was not patentable because similar knitted footwear had existed as far back as the 1940s. The legal back-and-forth would continue with mostly inconsequential results, as both brands continue to sell their knitted products globally.

As of this writing, the Flyknit Racer is not currently in production by Nike—although certain pairs can be found discounted at select retailers. But even though new pairs aren't being made, traces of the Flyknit Racer's sleek shape and sock-like construction can be seen in nearly every corner of the footwear industry. From the basketball hardwood to the fashion week runways and beyond, knitted sneakers aren't going away anytime soon.

Honorable Mention
Nike Roshe Run

No amount of revisionist history can erase the impact of the Nike Roshe Run. Today, the model is a meme, its relatively plain silhouette a marker of minimal effort on behalf of the wearer rather than on minimalism. But recent portrayals of the shoe as inherently basic and a choice of broke boys ignore just how bold and different the zen-inspired sneaker was when it debuted.

The Roshe was, at first, not a hyped sneaker. It was not a model that enjoyed any sort of press release communicating its arrival. There was no detailed breakdown of all the cutting-edge Swoosh innovation the shoe took advantage of. To be fair, there wasn't much cutting-edge Swoosh innovation. Instead, the Roshe sort of appeared out of nowhere, a humble $70 offering in plain, singly blocked black and red colorways that trickled into bargain stores like Nordstrom Rack when it first dropped in March 2012.

by Brendan Dunne

The sneaker was an antidote to the more overwrought styles that marked the first years of the new decade. It sat opposite the spectrum of shoes like the Nike Air Yeezy 2, a celebrity sneaker with straps, Air bubbles, faux animal skin, and glow-in-the-dark soles that demanded $245. The Roshe did the most with the least, using an airy mesh upper and coming courtesy of Dylan Raasch, a Nike designer who was relatively unknown at the time. He'd first presented the Roshe internally at Nike at the end of 2010 to no significant praise. After more than fifty upper revisions, and over a year later, the sneaker finally arrived.

The Roshe Run was important for its shape and its unusual release at retail. The former presented a sharp new view of casual footwear, one that would eventually contribute to the athleisure trends that took over at the end of the decade. The sloping toe-toward angle was perfectly timed for the advent of Instagram, a platform on which the sneaker flourished. Vintage shoe collectors had long looked for original silhouettes that had a proper slant toward the front of the foot—the Roshe provided this, but without all the crumbling that comes with deadstock purchases.

The quiet launch allowed the shoe to feel genuinely special, despite it showing up in the era when a months-long hype cycle felt like a prerequisite for the sneakerhead stamp of approval. The model was immediately the kind that people had to hunt for, which gave it a slightly mythological air. That's since been diluted by the millions of pairs produced, but anyone who tracked down the original "Iguana" or "Calypso" colorways can attest to its initial allure.

2013 Balenciaga Arena

It would be hard to argue that the Triple S isn't Balenciaga's most impactful sneaker design, stomping its way into fashion history as an icon of the ugly footwear movement that characterized much of what the major design houses released during the tail end of the 2010s. It was loud and heavy, as impractical and polarizing as it was pricey and unavoidable. *GQ* called it "insane-looking"; restocks sold out routinely for months. But Balenciaga had been experimenting with unconventional sneakers for years by the time the Triple S and its many knockoffs were infiltrating the mainstream in 2018. At the start of the decade, the house was already quietly courting men with money to spend on luxury sneakers. Quietly, that is, until the label's Arena sneaker truly took hold, in 2013, three years after the silhouette was introduced.

by Steve Dool

Suddenly, Balenciaga was a player in the lucrative men's footwear market. And somewhat unexpectedly for a label that had not previously moved the needle very much in men's fashion—let alone in sneakers—the Arena was at the center of a cultural shift that would influence for years thereafter how men dress to show off their assumed wealth.

It helps to understand the context of where we were in 2013 to piece together why, in hindsight, the Arena hit the way that it did. Compared to what came before and what would come after, optimism was relatively high. Barack Obama was in his second term, the pope was progressive, and Bitcoin was minting millionaires in ways most of us probably didn't fully understand.

Unlike several years prior, when the economy was down and it was poor form to consume conspicuously, 2013 was a comfortably post-recession open season for big-ticket purchases. Instagram, launched in October 2010, had only recently created the Explore page feature, driving up the potential for anyone to build a follower count beyond their immediate social circle and motivating the extra thirsty to be even thirstier.

Pop culture was flooded with men who visibly placed a premium on the clothes they wore. And they spoke about it, too. These were peak *Mad Men*, *Boardwalk Empire*, and *House of Cards* times, providing ample fodder for people entertained by impeccably suited men behaving badly. Beyond bespoke tailoring, though, there was also a noticeable move toward integrating high-end items and upscale finishes into even the most casual looks. 2013 was high-low season.

For celebrities, even if the price point wasn't shifting, the aesthetic was. Fresh off a marathon world tour with Jay-Z in support of *Watch the Throne*, Kanye West was ditching the baroque, gold-leafed excess of his Riccardo Tisci–designed stage wardrobe for a *Yeezus*-era look that was still luxe, but militant and monochromatic, distressed and topped off with crystal Margiela masks. Justin Timberlake was singing about wearing a suit and tie (and remained faithful to his Air Jordans), and LeBron James had mastered wearing both custom tailoring and streamlined streetwear pieces that came with similar price tags.

Images of burgeoning style icons and their fits were posted on sites like Complex and UpscaleHype and shared across social media early and often, marking the beginning of a fashion arms race. He who has the most likes wins.

High-end men's designers were also pulling from streetwear influence more explicitly than before, led by younger creative leads in high-profile roles, like Tisci at Givenchy and Kim Jones—who grew up loving Nike and basketball and listening to hip-hop—at Louis Vuitton.

"I think designers always looked to what was happening on the streets, and streetwear as a definition always existed—just its qualities and perceptions as a term have changed," Julie Ragolia, a veteran editor, stylist, and menswear expert, explained. "And as brands became more savvy at marketing than ever by way of social media algorithms, they just began chasing what they perceived as 'liked.'"

James Harris was a style editor at Complex in 2013 and remembers that year as a key turning point in the evolution of how men find inspiration to dress.

"2013 wasn't the beginning of social media, but it was when social media and streetwear combined forces and blasted off," Harris said. "It was the start of the ubiquity of instantly shared imagery and paparazzi photos. It was a perfect storm for a single statement sneaker that was instantly recognizable as a status piece to become the biggest sneaker of the year." The genius of the Arena in 2013, whether intentional or not, was just that: it was easily identifiable as a specific item and as a signifier of luxury. In the world of sneakers, the Arena is minimalist—more Common Projects than, say, Off-White—free of overt logo branding or the bells and whistles other design houses frequently employ. The shoe sits on a thick rubber sole, most often done in the same color as the leather upper, although some versions included contrasting tones. The tongue is attached, padded, and folded under along the sides, giving it the appearance of being extra thick. There is some subtle toe cap stitching and some more on the heel counter. The high-top version also comes with a heel tab, which is the one true reference to function in a shoe largely driven by form. Maybe none of those features alone or combined would have actually been enough to make it instantly recognizable, especially not when taken in on the four-inch display of an iPhone 5. The key element that set the Arena apart from the crowd was the hardware: a textured lace plate and seven metal D-rings up each side of the high-top version (six on the lows), rather than a lacing system that makes use of eyelets. The D-rings gave the Arena an edge, toughening it up a bit and referencing inspiration taken from a hiking boot.

"Fashion had begun to embrace masculinity as stronger," said Ragolia, citing a ruggedness that had crept its way onto the runways in major fashion cities. "The Arena sneaker was a brilliant hybridization of the mountain shoe and a street sneaker."

Not that anybody would take the Arenas out on the trail. These were not performance sneakers in the slightest. They were, however, luxurious, done up in lambskin, suede, or wrinkled leather and lined in leather, too. They came in a wide range of tasteful colorways: white, black, red, navy, a deep green. James's stylist posted a pair on Instagram that had been custom-made for the Heat MVP in black woven leather; James would later wear another pair in olive for a spread in *GQ*, too.

The roster of celebrity fans of the Arena ran much deeper than just James, though. Rick Ross got himself Arenas in white for Christmas in 2012—a flex, as it was mostly sold out online at the time. Wale, a noted sneakerhead, had reds in his rotation, and Usher had them in blue suede.

Pusha-T was a fan, wearing them off camera and on the set of his "Trouble on My Mind" video, with his costar, Tyler, the Creator, donning a matching pair. Dwyane Wade slipped his on with a Lanvin tux and posed arm in arm with Gabrielle Union on the red carpet at the ESPY Awards.

In January 2013, Grammy-winning producer Hit-Boy told Complex he had eleven pairs of all-white Arenas. "I like how sleek they are," he explained. "They just look like a men's shoe. It's a prime example of what a men's shoe looks like."

Hit-Boy confessed he first noticed Arenas on the man who was undoubtedly the sneaker's most notable and most visible fan. "A couple years ago, when I saw Kanye rocking them, I was like, 'What the fuck are those?'" he said in the same interview. "I had never seen them before."

West had been a vocal, longtime lover of luxury fashion by the time fans and friends noticed him wearing Arenas, from his days as the self-styled "Louis Vuitton Don" to when he famously wore a Céline blouse during his Coachella performance in 2011. And while some may have been turned off by his constant reminders that he is a tastemaker—a tendency encapsulated perfectly in his 2013 *New York Times* interview in which he demanded people respect his "trendsetting abilities" before referring to himself as the Steve Jobs of "internet, downtown, fashion, culture"—the fact remains that, especially at the time, what he wore mattered.

West wore the Balenciaga Arenas—and he wore them all over. He put on a white pair for lunch with his then-girlfriend, now-wife, Kim Kardashian, at L'Avenue in Paris; a black pair while house hunting in Beverly

Hills; some red ones at a hotel in Miami. He paired them with a Givenchy kilt at a Hurricane Sandy relief concert and with a field coat in New York City's SoHo. By the time 2013 came around, if you were inspired to buy Arenas after seeing someone other than West wearing them, the odds are pretty good that person came to them via Kanye West.

"Celebrities have always been influential in furthering a brand or an individual piece," said Harris. "But at this time, right around *Yeezus*, Kanye said rappers are the new rock stars. More than ever, that was right when rappers started becoming accepted beyond their core fanbase as stylish guys."

West wasn't the only rapper with a flair for designer goods influencing men's style at the time. On his major-label debut, *Long.Live.ASAP*, released in January of that year, ASAP Rocky was rapping about outfits from *Vogue* and Goyard bags, making a name for himself as a new style god. But West—in the midst of a clean, forward-looking style evolution that was taking him miles away from his previous shutter shades and ducktail hair—was embracing fashion as a lifestyle and a worthy artistic pursuit, speaking of his favorite designers in lofty tones that gave fashion credibility as something worth researching and investigating in the eyes of his fans.

In effect, he was positioning himself as an arbiter of elevated good taste, a worthwhile angle for him to pursue as he set his sights on building his own fashion empire. Other rappers and celebrities might splurge on Louis Vuitton luggage in a monogram print to telegraph their wealth as so many have done before, but West, the fashion expert, was going logoless, right down to his minimalist, hiking-inspired sneakers.

The result was a more grown-up way to show off that looked fresh and, even more significantly, looked expensive. (A pair of Arenas would set you back $545 or more at the time.) Writing about the sneakers in a piece published on Complex.com that June titled "What Your Favorite Sneakers Say About You," writer and sneaker historian Russ Bengtson characterized an Arena wearer in much the same way as you would the best-dressed people of the year: "I have simple taste and an extravagant budget."

Or at least the illusion of disposable income. Part of the widespread adoption of the Kanye look of the time was that, without logos, it could more or less be re-created on a budget. Replace a Balmain hoodie with one from American Apparel, A.P.C. denim with a pair of Levi's, and you might have enough left over to pick up the real-deal footwear, the easiest part of your wardrobe for others to authenticate on sight. Get the Arenas, and you might be able to fudge the rest.

Whether or not fashion industry gatekeepers bought into West as a visionary, his fans and admirers did. And West, for what it's worth, noticed. "Listen to what I'm saying, me, as Kanye West," he told *GQ*. "I guarantee you, I'm more than 50 percent responsible for every men's shoe that they sell. Me, the singular person. More than 50 percent responsible for every Balenciaga shoe they sell."

Such a precise number would be impossible to prove definitively, but more impressive than sales figures might be that West exerted enough pull to get more than a handful of men to even consider a shoe—or anything at all—from Balenciaga in 2013.

"There definitely were guys who knew about Balenciaga, but generally speaking, no," Harris remembered. "At the time it was more about Saint Laurent, Rick Owens, Raf Simons, Givenchy through *Watch the Throne*. Riccardo Tisci. Even Marcelo Burlon."

The foundation of what would become Balenciaga began with a boutique opened by couturier Cristóbal Balenciaga in San Sebastián, Spain, in 1917; he would go on to relocate to Paris at the beginning of the Spanish Civil War. Balenciaga the man was a creative visionary when it came to his designs for women's dresses and coats, favoring dramatic silhouettes in heavy fabrics, often with signature padding around the hips or exaggerated waistlines. He was a designer's designer, inspiring Christian Dior and Hubert de Givenchy and employing legendary names like Oscar de la Renta before they ventured out on their own. His work is hallowed among fashion lovers—but his legacy is firmly on the women's side of the industry.

So much so, in fact, that Balenciaga the label didn't even debut a ready-to-wear menswear collection until 2004, a solid eighty-seven years after its namesake established his business and a good thirty-two years after he died. When Balenciaga unveiled men's clothing for the first time, the house was led by designer Nicolas Ghesquière (who, after his fifteen-year stint there ended in 2012, would later go on to head up womenswear at Louis Vuitton). Like Balenciaga, Ghesquière was praised as a wunderkind for his women's designs, which were lauded for being innovative and modern, but still reverent toward the label's history. The men's collections, in contrast, were a mixed bag.

"Balenciaga menswear felt a bit more like an afterthought," said Ragolia. "Looks were more commercial, and there was a severity to that styling that didn't necessarily ring of viewpoint or story."

The lookbook for the Spring 2008 collection, for example, featured models wearing fairly straightforward suits, save for the fact that some had their pants tucked into gladiator sandals, or were not wearing pants at all—just a jacket and tie, silk boxers, and combat boots. Whereas women with the means were buying Balenciaga, the brand couldn't seem to connect to what a male consumer wanted, and over-the-top styling quirks weren't helping as menswear was winding down into minimalist sophistication.

The Arena, however, began to solve some of those problems. The silhouette, with its padded tongue, was striking in the way that Balenciaga's classic baby doll dresses were: exaggerated and memorable. But guys didn't need to know the brand history in order to understand the sneaker's appeal—it was still a simple enough design that you could wear it with your En Noir leather joggers or integrate it into your streetwear-heavy wardrobe for the high-low look that was gaining momentum.

"Back then, as a younger and more streetwear-oriented audience was starting to become aware of high-fashion houses, a single item could become an entry point into the wider micro-universe of a designer brand," said Harris. "Kanye and Rocky were educating their fanbase that wasn't as in tune with fashion houses. People were gravitating toward entry-point items. Sneakers were for dudes what handbags were for women."

It helped that men across the board were dressing more informally, not just those driving the front end of trends. Strict dress codes at work were becoming antiquated, athleisure was on the rise, and there were fewer places where you couldn't feasibly wear sneakers. "Sneakers started to become an acceptable accessory to tailoring," Ragolia said. "Men stopped wearing shoes."

But if men who wore suits regularly were better primed to replace their oxfords and derbies with luxury sneakers as work attire relaxed, the real revolution represented by the Arenas came courtesy of the young people who weren't necessarily

clocking in at a white-collar job every day, but were now buying designer sneakers. In the 2013 edition of Complex's annual roundup of sneakers of the year, editor Joe La Puma noted the sneaker's undeniable impact. "Hate 'em or love 'em, this was the aspirational sneaker for sneakerheads this year," he wrote. "They really were a silo that kind of changed how true sneakerheads look at lux. It was the Arena, and then the Saint Laurent highs and lows later in the year, that had the biggest impact. But the Arena was the silo that set everything off."

Luxury labels had made sneakers before this one, but the proof of concept provided by the Arena was pivotal. Rick Owens x Adidas, a lasting entry in the fashion sneaker landscape, was announced in June 2013, the same month as the founding of Buscemi, the brand that has taken luxury sneaker price tags to six-figure heights. In the time since, we've seen Gucci and Alexander McQueen riff on low-profile Stan Smith–a–likes; Ferragamo release a running shoe; and Dior mix calfskin with a technical knit. The list could go on.

And, of course, the Arena is a clear predecessor to the rest of Balenciaga's late-2010s stable of successful sneaker silhouettes sent out into the world, for better or for worse, with buzz, press coverage, and sales in equal measure. Balenciaga creative director Demna Gvasalia, appointed to the role in 2015, has shepherded in smash sneaker hits like the sock-with-a-sole Speed Trainers, memorably name-checked by Cardi B in "I Like It," and the monster Triple S styles in all of their many iterations. His previous success as creative lead at Vetements, the irreverent design collective he cofounded with his brother Guram, had proven a demand for luxury fashion that is more overtly influenced by streetwear than it is haute couture. As he did with Vetements, which enjoyed a healthy men's business under his tenure there, Gvasalia continued to push Balenciaga's men's offering to the forefront, putting on the house's first men's runway show in 2016.

In the show, models wore Triple S sneakers with down jackets, slim-cut khakis, boxy suits, and velour track pants. The streetwear influences of the Arena era were still front and center in the brand identity, as was the casualization of tailoring and the mixing of high and low—in aesthetics, at least, as even those velour track pants came with a price that crept toward a grand. And the sneakers tied it all together, as the Arena first did for Balenciaga in 2013.

"When you think about it, and if you go back and read the blogs, it definitely played a huge role in bridging the worlds of streetwear and high fashion," Harris said. "There may have been a sneaker in the moment that created a bigger buzz, but it didn't have the lasting legacy that the Arena had."

Honorable Mention
Nike Flyknit Lunar 1+

"Would you like your Flyknits steamed?" That wasn't an uncommon question to be asked when the Nike Flyknit Lunar 1+ released in stores early in 2013. As though the shoes were shrink-to-fit denim, select Nike shops offered customers the opportunity to steam their new Flyknits to get a more tailored fit. After a customer purchased a pair, they were able to place them in a "sneaker sauna" for thirty seconds to heat and dampen the Flyknit fibers. Then the customer was directed to put them on while they were still warm and damp so that the Flyknit fibers conformed to their feet. The result was one of the lightest, most form-fitting running sneakers Nike has ever released.

After the brightly colored Racer- and Trainer-inspired frenzies in 2012, everyone wanted to get their hands on anything Flyknit. Thanks in part to the success of the Volt train-

By Drew Hammell

ers that were on the feet of every Team USA athlete who stood on the medal podium at the Summer Olympics in London, word spread about this new shoe that featured an upper without precedent.

It was only a matter of time before Flyknit uppers would become the standard for running, basketball, and training sneakers because of the technology's many advantages.

The Lunar 1+ was the next step in the Flyknit sneaker evolution. Designed by Rob Williams, the Flyknit Lunar 1+ featured a new upper design, along with an updated Lunarlon foam midsole. The Lunarlon sole was inspired by astronauts bouncing on the moon and offered the sneaker a pillowy feel. The brilliance of the Flyknit upper was that it was completely synthetic, which gave the shoe a lighter weight and plenty of breathability without much compromise on durability. Embedded inside the seamless upper were flexible Flywire cables for added support. The ultra-light sock-like shoe weighed just under 8 ounces, yet was sturdy and stable enough to run a 10K in. The limited materials used in the model were synthetic, since the shoe was designed with sustainability in mind.

The Flyknit Lunar 1 released in many bright colors and also got a Supreme collab in a black/dark grey colorway. The world-renowned streetwear brand rode the wave of the Flyknit movement by stamping "SUP" boldly on the side of the new model in the fall of 2013.

The Flyknit Lunar 1+ was the second iteration of what has become a complete transformation for sneaker uppers. Its sustainability, style, and remarkable light weight set the standard for what a twenty-first-century sneaker could be.

2014 Nike Air Yeezy 2 "Red October"

On February 9, 2014, at 1 p.m. EST, with one tweet, Nike grabbed the attention of every person worldwide who had even a passing interest in sneakers. Out of nowhere, after months of speculation and rumors, the Air Yeezy 2 "Red October" became available to the masses. It didn't matter that Kanye West was at Adidas by then. It didn't matter that it had been weeks since we had heard anything about the all-red high-top. And the internet—or at least the part of it frequented by sneaker lovers—broke for a few hours.

By Mike DeStefano

The hype started the previous April, when West hit the stage for a performance on *Saturday Night Live* to promote his highly anticipated album *Yeezus*. Most were focused on the flashing backdrops and echoing screams seen and heard during his renditions of the tracks "New Slaves" and "Black Skinhead." But anyone with a keen eye for sneakers noticed the bright red pair on his feet. The same day, Kim Kardashian showed off a pair on Instagram, positioned next to a mockup of the upcoming album's cover. When the polarizing project finally dropped that June, West teased us even more on the fourth track, "Hold My Liquor," when he rapped, "Yeezys all on your sofa / These the 'Red Octobers.'"

"[Kanye] rapping about the 'Red Octobers' was almost like Rick James's red leather boots. It was that same vibe. Having 'Red Octobers' on, standing on somebody's couch, you're lit. These shoes are really worth more than your couch," said rapper and *Full Size Run* cohost Trinidad James. "It was a great statement for music and fashion. The 'Red October' was an incredible ending to his time at Nike."

In the following weeks, a release date of June 18 was rumored. West would also announce a special contest to be held on his website in which fifty pairs would be raffled off. By August, only twenty-four raffle winners were named. The supposed June date had come and gone. More questions. Few answers.

A few months later, there was still no retail release. Former NFL quarterback Geno Smith was spotted in a pair that turned out to be fake as he sat courtside at the Barclays Center in Brooklyn. Macklemore tossed a pair into the crowd during his New Year's Eve performance in Times Square. West went on an infamous press run of his own around this time filled with plenty of memorable rants. Some of the banter even targeted then–Nike CEO Mark Parker—the seeds that would eventually lead to Kanye jumping ship from Nike in favor of Adidas. He announced the move during an interview at New York radio station Hot 97 with Angie Martinez. Of course, West would have to put the "Red Octobers" he was frequently lacing up for weeks back in the box. Out of sight, out of mind for the Air Yeezy 2, right? Not exactly.

The hype wasn't all that surprising. This is Kanye West we are talking about. The man's style had the attention of everyone at the time. If he wore a pair of Nike Flyknit Trainers, that shoe skyrocketed in value. A random colorway of the Air Max 90 celebrating Independence Day that was destined for outlets flew off retail shelves and became a hot commodity on the aftermarket once West was seen lacing it up. Hype was a driving force behind many limited releases, and with sneaker culture penetrating further into the mainstream, one of the biggest names in pop culture was the perfect person to move the needle.

This also wasn't the first time the public had lost its mind over the Air Yeezy 2. The "Solar Red" and "Pure Platinum" colorways were released back in 2012 for $245 each. The "Solar Red" pair was exclusive to East Coast accounts, while the "Pure Platinum" was reserved for the West Coast. Chicago, West's hometown, was one of the few cities in the United States that actually received both colorways. The launch was not exclusively online, like that of their brightly colored successor. There were no secrets about the day they were coming. Brick-and-mortar boutiques across the country had to deal with massive lineups. Some hopeful fans even sat in queues for days ahead of time for the best chance to get their hands on West's latest offering.

The black- and gray-based pairs fell more closely in line with the color palettes used on the Air Yeezy 1, released in 2009. But the design itself saw a noticeable overhaul. Nathan VanHook, a senior creative director at Nike, was the design lead. Like its predecessor, the Yeezy 2 borrowed from Nike's archive by sitting it atop the recognizable midsole from Andre Agassi's Air Tech Challenge 2. The rest of the standout elements didn't owe to a particular model in Nike's expansive catalog, but aided in further catapulting West's latest signature sneaker into a more premium space—faux-reptile-skin side panels, a ribbed rubber heel, a midfoot strap hiding "YZY" hieroglyphics on its underside, a glow-in-the-dark outsole, and gold metal aglets, to name a few.

This monochromatic look was a pleasant departure from the original two versions from 2012. It had not been used on a Yeezy up to that point, and the all-red design, which many fans might quickly connect to West's iconic "Runaway" outfit at the 2010 MTV Video Music Awards, was guaranteed to turn heads. It also made a subtle design tweak by replacing the reptile-skin paneling present on the first pairs with a spiky triangular pattern. This wasn't the

first time West had designed a red sneaker, though—the Louis Vuitton Don from 2009 holds that honor, but a luxury sneaker certainly doesn't resonate with as large of an audience as something bearing a Nike Swoosh. All of the hype remained, but one major problem clouded the future of the "Red October." West was now officially aligned with Nike's biggest competitor. Which brings us back to the Nike tweet that had the sneaker world, at least those lucky enough to have noticed, watching in agony as their phones and laptops froze on a Nike.com landing page due to the wild level of traffic the notification had produced. Nike held a true "shock drop" that February afternoon in 2014. There was no warning. If you weren't working within the company's walls, or very closely connected to someone who was, you likely had no idea it was coming. Boutiques around the world didn't stock pairs like they did for the prior two drops. Foot Locker, which at one point announced it would be releasing the sneaker in December 2013 with a tweet of its own, also ultimately didn't. The element of surprise tied to the release made the hype surrounding the pair even more unfathomable than it had been for months. Within a few minutes, the dust had settled. Most had accepted that they missed their opportunity to acquire one of the most talked-about sneakers ever to release.

Others were a little more vocal. Trinidad James laced up his pair to play some pickup basketball at the local gym. While he wasn't able to get them when they launched, stylist Renaldo Nehemiah and Atlanta-based designer Chris Newton hooked him up. LeBron James did the same thing, shooting around at a Miami Heat practice to flex his lifetime Nike deal on all of his teammates.

"Things like that, you don't plan. You just do it," said Trinidad. "I'm a big sports person. I like to cross mediums. So sneakers that were meant to be drip on the red carpet, I'm going to hoop in them. People know that's what I do."

During the February 23, 2014, stop of the Yeezus Tour, at Nassau Veterans Memorial Coliseum in Long Island, New York, West even signed a lucky fan's pair. It would later be discovered that the fan, whom the *New York Times* identified as Jonathan Rod-

riguez, would turn down a $98,000 offer from someone to purchase the shoes, which is a pretty big indicator of just how rare the signed item (and how big a West fan Rodriguez) was. The rapper also autographed a fake pair a few months later. West wasn't with Nike anymore, and a product with his name on it was still commanding levels of attention rarely seen in sneakers.

On a broader scale, the "Red October" was responsible for a shift across the sneaker market. Many people wanted the "Red October" Yeezy 2s. Few were lucky enough to cop a pair. So what did sneaker brands do? They made a bunch of budget-friendly, widely available alternatives in an effort to satisfy the craving. Red sneakers were ubiquitous for a while after the "Red October" came and went. Red Air Huaraches. Red Air Force 1s. Nike even made a Dunk High that fully mimicked the materials of the Yeezy 2, if what was happening wasn't obvious. And this is only a handful of the dozens of examples.

Joe Perez, the former lead art director for West's now-defunct agency DONDA, which worked on all West- and G.O.O.D. Music-related projects at the time, recalls that the bright red used on the "Red October" was much more calculated than most thought.

"It was [Kanye's] splash of color. He loved that red. And it wasn't true red. It was this interesting Pantone that was off-red that he kept referring to. What was crazy about Kanye and colors was even if it was off just by the slightest number of Pantone, it registered in his brain," said Perez. "I think that goes back to him having discussions about seeing colors with music. So he was just way more sensitive to a color spectrum than any other human I've ever met in my life."

Perez also had a small hand in helping design the sizing tag on the Nike box, as well as a handful of promotional materials, including a raffle site that never saw the light of day due to the whirlwind of confusion that came with this release. The hieroglyphic-style iconography and Egyptian bird god Horus on the tongue of the Yeezy 2 were elements with which West was particularly infatuated at the time.

"We were playing with hieroglyphs, and specifically the [Horus] head, for a while. It was just iconography that really registered with him as just powerful animals, and iconography that's been in different cultures throughout history. I think it was something that really just caught his eye, and he really responded to it," said Perez. "It's all going back to ancient Africa. It's in Egypt. There's something about that culture, the artwork, the jewelry, and the grandness of the temples that they created in the pyramids. That's always going to be inspiring."

The Air Yeezy 2 "Red October" is more than just a hyped-up sneaker from the 2010s. It's a symbol of the end of an era. Nike's partnership with one of the driving forces of music and pop culture had come to a close. Both parties would move on with continued success. A good number of people might link West to his extensive catalog of Adidas products at this point, with the Air Yeezy 2 and its predecessor becoming afterthoughts to them. But the attention this release commanded, and the fervor it inspired, may never be surpassed by another West sneaker.

Honorable Mention
Nike Kyrie 1

Kyrie Irving's first two seasons weren't nearly as glamorous as the years he has experienced since. Drafted in 2011 as the number-one overall pick after playing just eleven games as a freshman at Duke University, he was the sole bright spot on an otherwise lackluster Cleveland Cavaliers squad at the bottom of the Eastern Conference. That would all change in 2014, when LeBron James announced his return to Ohio and the Cavs transformed into a contender literally overnight. It would also mean that Irving's All-Star-caliber ability would finally matter.

That year, Irving became the first pro basketball player Nike had added to its signature team since Kevin Durant in 2008. Irving had been a Nike endorser his whole professional career, but his level of play proved that he was worthy of his own line.

by Mike DeStefano

The Kyrie 1 was simple in its appearance. Designed by Leo Chang, the mid-top featured a Hyperfuse mesh upper, neoprene tongue, and Zoom Air cushioning in the forefoot. It had a spiked heel panel, which gave the sneaker more of a lifestyle look inspired by luxury fashion, and shark-tooth-esque outsole tread that extended up onto the toe portion of the midsole—a nod to the architecture of the Sydney Opera House.

The model—priced at only $110 when James's shoes, for example, hovered around $200—gave basketball fans an affordable signature option. Its debut colorway, dubbed the "Dream," was well received by fans when it hit shelves in December 2014. Other color schemes took inspiration from things like Irving's birth country of Australia or Blue Devils alma mater. The most notable was probably the "Uncle Drew," a promotional version limited to 150 units, coinciding with a Pepsi ad campaign in which Irving dressed up as a senior citizen and schooled unsuspecting players in pickup games.

When Irving debuted the model on court at Madison Square Garden against the Knicks in December 2014, he recorded his then-career high of 37 points. Had a knee injury not forced him out of the 2015 NBA Finals, it also could have been the shoe the point guard won his first championship in.

Irving eventually became an NBA champion in 2016, hitting the clinching three-pointer in Game 7 to overcome a 3–1 deficit against the Warriors. His line, meanwhile, grew into one of Nike's most successful signature series to date, proving there were players beyond James, Durant, and Kobe Bryant worthy of carrying the torch for the brand.

2015 Adidas Ultra Boost

Adidas had modest goals when it released the Ultra Boost in 2015. It simply wanted to make the greatest running sneaker ever. At the time, it seemed like an even taller task, because Adidas was attempting a rebrand after it nearly ran itself into the ground in the 2000s. The vessel, or midsole, rather, that would make it all work was made up of beads.

By Matt Welty

Boost technology wasn't exactly new when it arrived in the Ultra Boost in 2015. It had been rolled out two years prior in the Energy Boost, a performance running shoe with a stretchy upper the brand called Techfit, in collaboration with the chemical company BASF.

"It was in 2006, 2007 when someone from our research, we call him Dr. Einstein, he's looking outside of the box. He came with these particles to me and said, 'What can we do with that?'" Martin Vallo, key account manager for BASF, said in a 2016 interview with Complex. "I met him in the coffee kitchen, and I said, 'Honestly, I have no idea.' The tricky thing was, 'What can we do with these particles? How can we bring them together?' Later on, the idea came to use equipment that we use to bind Styrofoam particles. We weld them together with steam."

The result was a midsole compound unlike EVA foam, which is commonly found in sneakers and starts off soft but breaks down over time. Instead, Boost has a softness and spring to it. It will bend, only to return energy to the foot. There was nothing like it on the retail market. While the Energy Boost had introduced runners to the concept, the sneaker had little to no crossover appeal to the lifestyle market. It took a casual silhouette, the Pure Boost, which released in 2014, to open up the consumer to the model. While it was a popular sneaker, it wasn't without its downfalls. The Pure Boost's sole was too soft, and the upper, which resembled a sock, stretched too much. With all that said, Complex named it the best non-retro sneaker of 2014. It was a sign that Adidas was moving in the right direction, creating product that resonated with people who may have turned their backs on the brand or hadn't checked for it in years.

Although the Ultra Boost was introduced to the world in 2015, the process of creating it started two years prior, in 2013.

"The aim was to do something new, something we hadn't done before. We wanted to create this emotional reaction with the new design," said the shoe's designer, Ben Herath. "We wanted to trigger a 'wow' with the look, but also a 'wow' when you try it on. These three things were what drove the whole process."

The process of creating the Ultra Boost didn't start in the footwear industry. Instead, the shoe's creators looked to the skies and used technology from aviation. "We had new testing equipment that was being used by Boeing," said Herath. "It measured how aircraft wings would move, the stresses and strains. We took that machine and applied it to the human body. That just opened up a whole world of science for us, because we could suddenly see what was happening to the foot when you run. Therefore, we could then take all of that and help make decisions around the design. It was a design fueled by the science of what we could do."

The Ultra Boost may be a sneaker born from science, but a portion of its popularity comes from its aesthetic. It's a simple shoe: a Continental rubber outsole, a Boost midsole, a knitted upper made from a technology called Primeknit, and a plastic cage and heel. All of that, however, was still informed by the research and development used to put it together. Performance drove everything about the sneaker's design.

"We started designing the shoe from the inside out. We looked at all the layers inside the shoe and we said, 'Do we need that?

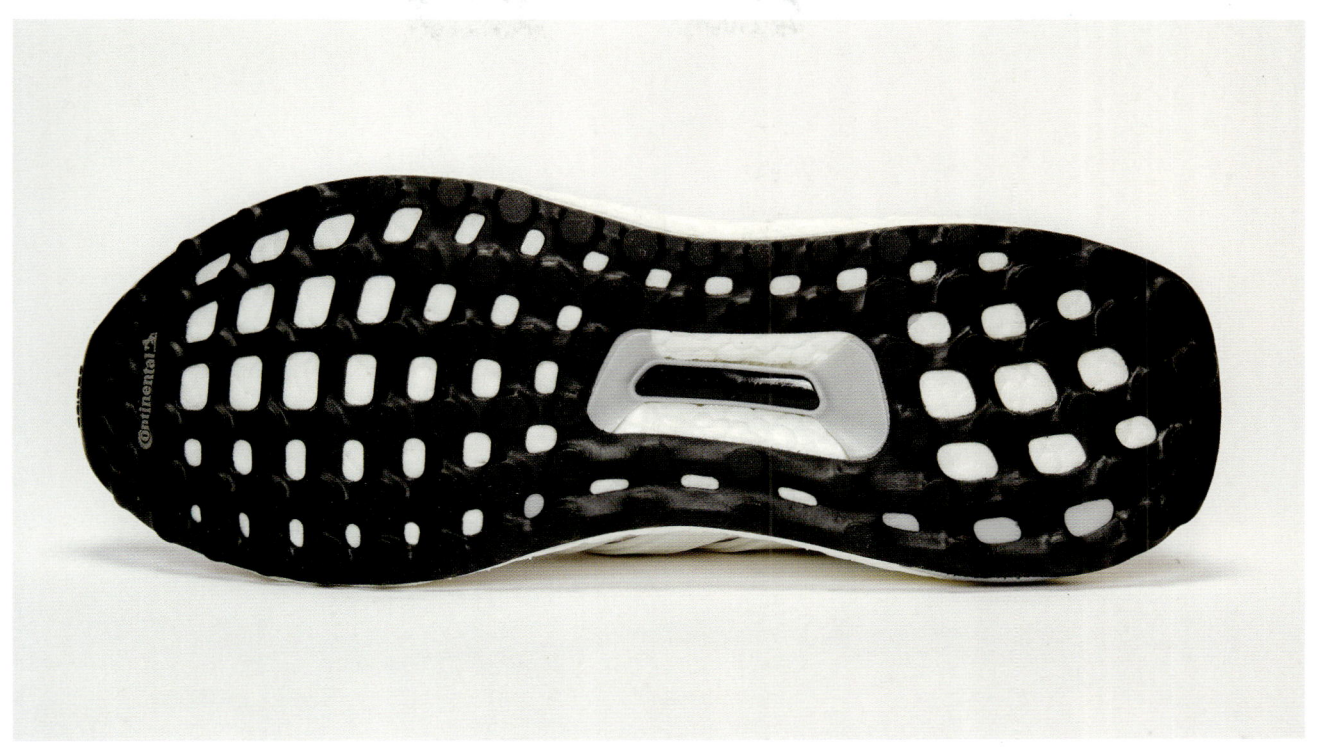

How do we make this part more comfortable? How do we make it lighter and make it work with the foot?'" said Herath. "It helped strip the shoe back and create what was essential to the design. It was a new level of simplicity we are able to achieve with pulling all these technologies together."

The story of the Ultra Boost doesn't stop with its design—in fact, it just begins there. Not only did the tagline of the "greatest running shoe ever" build high expectations for the sneaker, but so did the $180 price point. "We hadn't really created a running shoe for that price before," said Herath. "There was word of mouth, and I saw people discovering it, telling their friends about it, and getting excited and engaged by it. It did take time for that to happen."

While the Ultra Boost was billed as something that would generate buzz, it took some time for it to catch on with a mainstream audience, although sneaker connoisseurs were sold on it. "You had your pure sneaker people who looked at it and saw it for what it was," said Mike Packer, the owner of Packer Shoes, who collaborated on the Ultra Boost in 2019.

The Ultra Boost, however, was overshadowed by Kanye West, who was signed to Adidas and released his first shoe with the brand, the Yeezy Boost 750, during the 2015 NBA All-Star weekend. Over the course of the event, the brand did a limited drop of the high-top shoe from West, and Adidas and some in the industry thought it obfuscated the Ultra Boost.

The black and purple Ultra Boost, the first colorway of the shoe to hit the market, released on February 11, 2015, just three days before West's debut Adidas

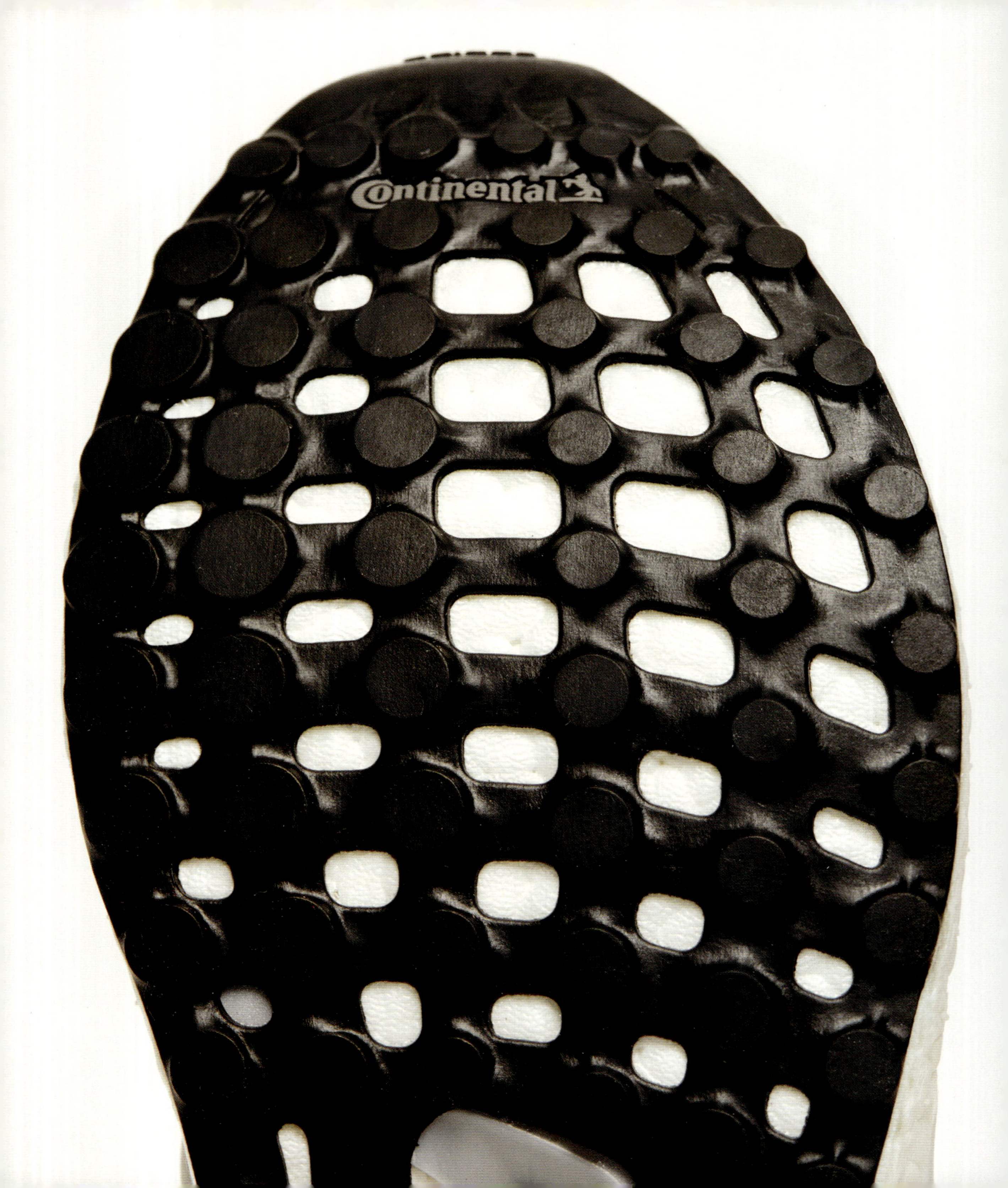
Continental

sneaker. "It was the same weekend that Yeezy dropped the 750s, and it went a little bit unnoticed by the masses. I mean, it was Kanye," said Packer.

In a weird twist of fate, casual observers eventually caught on to the Ultra Boost thanks to West. That same weekend, he was spotted in New York City wearing the original colorway of the shoe, complete with running tights, shorts, and a snorkel jacket. That moment planted the Ultra Boost into people's minds. But even more impactful: West wore an all-white version of the shoe during performances at the Billboard Music Awards and at Powerhouse in Los Angeles in May 2015. There was an immediate frenzy around the Ultra, and consumers ran out to buy a pair after that. Everyone needed them, and multiple pairs. The shoes flew off the shelves.

"It was great to see Kanye wearing it and introducing the Ultra Boost to people that might not have discovered this through running," said Herath. "He brought the Ultra Boost to a whole new audience, and it's great to see his level of engagement or excitement in the design as well."

The West cosign of the all-white Ultra Boosts not only brought sales to that specific shoe, but to the Ultra Boost in general. Sales all across the board for the sneaker started to rise as the public's interest in the design grew. "When Kanye wore those Triple Whites, it gets into the conscience of everybody saying, 'Hey, maybe this really is something,'" said Packer. "And then you got everybody going back, trying to get the original one that came out."

West isn't the only person responsible for the popularity of the all-white Ultra Boost—part of that belongs to someone

with a fraction of his influence. Derek Curry, the owner of Sneaker Politics, a sneaker boutique chain in Louisiana and Texas, wore the shoes in a now-viral picture. While West's photo shows him flying across a stage in the Ultra Boost, karate-kicking the air, Curry's is less dramatic. His bare ankles were enough to sell people on the shoe.

But how he got the shoes may be more important to the sneaker's trajectory, and his early belief in the model was something that some at the brand might not have seen. It all started during an Adidas preview in Las Vegas, where the sneakers caught his eye. "I walk into the women's room and no one was there. I was like, 'What is this?'" said Curry. "I texted the rep to see where they were at, and they asked me what I thought. And I was like, 'This shoe is amazing. It looks sick.' He was like, 'If you like it so much, just take it.' I wore it all the time. People were like, 'What is that?'"

He had the shoe for some time before its actual release, and he thought it was going to be a strong product. To ensure that the white Ultra Boost caught a buzz and he could move the pairs he had stocked in the hundreds, he asked Adidas for permission to post an early photo.

"Right before the launch, I was like, 'Do you mind if I release some photos to try and build up some hype?' And they said, 'Go ahead,'" said Curry. "I took a photo and it blew up and the whole world picked it up. Kanye wore the shoe, and that seven-hundred-pair order I put in was gone."

Curry called the Ultra Boost a classic in Adidas's archive, likening it to the Air Max 1, his favorite shoe from Nike. Packer echoed that sentiment, although he found a slightly different reference point for the sneaker. "That's their Air Max 95," he said.

After the success of the white Ultra Boosts, the sneaker caught a serious headwind in the retail world. Every pair sold out. Shop owners couldn't have been happier with the sales on the shoe, but they also couldn't get enough of the sneakers. They weren't being made on the mass level of other shoes. "They couldn't produce enough. They were limited," said Curry. "So when they come out with a color, no one could get it." Consumers who couldn't get their hands on the Ultra Boost, or didn't want to spend $180, started to find other offerings from Adidas that were similar in style. The sneaker had a trickle-down effect for the brand, and a lot of product started to take cues from it. "We have a very collaborative spirit here, and we're constantly sharing what we're doing," said Herath.

"I was constantly sharing with other creatives in other teams and seeing how we could take not just the technologies, but the comfort levels and learnings wrapped up in the Ultra Boost. You started to see other sneakers explore the shoe's technologies."

Not only were there other shoes from Adidas that mimicked the Ultra Boost, the shoe itself spawned offspring. There were Ultra Boosts without cages, ones without laces, and continued iterations of the design that would adopt the Primeknit upper's design pattern over the years. There were Ultra Boost collaborations. Germany's Solebox and Sweden's Sneakersnstuff were two of the retailers that created Ultra Boosts that went for large sums on the secondary market. Adidas-sponsored universities such as Arizona State and Miami received player-exclusive Ultra Boosts that found their way into the hands of those willing to shell out a chunk of change. The whole shoe itself was retooled in 2019 and is still marketed as a premium running model.

People have their opinions on where the Ultra Boost has gone and how it has strayed from its original form, but one thing is certain: the first version of the shoe remains a classic now, half a decade later. "It's something that you can wear and becomes part of someone's rotation," said Packer. "Which is something that's not here today, gone tomorrow."

Honorable Mention
Adidas Yeezy Boost 750

When Kanye West's endorsement deal with Nike finally ended in 2013 following two wildly successful Air Yeezys and multiple rants directed at then–Nike CEO Mark Parker during his Yeezus Tour, many were clamoring to see what the multi-hyphenate creator would come up with next. West would ultimately land at the most notable competitor to the Swoosh, Adidas, officially announcing the new partnership in November 2013. It would be a couple of years before the inaugural pair from the Adidas Yeezy line would surface. West spent the time in between wearing Stan Smiths, Y-3 sneakers, and newer models like the Energy Boost and Ultra Boost— a cosign that certainly played a heavy role in increasing the popularity of Boost in the lifestyle market.

by Mike DeStefano

Finally, images of what we now know as the Yeezy Boost 750 leaked courtesy of West's longtime friend and barber, Ibn Jasper. The model was polarizing. A high-top more similar to a boot than a traditional sneaker, it had a suede upper and featured a zipper running up each side panel, along with a large midfoot strap for lockdown. Of course, it sat atop a Boost-cushioned midsole, something that would become the norm for the majority of West's Adidas line. Admittedly, it wouldn't be easy for the average consumer to pull this sneaker off.

In February 2015, the Yeezy Boost 750—dressed in a light brown/carbon white colorway—finally released during NBA All-Star Weekend in New York City. New York locals were given the opportunity to reserve their pairs for pickup on the brand-new Adidas Confirmed app, the first major launch on the now-defunct sneaker reservation platform. West himself even stopped by the Adidas flagship store to surprise fans and hand out their new pairs. The shoe caused mass hysteria and sold out with ease despite its $350 price tag and the initial uncertainty from consumers.

The Yeezy Boost 750 would go on to release in only three more colorways after its debut: an all-black look, a gray pair with a glow-in-the-dark gum sole, and the "Chocolate" iteration that arrived in October 2016. The resale prices on all of these makeups remain high, with the gray exceeding $1,000. West's Yeezy line with Adidas would follow a much more sportswear-driven design language in the ensuing years, and the 750 would be put in the vault. Despite its short run, it marked the start of one of the most important partnerships in footwear history.

2016 Adidas Yeezy Boost 350 V2

"Eventually, everybody who wants to get Yeezys will get Yeezys." When Kanye West proclaimed this in February 2015 during an interview with Ryan Seacrest, it seemed like nothing more than an empty promise. At the time, West had only released one design with Adidas—the OG "Light Brown" Yeezy Boost 750—to the tune of just nine thousand pairs exclusively in New York City. Prior releases with Nike (the Air Yeezy 1 and Air Yeezy 2, each of which arrived in three different colorways) were arguably just as hard to come by and were among the most coveted sneakers of the era.

by Riley Jones

The idea that West and Adidas would follow through with such a grand vision and be able to produce enough pairs for everyone to purchase felt far-fetched. After all, the supply-and-demand effect of limited availability is a hallmark of the footwear industry and was a huge factor in the interest around West's aforementioned releases. If Yeezys really did become so available that anyone who desired them would be able to get their hands on a pair, would people actually still want them? We were about to find out.

By September 2016, the Kanye West–Adidas partnership had produced two sneaker models, the Yeezy Boost 750 and the Yeezy Boost 350, with a third arriving that month. Named Yeezy Boost for its use of Adidas's proprietary Boost cushioning, the 750 was a boot-like high-top with premium suede uppers, zipper closures, and a wide midfoot strap. In contrast, the low-cut Yeezy Boost 350 was a radical departure, instead opting for a sock-esque knitted upper highlighted by intricate patterns. It was this low-top variation that would serve as the blueprint for the third model and the shoe that would ultimately make good on West's promise, the Yeezy Boost 350 V2. As its name suggests, the model was an update to the original Yeezy Boost 350, which had been completely overhauled from the inside out. Aesthetically, the V2 saw the addition of new patterns that were even more striking than the first variation. It introduced a bold, contrasting stripe down the lateral section—a detail that would become tonal and even translucent in later versions—along with "SPLY-350" branding, a reference to West's Yeezy Supply e-commerce site. The shape of the shoe was redesigned, as was its midsole, which

featured more pronounced grooves. From within, the shoe was also tweaked for both durability and stability through the addition of a rigid material at the toe. It debuted on September 24, 2016, in a gray and orange "Beluga" colorway for a retail price of $220, which was $20 more expensive than the original Yeezy Boost 350 (but not as expensive as the $350 price tag of the 750).

Initial runs of the Yeezy Boost 350 V2 were relatively scarce. Aftermarket resale values weren't quite as inflated as they had been for prior designs, either—early averages for the "Beluga" style settled at roughly $700, around what the sneakers cost today—but Yeezys still weren't easily accessible by any stretch of the imagination. The limited

nature of the releases meant many fans were still left empty-handed, leaving West's promise unfulfilled more than a year after the fact.

With interest in the Yeezy Boost 350 V2 remaining steady among consumers, a handful of Holiday 2017 releases would follow before the model took a brief hiatus, resurfacing with the "Butter" colorway in June 2018. Then what was once unthinkable happened. In September 2018, Adidas rolled out what it described as "the most democratic drop in Yeezy history" with a relaunch of the "Cream White" (now known as "Triple White") style. "For the first time, a Yeezy sneaker will be released in mass quantities, giving an unprecedented number of fans worldwide direct access to Yeezy at retail price," read the brand's official press release. Notorious internet leakers Yeezy Mafia (no official affiliation with Kanye West) tweeted that "millions" of pairs were up for grabs during the restock, and while Adidas will not confirm exact units, consumers saw considerably more success than they had on any Yeezy drop prior. Pairs lingered on Adidas's official web store through the afternoon, offering plenty of opportunity for anyone who was interested in the sneakers to pick them up. And with that, West's once improbable promise was solidified—everyone who wanted Yeezys could get them. But what did that mean for the Yeezy Boost 350 V2 in the big picture?

Following the widespread "Triple White" launch, the sneaker went back into hibernation for a bit, returning in November and later switching things up with its now-signature translucent side stripe.

Eventually, Adidas pulled the reins back in, introducing region-exclusive Yeezy Boost 350 V2 drops that could only be purchased in certain countries, as well as hyper-limited reflective colorways. The strategy has more or less paid off, resulting in the return of sold-out releases and an upswing in aftermarket interest. More than three years after the Yeezy Boost 350 V2 first appeared on the scene, it's alive and well.

From a cultural standpoint, the Yeezy Boost 350 V2 reverberated in ways that few sneakers do. Its ever-increasing production numbers caused the shoe to become truly mainstream, appearing everywhere from the runways of West's Yeezy Season fashion shows to college campuses. Its sporty, sock-like design was in line with athleisure trends and made it instantly wearable, and there's hard data proving the shoe was right on time. In 2018, for the first time in the history of West's sneaker designs, the Yeezy Boost 350 V2 was among the best-selling athletic models, putting it into rare company with household names like the Air Jordan XI, Nike Air Force 1, and Converse Chuck Taylor All-Star (according to market research firm NPD Group).

The sneakers even found their way into one of the most high-profile rap beefs of this generation when Drake took aim at West on French Montana's track "No Stylist," rapping, "I told her, 'Don't wear no 350s 'round me.'" West would later express his frustrations over this line on social media, tweeting, "Still need that apology for mentioning the 350s and trying to take food out your idols['] kids['] mouths."

Of course, it wouldn't be a hit sneaker without its share of imitators, and the Yeezy Boost 350 V2 had many. Brands

like Skechers and Zara were quick to jump on the hype train and try their hand at similar designs, and even Adidas was guilty of regurgitating the Yeezy DNA across its main line. Counterfeits of the Yeezy Boost 350 V2 eventually became problematic, too, with replica makers dialing in their methods and using sites like Reddit to peddle their knockoffs. Yet, through it all, demand for the real thing has remained.

Honorable Mention
ADIDAS NMD Hu

By 2016, Adidas had all the momentum in the lifestyle market. The Ultra Boost and NMD were two of the most popular sneakers in the space at the time, and Kanye West's Yeezy line was still causing a frenzy with each release. But West wasn't the only superstar musician endorsing the Three Stripes. The brand was also home to Pharrell Williams.

Williams's deal with Adidas was officially announced in December 2014. The line started off with a handful of Stan Smith collections that hit retailers that year, ranging from monochromatic options with matching tracksuits to bright felt pairs made to resemble tennis balls. More collections prominently featuring the iconic tennis sneaker would follow in 2015, along with colorful Superstars and even the artist's first

by Mike DeStefano

original silhouette, the Elastic, in both laceless and laced versions. But it wasn't until July 2016 that Williams and Adidas released their biggest hit to date, the NMD Hu. The simple design was a take on the original NMD and came at a time when sock-like sneakers were arguably the biggest trend in footwear. The stretchy Primeknit upper featured a minimalist lacing system involving TPU cages on each side panel and a leather heel tab. The shoe sat atop a full-length Boost midsole with block inserts at the toe and heel similar to the original NMD design. Its signature details were the words "Human" embroidered in bold lettering on the right foot and "Race" on the left. As the line continued, the embroidery would change, with various logos, words, and symbols appearing on it.

The NMD Hu quickly became a hit for Adidas and Williams, and its original colorways from 2016 still hold value on the resale market. Williams's line has continued to expand, with multiple silhouettes joining the fold, but the NMD Hu remains a constant from the partnership. It has been the vehicle for plenty of special collections and collaborations, too, among them powder-dyed pairs to celebrate the Hindu festival of Holi in 2018, various projects with Billionaire Boys Club, a rare N*E*R*D version that was raffled exclusively at ComplexCon in 2017, and an even rarer collab with Chanel (limited to 500 pairs) available via raffle at Colette before the iconic Paris boutique permanently closed its doors in December 2017. While the hype behind the NMD Hu has dwindled more recently, the model cemented itself as one of the best lifestyle releases at the time and remains the highlight of Williams's work with Adidas.

2017 Nike Zoom Fly

In 2017, Nike found itself in unfamiliar territory. Riding off the success of Ultra Boost, Adidas dominated the conversation surrounding running shoes, the footwear category where Nike got its start. As its market share began to slip, the Swoosh needed more than just another cool-looking shoe with technology destined to be phased out in a year's time. Enter the Zoom Fly, a model that married performance tech with forward-thinking design.

by John Gotty

Nike introduced the Zoom Fly adjacent to the Breaking2 project, the company's push to have a runner achieve a world record for the first sub-two-hour marathon. Breaking2 was the culmination of a multiyear initiative, and Nike made a marketing moment out of the whole experience leading up to the actual attempt in May 2017. It equipped three select runners with custom versions of a new model called the Zoom Vaporfly Elite, whose energy-return properties it hoped would lift the athletes to shatter the record. The Vaporfly Elite featured super-squishy, responsive foam soles, called the ZoomX, and a full-length carbon-fiber plate. The shoe—highly technical and more advanced than most runners would ever need—wasn't made available for retail at the time. It was a warning shot to anyone who thought the company was asleep at the wheel while the competition caught up.

Ultimately, none of the three runners shattered the two-hour mark—Eliud Kipchoge missed it by twenty-five seconds. But the whole Breaking2 experiment generated enough attention to pique the interest of the footwear world. The momentum trickled down in a halo effect to a trio of new running models—the Nike Zoom Vaporfly 4%, Nike Zoom Fly, and Nike Air Zoom Pegasus 34—each dressed in a cool "Ice Blue" colorway accented by bright crimson and red nearly identical to those of the Zoom Vaporfly Elite. Of the three, the Zoom Fly was better suited to—and better priced, at a retail ticket of $150, versus the Vaporfly 4%'s $250, for—more casual running and lifestyle pursuits.

The Zoom Fly looked unlike any running shoe before it and came loaded with tech. A lightweight knit made up the upper, and Nike implemented Flywire technology to create a lockdown effect for the midfoot. An oversize Swoosh stretched down the lateral side, giving the shoe a sleek, swift look while making sure anyone glancing from a distance knew what brand the wearer repped. Other elements, like the angled cuts in the thin tongue and the sculpted heel, stood out upon closer inspection. But none of the above detracted from the model's most distinctive element: its sole.

The shoe arrived at a time when chunky soles were in vogue. Nike managed to craft a model that was perfectly in sync with the times yet didn't conform to the trends of the moment. The Zoom Fly's beefed-up soles served a purpose beyond aesthetics. The Lunarlon foam provided lightweight, durable cushioning and housed a carbon-infused nylon plate whose job was to help propel the runner forward. Whereas most running shoes opt for a low-profile approach, the Zoom Fly's rocker-shaped soles clocked in with a thirty-three-millimeter heel stack height and a ten-millimeter heel-to-toe drop, a descent akin to losing your stomach on the first steep hill on a roller coaster. Adjusting to the propulsion sensation took some getting used to, initially, while running or even walking. But the uncertainty lasted only a short spell. After that, the Zoom Fly helped the wearer realize how shoes should ideally engage with the foot no matter what they were doing.

The Zoom Fly came into existence for performance, but trendy takes introduced it to the masses. Nike delivered several special editions of the new model to help push it to cool status. Released in mid-May 2017,

306 Nike Zoom Fly

the NikeLab Zoom Fly SP "Breaking2" pair commemorated the namesake marathon event and instantly shot up in value on the resale market.

The SP version introduced a translucent nylon upper—a material used on multiple pairs thereafter—and featured graphic touches inspired by early prototypes and included callouts to Nike's running history. "Performance running hadn't had a layer of detailing beforehand, so that's what I wanted to bring to the table, hence the return of the pinwheel [logo]," designer Erick Goto shared in a 2018 interview with *Tempo*. "We basically colored it in off-white instead of white to make it look more like a prototype. The only pop of color was showing the lines of the carbon-infused accelerator plate. Then we put the infographics on there because they're real; this is the data that we're using to make a shoe."

The Zoom Fly SP stuck to its running roots via a small number of editions dedicated to top marathons and their respective host cities, with Chicago, Boston, Tokyo, and other locales receiving special colorways. But the shoe saw one high-profile iteration when Virgil Abloh and his Off-White imprint included the Zoom Fly SP in "The Ten" collection, the designer's take on ten select shoes important to Nike's archives.

Abloh appreciated how cutting-edge the new model was, just like the Air Max 1, Air Max 97, and other running shoes were in their heyday. As he discussed in *The Ten Textbook*, Abloh understood "so much running innovation and top-of-the-line progressive design is embedded in the chassis of this shoe." He tasked himself with bringing those elements to the forefront, using his familiar deconstructed approach. Like all of the shoes in the collection, obtaining a pair amounted to a near-impossible task, and soaring prices on the resale market didn't make things any easier. Monetary value aside, it says a lot that a fresh, new model is placed alongside iconic silhouettes like the Air Jordan 1, the Converse Chuck Taylor All-Star, and the Air Force 1 in Abloh's collection. Each of those models represents the peak of its respective period. Abloh's decision to include the Zoom Fly as one of the few modern models in the collection signals the position the shoe may one day hold.

The Zoom Fly and VaporFly 4% never emerged as the "Boost killers" many pegged them to be. Nike likely never intended for the shoes to compete with existing products in the athleisure niche. Various React and VaporMax models released around the same timeframe could handle that battle much better.

But the Zoom Fly represented the Swoosh's return to successfully innovating and creating products to benefit athletes, a hallmark of the company throughout its first few decades of existence. Customers expected Nike to dictate the direction of footwear on multiple levels through inventive and expressive design. The Zoom Fly reaffirmed that the company—which in recent years had lost its touch in performance categories like running and basketball—could make a shoe that performed well *and* looked good. Substance took rank over style, or vice versa. The Zoom Fly landed in a sweet spot, meeting both needs.

Honorable Mention
Adidas Yeezy Boost 700 "Wave Runner"

Kanye West is a father of four, so it's only right that his signature line with Adidas has gone from flimsy sock sneakers to chunky dad shoes. That progression started in late 2017 with the release of the Adidas Yeezy Boost 700 "Wave Runner," a model that's been updated and iterated upon since. The shoe was a departure from his previous models like the Boost 350 and Boost 350 V2, the latter of which remains the most popular shoe in his Yeezy line. The "Wave Runner" had a thick sole and suede and mesh on the upper, and was more color-blocked in its design. It also helped shift the direction of the sneaker industry.

From 2013 to 2017, much of the footwear industry was focused on minimalist designs that more closely resembled

by Matt Welty

socks with soles than proper sneakers. This trend dates to the Nike Roshe Run in 2013, was furthered by the rerelease of the Nike Sock Dart, and took off with the Adidas NMD, an amalgamation of three archival designs with a Boost sole. Those shoes flew out the door, colorway after colorway. The trend was also heightened by the popularity of the Yeezy 350, a limited-edition design few could get their hands on. Every other brand tried this formula—and it got tired after a while.

When people saw West wearing the "Wave Runner" for the first time in early 2017, no one was quite sure what it was. An Adidas sneaker? A high-fashion shoe? Some even guessed it was a rip-off of an early-2000s skate model. What it was, though, was a new design direction for the Yeezy line brought on by footwear veteran Steven Smith, whose long and varied résumé includes silhouettes like the New Balance 1500, Reebok Instapump Fury, and Nike Air Max 2009.

West's desire for a sneaker like the "Wave Runner" came as a surprise to Smith. "I didn't exactly know what he was asking me to design because the market was way over here in 350 land, and Roshe, and simple, and cheap, minimal parts, all seamless, and here we were designing this thing that's going to be a bazillion pieces stitched back together," he said in a 2020 interview with Complex. "I'm like, 'This thing's going to cost a fortune.' And he's like, 'Don't worry about price, bro. We'll just make it and we'll figure it out.'"

Recent history confirms that they made the right decision. After its initial release in 2017, the 700 saw broader distribution in 2018 and quickly put the public on notice that West and Yeezy were much more than the 350.

2018 Nike React Element 87

For those who came of age around the time of the release of the shoe that leads off this book—the Air Jordan 1—there was a shared adolescent conception of what the future would look like. Looking ahead to the year 2018 from the year 1985, it was easy to imagine a world filled with robot housekeepers and flying cars à la *The Jetsons*.

by Justin Tejada

As for sneakers, it was hard to even comprehend what footwear might look like thirty-plus years in the future. For those who did dare to imagine, their thoughts likely tended toward the Nike Mag they saw in *Back to the Future Part II*, with its power-lacing capabilities. One thing is certain: no one in 1985 thought that the Air Jordan 1, with the simple addition of a backwards Swoosh or a zip tie, would still be one of the most popular shoes as the second decade of the twenty-first century drew to a close.

That's what made the release of the Nike React Element 87 so refreshing. Here was a shoe whose aesthetics were more akin to what kids in 1985 envisioned futuristic sneakers looking like. Here was a shoe that felt like it could be a reference point and design inspiration for a shoe that comes out in the year 2055. Here was a shoe that felt new in a bold way, that planted a flag in the sand.

Even the way the React Element 87 was revealed reflected its boldness. In the overwhelmingly male domain of sneaker culture, the first public glimpse of the React Element 87 was on the feet of a woman.

A light rain and fog fell on Paris as day broke on the morning of March 2, 2018. But by midday the sun was peeking out when Jun Takahashi sent his Undercover Fall 2018 ready-to-wear collection down the runway. The fashion show took place in tents at the Pavillon Ledoyen, one of the oldest restaurants in Paris, dating back to the late 1700s. Situated near the Seine, the Champs-Élysées Garden, and the Place de la Concorde, Pavillon Ledoyen is rumored to be where Napoleon met his first wife, and it was a favored haunt of artists such as Monet, Degas, and Flaubert. More recently

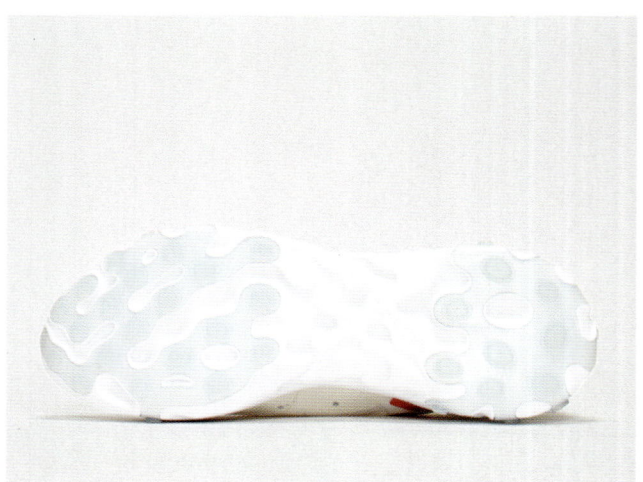

it has been operated by renowned chef Yannick Alléno and has three Michelin stars.

But the menu wasn't what people were admiring on that second day in March. Instead it was the feet of actress Sadie Sink, who led off the Undercover show. As the music of crooner Paul Anka played, Sink, who portrays Max on the Netflix show *Stranger Things*, strode down the runway in a red hoodie, track pants, and beanie that framed her red hair. On her feet were a pair of React Element 87s in a chameleon-like colorway.

The choice of a *Stranger Things* cast member was fitting for the Undercover collection, which had undercurrents of both adolescence and things not being what they seem running through it.

The phrase "Total Youth" featured prominently on many garments, and the denim on what appeared to be a ripped pair of jeans was revealed to be a dyed sweatshirt jersey fabric.

This sense of youth and revelation came through on the React Element 87s that went down the runway as well. The colors seemed to be pulled from the loudest options in

a Crayola box. And what seemed at first glance to be a traditional upper material was, in fact, translucent, allowing the colorway to morph to that of whatever socks the wearer had on underneath.

The brashness of the "Undercover" colorways was contrasted by the staid nature of the first inline versions to launch, a creamy "Sail" and a black "Anthracite." But, in a testament to the overall design of the React Element 87, the black and white versions were no less hyped and coveted.

As bold as the React Element 87 was on that first Parisian glimpse, the shoe does contain design cues that are familiar in the recent oeuvre of Nike's hype-register footwear. The translucent upper comes in the wake of Virgil Abloh's 2017 "The Ten" project, which saw similar treatments to sneakers. (The see-through trend was also seen on various sneakers in the 2000s.) Even the low-slung Swoosh has a precedent in the avant-goofy branding seen on the uber-hyped Tom Sachs x NikeCraft Mars Yard model.

But for a shoe that debuted on one of high fashion's biggest stages, the React Element 87 started off rather humbly. "The whole concept behind this was, 'How do we make a basic staple jogger feel more comfortable?'" said Darryl Matthews, the Nike Sportswear Innovation Designer who led the project.

One of the most distinct characteristics of the shoe is the tooling on the midsole and outsole. But in an age when 3D printers and CAD designs are incredibly accessible, members of Nike Sportswear's special projects team went with a more rudimentary and tactile approach.

It was as simple as a block of foam and a Dremel tool.

"The whole process was really a back-to-basics exercise that taught us new ways to make a shoe look and feel great while also harnessing the power of cutting-edge computation design," Matthews said.

After developing pressure maps of people who spent a lot of time on their feet, designers literally just started boring holes into foam in an attempt to provide support where the foot needed it and remove it where it didn't. While the drilling was designed to serve a very practical purpose, it had the added benefit of looking incredibly cool.

But drilling alone wasn't going to cut it. Matthews and his team developed an algorithm that was used to take what they'd learned about foam densities from the drilling and scale it across all the different sizes that would be required to make a full production run, although shipping a shoe to customers wasn't a top-of-mind consideration.

"This wasn't a project that was going to market at this point. This wasn't even a React project," he said. "This was just an exploration of how to change the durometer of basic EVA foam, to make it more comfortable."

The futuristic-looking midsole was paired with an equally avant-garde upper, which also had a very DIY origin story. On a plane to South Korea, Matthews sketched his idea on a Post-It note. He had none of the tech specs required to turn his drawing into an actual prototype but was able to work with the factory to get something created in a week.

While it may be difficult for the untrained eye to spot, the React Element 87 was inspired by the 1983 Nike Internationalist, in a move that was driven by office politics as much as by design. Matthews knew that then–Nike CEO Mark Parker, who would need to sign off on the React Element 87, had created the Internationalist. So Matthews shrewdly incorporated elements of Parker's creation, such as the height of the collar, the vamp length, and the tongue shape, into the design in hopes that it might help get the project approved.

"I wanted to have an element of the past for the future," Matthews said. "So you get this nostalgic futuristic look, which at the time wasn't really happening, and it landed right at the sweet spot. You could take the Swoosh off this, and this would [still] be a Nike shoe."

Yet for all the nods to the Internationalist, the React Element 87 doesn't look like anything that came before it, and that's an important part of what makes it so special. It feels like the trunk of a new family tree rather than an outer branch of an existing one.

It isn't so much that each of the, ahem, elements of the React Element 87 is unique. Nike had made shoes with translucent uppers previously. Ditto for cork insoles and exposed zigzag stitching. But it's in the mix that the greatness of the shoe is revealed. It's a sneaker that feels both deconstructed and completely polished. The asymmetrical design of the tongue makes little sense, but somehow on the React Element 87 that quirky, design-for-design's-sake whimsy comes across as a feature, not a bug. And even though the tongue shape may not lead to the most comfortable sneaker collar, somehow it feels worth it.

Initial feelings about the shoe internally were mixed. It didn't resonate with some of the older executives at Nike, but after brand collaborators such as Tom Sachs, Undercover, and Abloh started expressing their fondness for the React Element 87, moods shifted. Matthews says Abloh even wanted the style to be part of "The Ten."

"We knew we had a banger, but we never knew it would be received in this way," Matthews told *Sneaker Freaker* in 2018.

He also didn't know his creation would be showing up in that fateful Undercover show. Someone at Nike had given the React Element 87s to Undercover without being certain they were cleared to go down the runway. As testament to the improvised nature of the entire process, parts of the shoe were actually painted on, which helps explain why the runway versions were different from the eventual production ones. When someone sent Matthews a picture of his creation on the runway, he was shocked. "But you know what? It helped. It brought a lot of attention," he said.

That early attention, however, meant sneaker fans had to wait a long time to actually get their hands on a pair. Nike likes to showcase new innovations in performance silhouettes. While React foam had already been used in Nike Basketball styles, the brand wanted to make a bigger splash around its release in a running shoe. So even though React Element 87 was ready, it couldn't be released. It needed to wait in line until the Epic React Flyknit performance running shoe was completed.

Once the React Element 87 did come out, people who got their hands on a pair were treated to another surprise: the translucent textile used on the upper gave the wearer's foot an important role in the overall look of the shoe. That role hinges on whether someone is wearing the shoes barefoot or with socks. With the React Element 87, it's possible to wear the same shoe ten days in a row and have it look vastly different each day.

"I wasn't really aware of the transparent nature of the upper until it was in hand," said Ben Jacobs, brand director at Stadium Goods, echoing a sentiment shared by many early adopters. "So having to think about how the color of my socks would change the appearance of the shoe definitely took it to a whole other level in terms of wardrobe coordination."

"People are drawn to the shoe because it has layers. It's not a flat shoe," said Matthews, who in hindsight wishes he'd included a pair of socks with each pair. "It's like when Nike exposed the Air bag, except now we're able to expose the inside of the shoe, too."

Given the sneaker's age, it's important to remember that the impact of the React Element 87 won't be felt for years to come. If you look at some of the other hyped sneakers that came out in 2018, the majority of them were either actual retros, like the "Black/Cement" Air Jordan III, or reinterpretations of retros, like the Diamond x Nike SB Dunk Low "Canary" and the Sean Wotherspoon x Nike Air Max 1/97. That isn't a knock on any of those shoes. They are all memorable in their own way and are sure to have an enduring appeal. But they don't mark time the way a new sneaker silhouette does.

Shoes like the React Element 87 or the Nike Air Fear of God 1, which also dropped in 2018, bring something unique to the table with their newness. For starters, it renders moot arguments from so-called "old heads" that new styles—an Off-White Air Jordan 1, for example—can't compare to the OGs. The initial colorways of the React Element 87, both the Undercover collaboration and the

quieter black and white iterations, are the OGs for this silhouette. They are the styles that kids who came of age in the late 2010s will be nostalgic for when they reach their 30s. And they will belong solely to them. They won't be driven by their nostalgia layered on top of another generation's nostalgia, as is the case with many retros.

Another refreshing thing about the React Element 87 is that for all the attention that the Undercover collaborations received, the "Sail" and "Anthracite" colorways captured the imagination just as much. It was nice to see a shoe succeed on its own merits and not because of cosign from a hot artist or designer.

"It's something that is few and far between these days. It generally takes a collaborator to help companies take risks and think outside of what's expected," said Jacobs. "It's nice to see that they can continue to innovate and push boundaries, and create something that's new and different but also feels right on time for the era."

Talking about "purity" in sneakers is a fool's errand these days, but the excitement around the React Element 87 did seem driven more by consumers genuinely liking and wanting the shoe and less by a desire to make a quick buck on the resale market. Although, more than a year and a half after the shoe's initial release, it is still selling for above twice its retail price on the aftermarket.

It's unclear how sustainable that demand for the shoe is. No subsequent release has achieved the acclaim of the debut colorways. In 2019, Kendrick Lamar developed a version of the sneaker's opaque—and arguably more comfortable—cousin, the React Element 55, that featured a marbleized upper that caused some ripples but didn't turn into a full-fledged hype phenomenon.

But that does nothing to diminish the status of the React Element 87. It may be a one-hit wonder, but that one hit was pretty damn good. It may be a shoe that is destined to become a cult classic in the way of a style like the Nike Air Spiridon, whose fans may never eclipse a Jordan 1 in number but whose passions run no less deep. Or it may just be that the React Element 87 was ahead of its time. And it may take the rest of the world a little longer to catch up.

Honorable Mention
Nike Air Fear of God 1

Collaborating with Nike on a colorway of an existing sneaker is a milestone in any designer's career. But Fear of God's Jerry Lorenzo took it a step further, with the brand allowing him to create original silhouettes for it, an opportunity few receive.

Details of the Air Fear of God 1 started surfacing during the summer of 2018, and the model was finally revealed that September, in a short film teasing Lorenzo's forthcoming Nike collection.

Lorenzo worked with Nike Basketball footwear design director Leo Chang on the shoe, which, in addition to borrowing from an existing Fear of God silhouette, was indebted to the Nike Air Huarache Light, alongside the Air More Uptempo, the Air Pressure, and the Air Max 180. "His attention to detail is insane," Chang said to Complex in 2018. "He took us to another level with the craft, with just sweating every single thing."

by Ben Felderstein

Lorenzo can't reasonably claim his design's merits come from Nike innovation. He's described the FOG 1 as a performance shoe, but this is not a sneaker that's been through the Nike Sports Research Lab-level of testing. Instead, as with his clothing designs, the solution is in the shape—the designer flew in his own last from Italy to get the lines just right. Regardless, Lorenzo sees it as a model without compromise.

"You're gonna be able to go to the club in that and dunk on somebody, and both at the highest level," he told Complex in 2018.

With the latter in mind, P.J. Tucker, the Houston Rockets forward renowned for his sneaker collection, laced up a pair for the first half of a November 2018 game against the Brooklyn Nets, heightening the anticipation for the model's release.

But despite its appearance on an NBA court, the FOG 1 is a luxury sneaker, which is why it comes in a premium orange box, accompanied by dust bags, alternate-colored laces, toggles, and a tote. All of that, combined with the shoe's premium build, amounts to a retail price of $395. Since its initial release, in black, the model has arrived in hues ranging from the bright and bold "Orange Pulse" and "Frosted Spruce" to the more muted "Sail" and "Light Bone." Nike's basketball division has also continued to work with Lorenzo.

"I was trying to propose something that makes a kid feel the same way I felt the first time I had a pair of Jordans," Lorenzo told Complex of his collaboration. "That's lofty, and that's beyond what maybe anyone would think of a Nike collab, but if that's ... If you're gonna get the opportunity, that's the chase. You don't want to fall short of that."

2019 Nike x Sacai LDV Waffle

In June 2018, Japanese designer Chitose Abe presented Sacai's Spring 2019 men's and Resort 2019 women's collections during Paris Fashion Week. "Freeform" was the theme: "To defy preconceived ideas of how clothes can be." There were fifty-seven looks in total, which included a one-sleeve fisherman knit sweater; a jacket that was part tailored pinstripe, part army green anorak; and blankets made in collaboration with Pendleton that morphed into kilts (and vice versa). The star of the show, though, was a reinvention of two running sneakers that no one expected in a high-profile designer collaboration from Nike: a hybrid of the Nike LDV and Waffle Racer with double laces, double tongues, and double Swooshes in bold "Green/Maize/Orange" and "Blue/Red/Del Sol" colorways. (Abe also debuted a Blazer.)

by Karizza Sanchez

The Nike x Sacai LDV Waffle quickly became one of the most anticipated sneakers of 2019. From the moment it hit the runway in Paris, the majority of the comments surrounding it, even from those who probably had no idea who Abe or what Sacai was, usually went something like, "These go hard" or "Instant cop." Blogs were predicting it "could be one of 2019's best releases." Even a delay—the sneaker was initially scheduled for a January 2019 release but was pushed back a few months, reportedly because Abe wanted to perfect it—only added to the hype.

Abe, who got put on with Nike through a friend who worked at the brand (her first collaboration launched in 2014), says she didn't initially recognize the fervor around the sneaker. "I was aware that the sneakers were being featured in the press and included in sneaker blogs," she said, "but it wasn't until I prelaunched the sneakers through my pop-up store in Paris in January and seeing the long queue outside, hours before the store opening, that I realized that they were a hit." To everyone else, though, it was pretty clear.

When the sneaker finally dropped on March 7, lines snaked down blocks and the shoe sold out everywhere.

On the secondary market, it was being resold for as much as $1,456, nine times the retail price ($160)—though Abe doesn't exactly support this. "It's flattering to know that there are people out there who like the sneaker to that extent, but I'm a little conflicted about this," she said. "It was really important for me that the sneakers were priced at an accessible price point."

"I think that's the most beautiful shoe, and I never get tired of looking at it—ever,"
Lil Yachty said during Complex's 2019 "Sneaker of the Year" panel at ComplexCon. "I love the Waffle, and I love the shield around the sole, you know what I'm saying? I love the mesh. When you look down on the toe, you could see your sock … That shoe is hard. That's the best shoe."

It would be hard to argue that the Nike x Sacai LDV Waffle isn't the best sneaker of 2019. But it's true: Abe and Sacai don't come from a sneaker background. So how'd they pull it off?

Hybridization is an essential part of Abe's work. It's a concept she came up with while she was on maternity leave after the birth of her daughter, Tohko. Abe, who earned her degree in fashion design in Nagoya, moved to Tokyo and cut her teeth at a large apparel company, World Co., Ltd., before eventually working at Comme des Garçons as a pattern maker and, later, Junya Watanabe's label. She quit her job at Comme des Garçons after eight years to raise her daughter, but it wasn't long before she needed a creative outlet again. So, at the suggestion of her husband, Junichi, whom she met at Junya Watanabe and who now has his own brand, Kolor, Abe launched Sacai (a play on her maiden name, Sakai) in 1999 and began developing what would become her signature aesthetic. "All I was wearing were jeans, chinos, V-neck sweaters, T-shirts, polo shirts," she wrote in *Sacai: A to Z*. "I thought, is this it? I started to experiment to see if I could maybe fuse two garments—say, a sweater with a shirt."

Sacai started with five hybrid knits, including a sweater mixed with a shirt. "I don't think those kinds of knits existed at the time," she told SSENSE. "Now, there's a ton of hybrid knits and other clothes, but

at that time, knits were nothing more than knits. I was really only thinking about creating unique pieces, even when I first went overseas." Since then, the label has evolved to include other ready-to-wear pieces, accessories, bags, footwear, and menswear. But what's remained consistent—and what Abe's famous for now—is her ability to splice together unusual combinations to create something entirely new.

The Nike x Sacai LDV Waffle runs through that same filter. From the jump, Abe knew she wanted to "combine two different Nike sneaker styles into one. No matter what the category is, whether it be clothes, accessories, and even the interiors of my stores, the concept of hybridization is crucial to my design philosophy," she said. "So when it came to the collaboration with Nike, the impetus was to create everything—the apparel, the sneakers—in unexpected ways and playing with the silhouette. This time, with the sneakers, I wanted to highlight Sacai's hybrid method."

According to Nike's Reba Brammer, Designer II, Footwear Innovation (NSW), they suggested exploring different BRS models. "[Chitose] has a real interest in vintage Nike," she said. "We pitched the idea of using different BRS models because we were interested in them at the time. We were thinking of bringing those models back and how that would work really well." They looked at old Nike Japan catalogs and various '70s running shoes, including the Daybreak and the Moon Racer. "They were all sort of within the Prefontaine era," said Brammer. They also referenced *kintsugi*, the centuries-old Japanese art of repairing broken pottery, and tried combining different shoes. "We did a lot of collaging, glitching shoes, and Photoshop," recalled Brammer. In the end, they landed on the LDV and the Waffle Racer.

One day, while Abe was working in her studio in Japan with the Nike design team, the idea to combine these two silhouettes occurred to her. She grabbed two photocopied pictures—one of the Waffle Racer and the other of the LDV—and ... simply folded them in half and put them on top of each other. Abe designs based on intuition, and when she knows, she *knows*. "I wanted the new pair to have the essence of both shoes equally, half and half." From there, they developed the defining characteristics of the shoe: double tongues, double shoelaces, double Swooshes, and a heel accent that gives the impression of a double-stacked sole.

"We wanted to marry the two toolings to the two bases of the shoe," explained Brammer. "And if you're going to put those together, why not have two tongues and two laces? I think Chitose might've actually suggested the second shoelace. I don't think we had the second shoelace at the beginning, but we already had a double tongue."

There were four or five samples of the sneaker (a relatively small number in the world of shoe design), but the first prototype was pretty close to the final product. "We always go through several samples for wear testing and stuff like that, but the initial sample looked pretty good," said Brammer. The bold retro colorways—another distinct element of the shoe—didn't change much, either. They went through roughly three different rounds of color combinations, but the "Green/Maize/Orange" colorway, for example, was always one of the original options. "[Chitose] really wanted to reference back to the vintage models, so bringing those vintage colors together in the right way just really worked," said Brammer. "She stuck with vintage colors from the catalog."

To some, the LDV and the Waffle Racer may have been unexpected choices. The Waffle Racer was famously designed by

Nike cofounder Bill Bowerman, who used his wife's waffle iron to create a new kind of running shoe to help runners go faster, in 1972, and was successfully marketed and released a year later. The sole had small protruding squares and was lighter and provided extra grip and rebound. It changed running shoes forever and was the first major innovation from Nike. The LDV, originally released in 1978, was the first long-distance running sneaker that had a breathable mesh upper, which kept the shoe lightweight, and a waffle outsole that worked for any trail. While both models are pivotal in Nike's history, neither was exactly at the top of people's minds, especially in 2019. But for Abe, a fan of vintage Nike, the choice was simple.

"I enjoy mixing elements from multiple different and familiar items and creating something completely new," she explained. "I noticed that many people enjoy wearing the LDV, while they may also sometimes wear the Waffle Racer. So I thought, what if one could enjoy both styles at the same time, in one pair? I thought that it would be something unique and special."

Design elements aside, though, what also made the LDV Waffle special was that it transcended the sneaker world. Sneakerheads and OG collectors wore the shoe, no doubt. But fashion people who rarely wore athletic footwear were into it, too. In a way, it's indicative of where streetwear and sneakers are today. Streetwear *is* high fashion. Sneakers is a multibillion-dollar industry. And the luxury space is finally grasping the power and influence of streetwear and sneaker cultures. It made sense, then, that the silhouette debuted during Paris Fashion Week—where streetwear shifted.

Nike has gotten good at working with fashion designers and fusing fashion with sportswear. In the last few years, it has added the likes of Alyx's Matthew Williams, Ambush's Yoon Ahn, Martine Rose, and Cactus Plant Flea Market's Cynthia Lu to its roster. And through projects with these names—creatives who have their pulse on the zeitgeist, and often dictate it—Nike has turned collaborations into pop culture moments. Still, no other fashion sneaker collab from Nike or any other footwear brand, save maybe for Virgil's Nike x Off-White "The Ten" or Kanye West's Yeezy releases, has captivated both the sneaker and fashion worlds quite like the Nike x Sacai LDV Waffle did.

Sacai and Nike have since released new colorways of the LDV Waffle—"Pine Green/Clay Orange-Del Sol-Orange," "Black/Anthracite-White-Gunsmoke," and "Summit White/White-Wolf Grey-Black." They were well-received, like the first round, but by that point the hype had died down a bit. In January 2020, the Japanese label also debuted a new Nike collaboration, the Nike x Sacai Pegasus Vaporfly SP (a hybrid of the Pegasus and Vaporfly running silhouettes) at its Fall/Winter 2020 runway show in Paris. The feedback was mixed: some thought it was a strong follow-up, while others said the original release eclipsed this one.

It's hard to predict (at least at the time of this writing) how well the new Nike x Sacai Pegasus Vaporfly SP will do, and if it will surpass its predecessor. But what's undeniable is this: Sacai, a brand without formal ties to the sneaker world, made the best sneaker of 2019.

Honorable Mention
Air Jordan 1 High "Travis Scott"

The sneaker scene in the 2010s looked vastly different than it did in the 2000s and 1990s. Rather than athletes, the biggest names in hip-hop were the ones setting industry trends. And while the shift didn't begin recently—Jay-Z and 50 Cent had signature Reeboks in the early 2000s, and Run-DMC was synonymous with Adidas decades before—it crystallized with figures like Kanye West and, then, Travis Scott releasing their own models and putting their stamp on existing fare.

    The latter, a Houston rapper whose ascent began in the early 2010s, is central to the conversation today. Scott has moved the needle repeatedly with products from Nike and Jordan Brand. No release bearing his name, however, is more

by Ben Felderstein

celebrated than his Air Jordan 1 Retro High. Being entrusted with a model as highly regarded as the Jordan 1 is a true sign of a collaborator's influence, and his version is among the most popular of recent years.

In 2018, Scott teased the sneaker on Instagram, writing that it was "still cooking." As with any AJ 1 collab, hype around the Cactus Jack head's newest sneaker project instantly sky-rocketed. It continued to rise as Scott wore the model during his Astroworld: Wish You Were Here Tour, in support of his Grammy-nominated *Astroworld* album. The model itself bore a reversed Swoosh on the upper, along with a hidden stash pocket around its ankle collar and Cactus Jack branding etched into its heel. Eventually, an official release date surfaced: May 11, 2019. While the shoe was sold via Nike's SNKRS app, the release was not without incident, with buyers unable to check out as a result of bugs in the system. The chaos only fueled the hype, and the sneaker would soon fetch quadruple-digit figures on the resale market.

But that, of course, is not the final marker of a shoe's success. Why, secondary-market prices aside, is Travis Scott's take on the Jordan 1 so successful? Part of it has to do with the rapper's prior sneaker output, which gave him a long runway to test out ideas. The Air Jordan 1 is bold, with its horizontally flipped Swoosh, but it arrived after Scott put out tamer Nike work, like his Jordan IV, that was a bit more respectful of the original palette. Essentially, he did some playing by the rules before going against them. It also arrived as part of a branding conversation—remember, he was flipping Swooshes way back on his Air Force 1 project that debuted in 2017.

2020
Off-White x Air Jordan V

The directors at the factory couldn't believe it. They felt trepidation in presenting the project. *Was this really what Nike's designers envisioned?* They'd executed the ask, but the final product appeared not so final—it was raw, with exposed foam and stitching that made it look like it was falling apart. The designers were ecstatic. The factory team was confused. That shoe, the original Off-White x Air Jordan 1 collaboration that was released as part of designer Virgil Abloh's "The Ten" collection in September 2017, redefined a footwear icon and helped reestablish Nike's dominance at the end of the decade. The overarching project, Abloh's reinvention of the brand's retro catalog, is still unfinished.

by Brendan Dunne

It is not easy work. Critics of Abloh—the vastly influential artist whose various and sundry positions include CEO of his own Off-White label, men's artistic director at Louis Vuitton, and impossibly prolific DJ at nightclubs across the globe—will claim slapping his signature quotation marks on any product is a shortcut to hype and resale market buzz. But this complaint ignores the delicate equation of his sneaker portfolio under the Nike umbrella. The Off-White x Air Jordan V, released in February 2020, is the smartest example of this work.

The success of the ten-shoe range that contained his first Jordan 1 owes to its balance of reverence for genre staples and willingness to reinterpret them. This means confounding factories by making them rethink what an Air Jordan should look like. This means challenging stodgy sneakerheads who cling to the idea that the present and future have nothing to add to the models from the past that they love.

"It's tough to do that, knowing how sacred these are to these kids," said Gemo Wong, senior designer of special projects at Jordan Brand.

The Nike sub-brand trades heavily on nostalgia and retro product, so it makes sense that its most devoted consumers flinch at the idea of altering an icon. For it to do so successfully, it needs the license of a collaborator like Abloh. The whole idea of collaborations was an extremely tired one by 2020, the era of Everyone x Everything, but in this case the outside partner is truly doing something the brand can't on its own. And he's doing it with a careful eye toward tradition—remember, Abloh grew up just outside of Chicago while Michael Jordan was at the height of his powers.

"He's always been respectful of retro colors, and he adds just that little twist," Wong said of Abloh. "We'll always look at an original colorway and how we could respect it yet push it in other ways—whether that's form or material."

That pushing is crucial to the Off-White x Air Jordan V, a shoe created to make it look like a time capsule from the future landed in 1990, the year of the original Jordan V's release, and aged to perfection for thirty years. It is a love letter to that model, written in Abloh's idiolect. There are white laces, just like how Jordan wore them. The soles arrive pre-yellowed to mimic natural aging, making them look like they came out of a collector's closet after years-long hibernation. The dingy tint was a challenge to Jordan norms; in the earlier part of the decade, the brand worked hard to make sure the translucent rubber bottoms on shoes like the Jordan V wouldn't turn color with age. As part of the solution, it injected them with an icy blue. Abloh tossed that progress out, opting for a patina that veteran collectors know well.

How else did he twist the formula? He literally poked holes in the Jordan V—the shoe has circles on its upper where the materials are cut away, with only a thin film layer left. The Swiss cheesing of the silhouette is meant to evoke the magic of Nike's Air technology embedded in the soles. Where Tinker Hatfield, the silhouette's original designer, made that cushioning visible with windows in the midsoles of shoes like the Air Max 1 and the Jordan V, Abloh extended it by allowing even more air in.

"The circles, to be honest, were supposed to be fully cut out on the medial and the lateral. I made the call to not do that full

cut-out," said Wong, explaining that he put the onus on Abloh to extend the conversation around the design once it came out.

The Off-White designer did so by posting a video of himself carving out those circles. If his first Nike releases looked unfinished, this was Abloh communicating that his latest Jordan was the same way and empowering those lucky enough to buy the super-limited shoes to finish the job. Not only did he have the audacity to alter a shoe many consider perfect, he was telling followers on social media to take a knife to it.

Is that blasphemy? Is it heretical to try to recast the creations of Jordan and Hatfield, both gods of their fields? For Don C, who is three years Abloh's senior and thus spent more time worshiping the Chicago Bulls, yes. But, he adds, that's what makes Abloh a great designer.

"I'm so embedded, it's like a religion, almost, to me," said Don, a fellow Chicago-area designer, longtime friend of Abloh, and member of the same extended circle of Kanye West–adjacent creatives. "When you a religious person, you're not gonna wear a T-shirt of Jesus Christ upside down. You just ain't gon' do that. That graphic might look cool, though. That hindrance is what makes me not that good of a designer."

Don says that, by contrast, Abloh is so successful because he is less precious with such idols. That's what allows him to take a Jordan V and strip the original padding away, hollowing out the chunky collar and creating something slimmer and more modern. That's what makes Off-White's Nikes more striking and resonant in 2020 than, say, the work of Hiroshi Fujiwara's Fragment Design label. Was the

Fragment x Air Jordan 1 from 2014 an elegant update to a classic sneaker? Yes, but it was too elegant, perhaps burdened by Fujiwara's own long and deep history in sneakers. Abloh's sneakers do not operate under the same pressure.

"He has all the input, and he's the teenager during the Jordan era and everything," said Don of Abloh. "But he wasn't as into it as I was, so it doesn't mean as much to him. He can be more free with it."

Does that put a retro-focused entity like Jordan Brand in a difficult position when it comes to liberties like these? Definitely. Wong admits to worrying about letting someone tweak something held in such high regard. But the process is not without checks and balances, and Abloh's Off-White x Air Jordan V sneaker did receive perhaps the most important cosign during its incubation.

"Getting MJ's thoughts on it was huge," Wong said. "He blessed it, thank God."

If the Jumpman himself blessed it, surely it should be good enough for the formalists in his congregation. Showing such a reworked shoe to Jordan, who originally made it iconic, is a bold move, but none of these shoes were first designed with a particular respect for tradition. None of the great steps forward in sneaker design were prompted by an adherence to old rules. Tinker Hatfield was not a sneakerhead. Just like Abloh, actually, he studied as an architect before switching careers.

Abloh is still switching them—with each new quarter, it feels like he is involved with a new discipline. The extremely busy schedule he keeps (on the advice of his doctor, Abloh had to slow himself down in late 2019 and cancel all travel for three

months) means that he doesn't have enough hours in a day to be a full-time sneaker designer. Wong says Abloh hasn't really been working at Nike and Jordan Brand's world headquarters in Beaverton, Oregon, since the original "The Ten" project years ago. These days, he trades feedback remotely, via WhatsApp. Abloh has spent enough time sharpening his vision to be able to design from a distance.

"What I love about Virgil, he's created such a design code," Don said. "He doesn't even have to design."

This code allows him to maximize his reach and pace. It's what lets him go from launching one of the most hyped Nike collections of all time to releasing a furniture range with Ikea to making a custom Patek Philippe watch for Drake in an impossibly compact time frame. It is Bauhaus in spirit, spreading Abloh's art via mass production. Well, relatively speaking—"mass production" may be an odd term to connect to relatively limited affairs like his Nikes, but even Abloh has said he has no interest in making his product so scarce. His practice in projects like the Off-White x Air Jordan V is to give this code to a capable team and trust it to deliver.

The people entrusted with that duty at Jordan Brand included Israel Mateo, a Swoosh veteran who rose through the ranks at hyper-cool Nike retail spots like 21 Mercer, and Paul Savovici, a relative newcomer who didn't have much of a sneaker background before starting at Nike in 2013. Their job was essentially to translate Abloh's ideas to sneaker form.

The designer had a prescriptive notion about creating a project that was "retro future." For the first part of the term, Mateo and Savovici made trips to the Department of Nike Archives, where the brand houses its most treasured relics, to study the aging processes of original Jordans. With the second in mind, they rebuilt the shoe with transparent materials so it would appear even sleeker. Time was of the essence, both in the project's theme and in practical terms—changes were made on the Off-White x Air Jordan V right up to the last minute.

The team of Mateo and Savovici on the task is something like a Venn diagram, the intersection of their work on the collaboration reflecting Abloh's background. Mateo, although he shuns the term, is the sneakerhead of the two. His name stayed scrawled on a wall in the stockroom of a Foot Locker in Menlo Park, New Jersey, well after he left the retail chain. Savovici (who left the brand in 2020) came to Nike, and eventually Jordan, fresh off a NASA internship after studying industry and product design at the Rhode Island School of Design. One is fluent in the importance of various coveted Nike styles from the 2000s. One is not weighed down by too many inhibitions about why those styles, or ones from years before, shouldn't be touched. Abloh, through the balance and equation of work like the Off-White x Air Jordan V, is both.

The project is about maintaining the integrity of the original Jordan V idea while working past preconceptions and inhibitions. It proposes, audaciously, that, with the right alterations, the timeless shoe could be even better. It exists outside the more rigid inline catalog of Jordan Brand, employing an openness—quite literally, thanks to those holes—not possible without a partner like Abloh. It doesn't, however, lose sight of the designer's affinity for Air Jordan history. The combination of the original black and metallic colorway remains, filtered through a diaphanous treatment that reads like a lens looking back in time. The directions of backward and forward were there on the original Jordan V, too, an innovative design in 1990 that looked to World War II fighter jets for inspiration.

The Off-White x Air Jordan V suggests that the sneakers we love are to be viewed as dynamic, and not static, pieces of design. It says that even after the work of a shoe's creator is over, the work might still be unfinished. There are collars to resculpt. There are still holes to cut out. There are visions from the future that can alter how we see a particular retro. Even when we cross the finish line, there may still be a ways to go. In fact, if a certain Nike adage is to be believed, there is no finish line.

Honorable Mention
Nike Air Zoom Alphafly NEXT%

The Air Zoom Alphafly NEXT% changed the way we think about sneakers. That's not sportswear marketing hyperbole. The design, a high-tech model made specifically for marathons, challenged notions of just how much footwear should be allowed to enhance the abilities of the wearer. It had Nike's competitors questioning the ethics of creating something that really could make you run faster. It was almost banned from competitions in the process.

The story of the shoe goes back to May 2017 at Nike's Breaking2 event, a three-man race engineered with the goal of recording the first sub-two-hour marathon. None of the participants managed to beat the two-hour mark, but Kenya's Eliud Kipchoge came close, at 2:00:25. They all wore the Zoom

by Brendan Dunne

Vaporfly Elite, which used a controversial carbon-fiber plate in the midsole to maximize energy return. Nike never gave that model a proper release, but it crafted a whole line around the silhouette that reshaped the look of its running shoes. The Zoom Vaporfly 4% from 2017 and the 2019 Zoom Vaporfly NEXT% started dominating marathons, leading many to complain that Nike had taken running shoe technology too far.

Then the impossible happened. Kipchoge did it. In October 2019, he completed a marathon with an astonishing time of 1:59:40. (Like his Breaking2 time, it's not technically a world record, as it wasn't run in standard marathon conditions.) He ran in a prototype version of the Alphafly NEXT%, logging a time so bold that detractors suspected that the international governing body of track and field would ban the shoes—especially considering the unfair edge they could give Nike runners in the 2020 Summer Olympics.

The Alphafly NEXT%, which got a limited release in February 2020, is even more advanced than its predecessors. When purists said Nike took things too far, the brand went even further. Working in unison with the carbon-fiber plate on the new shoe was a set of Zoom Air pods on the forefoot. The foam looked chunkier. Still, it escaped being halted by history. When new rules around competition-acceptable running shoes were announced in January 2020, the Alphafly NEXT% was safe. The sneaker didn't enjoy the grand stage it was meant for in 2020—COVID-19 pushed back the Olympics to 2021, and any sort of outdoor activity was rendered risky. That's OK, though. A shoe that was always a step ahead can probably afford to wait until next year.

ABRAMS

Samantha Weiner, *Editor*
Mike Richards, *Managing Editor*
Diane Shaw, *Art Director*
No Ideas, *Designer*
Robert Engvall, *Illustrator*
Larry Pekarek, *Production Manager*

COMPLEX

Donnie Kwak, *GM, Complex*
Joe La Puma, *SVP of Content Strategy*
Ryan Dunn & Wyeth Hansen, *Executive Creative Directors*
Gina Batlle, *Associate Creative Director*
Lucas Wisenthal, *Director of Content Development*
Karizza Sanchez, *Director of Content Strategy*
Brendan Dunne, *GM, Sole Collector*
Matthew Welty, *Senior Editor, Complex Sneakers*
David Cabrera, *Staff Photographer*
Taylor Korsak, *Associate Director of Publisher Development*
Marlon Calbi, *Former Director, Strategic Partnerships*
Gerald Flores, *Former Editor-in-Chief, Sole Collector, and Deputy Editor, Complex Sneakers*
Damien Scott, *Former Editor-in-Chief, Complex*
Rich Antoniello, *CEO and Founder, Complex Networks*
Michael Hermann, *President/CEO Wicked Cow Studios*

Text copyright © 2020 Complex Media, Inc.
Photographs copyright © Complex Media, Inc., except the following:
Sneaker images on pages 37, 39, 45, 49, 53, 57, and 63 courtesy of Nike
Page 40, Getty Images/View Pictures
Page 54, Getty Images/Chicago Tribune
Page 55, Getty Images/Rich Clarkson
Page 233, Getty Images/Lester Cohen
Page 268, Getty Images/Marc Piasecki

All photos that are copyright © Complex Media, Inc. are by David Cabrera.

Cover © 2020 Abrams

Published in 2020 by Abrams Image, an imprint of ABRAMS. All rights reserved. No portion of this book may be reproduced, stored in a retrieval system, or transmitted in any form or by any means, mechanical, electronic, photocopying, recording, or otherwise, without written permission from the publisher.

Printed and bound in China
10 9 8 7 6

Abrams Image books are available at special discounts when purchased in quantity for premiums and promotions as well as fundraising or educational use. Special editions can also be created to specification. For details, contact specialsales@abramsbooks.com or the address below.

Library of Congress Control Number: 2020931088

ISBN: 978-1-4197-4579-9
eISBN: 978-1-68335-939-5

Abrams Image® is a registered trademark of Harry N. Abrams, Inc.

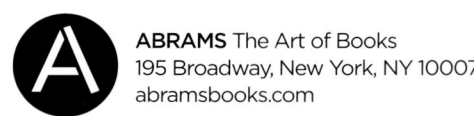

ABRAMS The Art of Books
195 Broadway, New York, NY 10007
abramsbooks.com